Working in the Middle

Working in the Middle

Strengthening Education and Training for the Mid-Skilled Labor Force

W. Norton Grubb

Jossey-Bass Publishers • San Francisco

Substantial discounts on bulk quantities of Jossey-Bass books are available to corporations, professional associations, and other organizations. For details and discount information, contact the special sales department at Jossey-Bass Inc., Publishers (415) 433-1740; Fax (800) 605-2665.

For sales outside the United States, please contact your local Simon & Schuster International office.

Manufactured in the United States of America on Lyons Falls Pathfinder Tradebook. This paper is acid-free and 100 percent totally chlorine-free.

Library of Congress Cataloging-in-Publication Data

Grubb, W. Norton.
    Working in the middle: strengthening education and training for the mid-skilled labor force/W. Norton Grubb.—1st ed.
      p. cm.—(The Jossey-Bass higher and adult education series)
    Includes bibliographical references and index.
    ISBN 0-7879-0258-6 (cloth : acid-free paper)
    1. Vocational education—United States. 2. Occupational training—United States.
3. Technical education—United States. 4. Labor market—United States.
5. Education—Economic aspects—United States. 6. Cooperative education—
United States. I. Title. II. Series.
    LC1045.G78 1996
    370.11'30973—dc20   96-9944

FIRST EDITION
HB Printing 10 9 8 7 6 5 4 3 2 1

The Jossey-Bass
Higher and Adult Education Series

Contents

List of Figures and Tables

Preface

Americans have placed great faith in education as a source of economic advancement. In his efforts to institute publicly supported common schools in the 1830s, Horace Mann described education as "not only a moral renovator and multiplier of intellectual power, but also the most prolific parent of material riches" (Mann, [1842] 1971, p. 147). The movement for an explicitly vocational component to formal schooling during the period from 1890 to 1920 similarly justified education as a mechanism for "learning to earn," and as the solution to problems of international competitiveness, poverty, and the integration of immigrants into the mainstream of society (Lazerson and Grubb, 1974).

More recently, a barrage of commission reports—starting with *A Nation at Risk* (NCEE, 1983), which called for education renewal as a way to restore "our unchallenged preeminence in commerce, industry, science, and technical innovation" (p. 5)—has promoted education reform as the principal solution to declining productivity, maintaining our economic position in an increasingly competitive world, and domestic problems such as poverty and inequality. The well-known relationship between years of formal schooling and earnings has supported our faith in the economic value of education and has served as justification to promoters of education ranging from politicians to educational administrators and parents.

At the same time, the belief in education has often been blind faith, with little evidence about why and how education should improve productivity, competitiveness, or individual well-being. As many have pointed out, education has often been considered a remedy for the social problems of the moment, but on closer inspection it has been a highly imperfect panacea (Perkinson, 1977). The details have often been missing as to how formal schooling contributes to employment, that is, how specific employment opportunities open up to better-educated individuals, and how more formal education results in higher productivity. Education has often not worked out along these lines, and the flip side of our faith has been disappointment when it doesn't. The obligatory newspaper articles about recent college graduates driving taxis, the horror stories of students defrauded by proprietary schools and defaulting on their loans, and "the case against college" (Bird, 1975) are all testimony to the ways that education can fail individuals.

The Mid-Skilled Labor Market

In this book, I examine a part of the labor market and the education and training "system" where the relationship between the two is not well understood. As I define it, *the mid-skilled, or sub-baccalaureate, labor market includes those individuals who have at least a high school diploma but less than a baccalaureate degree.* Some of them have a high school diploma, while others have some college education ranging from a two-year associate degree or one-year certificate to near-completion of a baccalaureate degree to one or two postsecondary courses. This group comprises a majority of the labor force, about 60 percent of all those employed. Growing rapidly, it covers the various mid-skilled occupations that form the heart of the economy. I therefore use the terms "mid-skilled" and "sub-baccalaureate" interchangeably.

For different reasons, the groups on either end of the educational distribution are quite unlike the one in the middle. High school dropouts typically are not considered by employers for mid-skilled occupations and instead are relegated to unskilled positions with unstable employment conditions and lower earnings. At the other end, individuals with baccalaureate and graduate degrees have access to many professional and managerial occupations denied to those with sub-baccalaureate credentials, occupations for which formal schooling is an absolute requirement in ways it is not for sub-baccalaureate positions.

These mid-skilled occupations, and the education and training institutions that prepare individuals for them, are therefore betwixt and between. They fall intermediate between the unskilled labor market, where education makes little difference, and the baccalaureate-level labor market, where formal schooling makes all the difference. This is a segment of the labor market where formal schooling and training *can* make a substantial difference to employment options and earnings, although often it does not. The goal of this book is to help students and educators realize the potential benefits of education and training for the sub-baccalaureate labor force.

A bewildering aspect of the sub-baccalaureate labor market is that many different types of institutions prepare individuals for these mid-skilled jobs:

Community colleges

Technical institutes

Area vocational schools

Proprietary schools

Shorter-term job training programs

Firm-based training paid for in part by public funds

All of these institutions emphasize different occupations and serve different populations to some extent. But their purposes overlap considerably, and it is often difficult to disentangle the many programs, whether for students deciding which one to attend, employers wondering where to hire, or policy makers deciding how to improve workforce preparation.

The Centrality of Two-Year Colleges

In this book, I concentrate on two-year colleges, including both community colleges and their occupationally oriented relations, technical institutes. Most students who do not go beyond high school consider community colleges rather than four-year colleges as the alternative open to them, and these institutions prepare the largest proportion of those in the sub-baccalaureate labor market who do go beyond high school. Two-year colleges are nearly ubiquitous, and they provide access to postsecondary education to students who would otherwise be unable to continue. They have also been quite controversial, although in the absence of better information a kind of uninformed stand-off has developed. On the one side, numerous critics have castigated them for failing to live up to their promise as "second chance" institutions, and for tracking individuals (including many working-class and minority students) away from the higher rewards associated with four-year colleges. On the other hand, the defenders of community colleges have often acted as if two-year colleges can do no wrong, endlessly repeating slogans about the egalitarian virtues of the "people's college" and the superiority of the community college as a teaching institution.

My own view is that two-year colleges are institutions of great promise, but with both positive and negative consequences (as Kevin Dougherty has also argued, in *The Contradictory College*, 1994). The reasons for these contradictory effects are, in my interpretation, largely structural. The position of two-year colleges in the middle of the education system, between mass institutions of secondary education and the selective four-year colleges with their different traditions, causes various problems:

- Community colleges represent the most generous impulses in American society, the impulse to include everyone in education and the willingness to provide alternatives and second chances. But they also constitute the bottom level in a highly tracked postsecondary education system, with lower status, lower funding, and less public attention—problems not of their own making.
- Community colleges are given the most difficult teaching task in postsecondary education, since by design their students are the least well-prepared and the least sure of their intentions. But community colleges are given fewer resources to carry out this task than any other postsecondary institution.
- While many individual instructors are strongly committed to their nontraditional students, community colleges *as institutions* (like most other educational institutions) rarely support or reward good teaching.
- The students in community colleges face a number of challenges unrelated to cognitive development and classroom learning—including the need to find a life course, financial burdens, and pressures from family and community—that are

typically more difficult than for other postsecondary students. But community colleges are nonresidential institutions with limited resources for the noncognitive side of student development. Even though they include many nontraditional students, they largely act like traditional educational institutions: offering isolated courses instead of coherent programs, focusing on a narrow set of skills (especially cognitive skills), and cooperating relatively little with external institutions such as employers and high schools.

Given these structural problems, the task is to figure out what the institution of the two-year college does and then to improve it. Therefore much of the work presented in this book is empirical: it tries to determine what students in community colleges are like, what the labor market for mid-skilled positions is like, what the economic benefits are, where problems can be seen, and what kinds of solutions are being tried by innovative institutions. My emphasis in developing this empirical material is consistently on *improvement,* in the interests of students, employers, the taxpayers who support these institutions, and ultimately two-year colleges themselves.

In addition, this book looks at the shorter-term job training programs that attempt to provide access to employment for high school dropouts, the underemployed, welfare recipients, dislocated workers, and others in need of training and retraining, all individuals who would be unlikely on their own to find their way into two-year colleges. Typically, job training programs do not prepare individuals for the sub-baccalaureate labor market: their economic benefits are relatively small and short-lived, and they fail to place their clients in the kinds of mid-skilled jobs that can move them out of poverty or off welfare. Improving these programs is another priority, particularly since they consume substantial public funds. One way to do so—perhaps the only way—is to re-integrate *job training* with the kinds of *education* programs now provided in two-year colleges. This would then create a coherent system of education and training for the sub-baccalaureate labor market, in place of the current welter of uncoordinated and incomprehensible programs.

I am principally concerned in this book with *public* institutions, since the community colleges and technical institutes that dominate preparation for the sub-baccalaureate labor market are public rather than private, as are the job training programs that provide other second-chance routes into employment. Very often, however, federal and state policies have ignored preparation of the sub-baccalaureate labor force, as I clarify in Chapter Seven, and they often lack a good understanding of both the labor market and the institutions preparing individuals for it. Overall, the policy questions are still those that have been around since Mann declared formal schooling "the most prolific parent of material riches," and certainly since developments at the turn of the century made our educational system explicitly vocational: how best to design formal schooling to contribute to the economic well-being of both the country and its citizens.

While occupational preparation is important, I would never want to be interpreted as saying that it is all-important. One damaging consequence, throughout this century, of the increasingly occupational role of educational institutions is the great neglect of their earlier purposes: the political preparation of the citizenry, and the moral and intellectual development of broadly educated adults. These purposes live on, of course, and commission reports and reformers resurrect them from time to time. They usually aren't taken very seriously by students, particularly the ones who come to community colleges, often desperate to find a "way into the world," a route into well-paid, stable, fulfilling careers. But their interests will not be well served in the long run by narrowly constructed occupational programs. So I argue throughout this book for conceptions of occupational programs that are relatively broad, that encompass the "academic" and higher-order capacities increasingly necessary in the work world as well as the worlds of politics and community, that integrate occupational and academic capacities, and that pay attention to the personal capacities necessary to "get into the world."

The operations of the sub-baccalaureate labor market therefore affect a number of distinctly different participants: students, employers, education and training programs, and policy makers. But the interests of those groups affected by the sub-baccalaureate labor market are potentially quite different. The concern of students with gaining access to occupations with substantial earning power, stability, and future prospects is not necessarily the same as the concern of employers with obtaining skilled and reliable employees at low cost. Educational institutions are interested in strong reputations and in expansion, of course; they can earn their reputations by serving their students and employers well, but they can also survive through puffery and obfuscation, at least in a world where information about effectiveness is scarce. And policy makers are presumably concerned with serving their constituents well, including both students (or parents) and employers; but they too have independent interests and may be led by ideology or crude interest-group politics to make unwise decisions. In part, then, the task of this book is to clarify the options for various participants in this segment of the education system and the labor market, and to suggest how their interests can best be reconciled.

This book should be of use to everyone involved in the education and training of workers in the middle, both in business and educational settings. Indeed, improving the preparation of this critical workforce requires collaboration between those in both environments. Human resource professionals will find in this book strong evidence that building links with community colleges and other occupational or vocational institutes is the best way to develop technical and intellectual skills for mid-skilled jobs. Educational leaders in postsecondary institutions will gain a clearer understanding of a population of learners about whom they currently know very little; they will also find some powerful recommendations for implementing educational programs tailored to the needs of these learners and to the wider business and industrial environment.

Because the book contains important new data on the educational backgrounds and needs of a neglected segment of the American workforce, both educational researchers and specialists in labor policy will find the book useful for their own investigations and analyses. Academics in fields as diverse as economics, sociology, education, and political science will gain insights about the interaction between labor markets and education and training institutions. I intend this book, therefore, to be utilized in many quarters to build a much-needed network of development and support for a population of learners whose competence is critical to economic prosperity in the years ahead.

Overview of the Contents

Despite the importance of the sub-baccalaureate labor force, there has been relatively little analysis of how it operates, and the debates over such educational institutions as community colleges have often been ideological rather than empirical. The purpose of this volume, then, is to begin the task of *investigating*, rather than *assuming*, the nature of the sub-baccalaureate labor market and its implications for students, educational institutions like community colleges, and public policy.

In Chapter One I clarify the importance of the sub-baccalaureate labor market to the American economy. Using information from employers and educators in four local labor markets, I then examine the distinctive characteristics of these employment opportunities, including how they differ from both the unskilled labor market for high school dropouts and the professional and managerial labor market. These results clarify several characteristics having important implications: the local nature of the sub-baccalaureate labor market, the skills that employers value, the dominance of experience over formal schooling in hiring, and the varied ways education and training influence hiring and promotion.

In Chapter Two, I examine the different routes into the sub-baccalaureate labor market. Some individuals in this niche are high school graduates who elect not to continue in postsecondary education. Some enter two-year colleges and either complete their credentials or leave without credentials but with widely varying amounts of education. Others, surely the most disappointed in their aspirations, enter four-year colleges but drop out without completing a baccalaureate. Smaller numbers enter through area vocational schools, proprietary schools, and job training programs. The first part of the chapter describes these different groups, to clarify the importance of two-year colleges in preparing individuals for the sub-baccalaureate labor market. I then examine the debates about the role of community colleges within postsecondary education, particularly the charge that they "cool out" students who might otherwise have attended four-year colleges. Relying in part on interviews with students, I describe the variety of purposes held and decisions made among students in community colleges. This helps clarify the reasons for high rates of noncompletion, as well as the sense in which community colleges are occupational institutions for large numbers of students trying to find an appropriate career.

In Chapter Three I present the available data on the economic effects of sub-baccalaureate education, to see what happens in employment to those students described in the preceding chapter. These statistical results indicate that individuals who complete credentials benefit substantially, at least under the right conditions, though they also clarify that many individuals attending postsecondary education fail to benefit at all. These findings then help to shape the recommendations for improvement in Chapters Five and Six and the implications for public policy in Chapter Seven.

Chapter Four shifts attention away from educational institutions to the shorter-term job training programs that have proliferated since the early 1960s. While these programs are usually distinguished from educational institutions, they are (like community colleges) second-chance institutions preparing individuals for many of the same sub-baccalaureate occupations. Yet their economic benefits are generally small and temporary, and so they are largely ineffective in lifting individuals out of poverty, or allowing them to leave the welfare rolls, or gaining them access to careers with long-run prospects for advancement. To remedy this outcome, the chapter provides a vision of linking job training and education programs in "ladders" of increasing skill levels, using the community college as a crucial junction between the current training system and the education system. This approach provides a way of creating a coherent "system" of education and training for the sub-baccalaureate labor market from the current confusion of unrelated and incomplete efforts.

Chapter Five clarifies the implications of these labor markets for the instructional content of two-year colleges. Given the emphasis of employers on higher-order competencies, narrowly defined vocational programs are unlikely to provide the skills necessary for individuals to prosper over the long run. Therefore methods of enhancing the content of community college programs are necessary, including integrating academic and occupational education, strengthening remedial instruction, creating learning communities to accomplish these and other purposes, and generally reinforcing instructional missions.

Chapter Six turns to the organizational structure of community colleges and how they might strengthen their connections with employers to provide greater employment possibilities to their students. While community colleges have practices that potentially link them to employers, many of the practices need to be improved. This chapter describes the problems and possible solutions in a variety of such mechanisms: advisory committees, placement offices, placement by occupational instructors, student follow-up and tracking mechanisms, contract education, responsiveness to student demand, and licensing requirements. Given the special importance of experience in the sub-baccalaureate labor market, I outline the powerful advantages of work experience and co-op programs and illustrate the discussion with information on co-op programs in Cincinnati.

In Chapter Seven, I turn to public policies. Currently, policies related to sub-baccalaureate education tend to fall through the cracks, particularly at the federal level: community colleges and technical institutes receive little funding and scant attention from the most important federal policy toward postsecondary education, the student aid system. They also receive relatively little of the direct funding for the programs—for example, for vocational education, compensatory education, and bilingual education—that dominate K–12 federal policy, and so again there are few mechanisms that would allow policy makers to improve community colleges. Many states have only weak state policies, generally leaving community colleges to be governed by local boards and local concerns; the practice often thwarts the ability of states to improve the quality of local programs. Finally, at the local level, community colleges have often been more concerned with their "collegiate" role, the academic side with its transfer function, than with the occupational side. The preparation of the sub-baccalaureate labor force has therefore been neglected at all three levels of governance. In this chapter I examine areas in which federal, state, and local institutional policy could be strengthened, in ways that would improve the effectiveness of two-year institutions without impeding their abilities to conform to local economic conditions.

Finally, Chapter Eight examines the thorny question of the labor market's future. Forecasting has always been riddled with errors, of course, and the direction of labor markets and the institutions that educate students for them cannot possibly be known with any certainty. But it is important to avoid certain kinds of extremism. For example, the forecast of the SCANS Commission (the Secretary's Commission on Achieving Necessary Skills of the U.S. Department of Labor) and others that this country is moving toward high-skilled flexible production is contradicted by evidence of other employment patterns, including the continued growth of low-skilled employment and of temporary or "contingent" work. In addition, it is crucial to understand trends in the kinds of students entering postsecondary education; and institutions themselves have been changing, sometimes in ways that limit their effectiveness. This chapter therefore considers trends in students and in institutional structure, as well as in the nature of labor markets, so as to clarify some alternative futures.

Throughout this book I offer a number of recommendations. They fall roughly into three groups, defined by their role in the market arrangement whereby two-year colleges (and, secondarily, job training programs) prepare individuals for the sub-baccalaureate labor market, employment practices create demand, and the market links demand with supply. The three kinds of recommendations include the following:

1.   A large number of recommendations involve ways that community colleges and technical institutes (and, in Chapter Four, job training programs) can improve the preparation they provide their students. In particular, community colleges pride themselves on being nontraditional institutions for nontraditional students; but like all institutions they are the heirs of educational practices developed for another time, and they often act as traditional educational institutions despite having nontraditional students and facing a changing world of employment. A number of recommendations are therefore intended to help two-year colleges become a very different kind of educational institution; see in particular the recommendations in Chapter Five on new approaches to instruction, Chapter Six on linkages to employers, and Chapter Seven on state and local policies for two-year colleges.

2.   The dominant approach to education and training in this country is a market-driven system, in which individuals negotiate the complex of education and training offerings and find their own ways into a shifting and chaotic labor market. (In contrast, the

countries we often admire—especially Germany with its apprenticeship system—tend to have more institutionalized and less market-driven systems, where the occupations themselves and occupational preparation are more rigidly structured by organizations of employers, labor representatives, and educators, as shown by Soskice, 1994.) But because markets don't necessarily operate very efficiently, a number of my recommendations are intended to improve the operation of these markets. For example, we could increase the information available to all participants, improve the relationships between educational providers and employers, and enhance the two-year colleges' responsiveness to labor market conditions and employment opportunities (see especially Chapter Six).

3. Institutionalizing a system of education and training is tempting, although it would require changes in employment practices that are difficult to carry out in this country. In Chapter Seven on public policies, I acknowledge the political limits on intervening directly into employment practices. However, a few recommendations—including those related to skill standards, work-based learning and co-operative education, and organizing small employers—represent small steps toward a more institutional system, with employment practices that are better organized or codified (just as many medical occupations now are).

In the end, the long-lived faith of Americans in the economic power of schooling can be realized only if certain outcomes are consistent among students, educational providers, and employers. If the economic benefits to further education are insubstantial or short-lived, then potential students will not reliably continue in postsecondary education, at least not in a society that stresses economic advancement over such noneconomic goals as political participation or cultural enjoyment. If employers do not benefit from hiring individuals with higher education levels, then they will stress other characteristics in their hiring practices and will not support local education providers; indeed, this appears to be the case within many sub-baccalaureate labor markets. And if educational providers cannot serve both employers and students, if they are rigid and unresponsive to the two groups that they serve as intermediaries, then over time they will become irrelevant and wither away, replaced by other forms of preparation such as firm-based training, short-term job training, or proprietary schools. The challenge, then, is to create this consistency, recognizing the mutual benefit in moving toward a future where greater certainty about effectiveness displaces a simple-minded faith in education.

Berkeley, California   W. Norton Grubb
May 1996

Acknowledgments

In the course of doing research for this book, I have piled up enormous debts. Much of the research has been supported by the National Center for Research in Vocational Education, of the University of California, Berkeley, through grants from the Office of Vocational and Adult Education of the U.S. Department of Education. The conventional disclaimer is appropriate, of course: the views expressed in this volume are not necessarily shared by others in the National Center or the U.S. Department of Education.

My research has involved time-consuming investigation of practices across the country; it has necessarily been highly collaborative, and I owe a great debt to all my colleagues. Much of the research on the nature of the sub-baccalaureate labor market was conducted with Torry Dickinson, Lorraine Giordano, and Gail Kaplan. A return visit to Cincinnati, to probe the interesting co-op programs there, was carried out by Jennifer Curry Villeneuve; parallel investigation of the exemplary co-op program at LaGuardia Community College was carried out by Norena Badway. (Both of these activities were supported by the Office of Technology Assessment of the U.S. Congress.) The examination of exemplary programs that integrate academic and vocational education was done first with Eileen Kraskouskas and subsequently with Norena Badway; both have contributed enormously to my thinking about innovations in community colleges.

For reasons now clouded in history, I became responsible for the National Center's investigations into the interactions among vocational education, job training, welfare-to-work, and adult education. My collaborators on these projects included Cynthia Brown, Phil Kaufman, John Lederer, and Denise Bradby. Judy Kalman, Marisa Castellanos, Cynthia Brown, and Denise Bradby carried out the fieldwork necessary to understand the role of remedial programs within vocational education and job training, and Judy Kalman was especially helpful in shaping my understanding of pedagogy. Lorraine McDonnell of the University of California, Santa Barbara, and I collaborated on several monographs and articles examining the overall shape of the education and job training "system"; in the fieldwork for these projects we were immeasurably helped by Liz Alpert, John Lederer, and Patricia Damiano. Much of this work has found its way into Chapter Four, on the job training system. My understanding of the job training system was also informed by a monograph commissioned by the International Labor Office in Geneva, for which I thank J. Gaude; this work is also being published by the Russell Sage Foundation. The interviews with community college students, summarized in Chapter Two, proved to be unexpectedly enlightening; Kathy Reeves headed this project, ably assisted by Ara Meha and Susan Newman.

At several points in this volume I refer to a study of teaching practices in community colleges and technical institutes, conducted during 1993–1995; my collaborators on this project included Chet Case, Stan Goto, Elnora Webb, Helena Worthen, and Jennifer Curry Villeneuve. I have mentioned a number of conclusions from this study, although we will begin writing up these results only in 1996.

In all these studies, however, the most critical and the least recognized contributors have been the hundreds of instructors, students, administrators, business representatives, and policy makers who gave freely of their time and insights. Almost uniformly, they were open about their institutions and practices, and their voices make up what I feel is the most important aspect of this volume. In many cases they have been able to comment on early drafts incorporating their contributions; I can only hope that I have gotten them right.

Some chapters in this volume rely on statistical analyses of complex data sets. For her patient programming of the NLS72 data, I thank Ellen Liebman; for his care with the SIPP data, I thank Bill Ponicki. Lew Oleinick analyzed the Current Population Survey data presented in several places (an extension of my earlier work with the CPS, carried out with Bob Wilson of the University of Texas at Austin), ably assisted by the programming of Starling Pullam. Various individuals at MPR Associates in Berkeley have been generous with their own data analyses and interpretations, especially John Tuma, Laura Horn, Bob Fitzgerald, Sonja Geis, and Alex McCormick.

Throughout the writing of this book, Marjorie Lovejoy and Anne Whitacre were patient and careful with many revisions, and I thank them for putting up with my fits of anxiousness. Brian Frazier and Kevin Adams were unfailingly helpful in tracking down source materials of all kinds.

I want to give special thanks to Gale Erlandson of Jossey-Bass Publishers; she saw the potential in an early outline (of a work intended for economists) for a volume addressed instead to educators and policy makers. In the process, she spurred me to write a more coherent book that includes more of my recent research on community colleges. I also want to thank a number of individuals who were helpful in commenting on early drafts of this volume, especially Arthur Cohen, Jim Jacobs, Paul Osterman, and two anonymous referees for Jossey-Bass whose comments were especially insightful.

Finally, I thank those people and places that have been sources of inspiration and comfort: my beloved wife Erica, SWMBO; my wonderful children, Hilary and Alex; visual artists and print-makers from many times, especially Helen Frankenthaler, Robert Motherwell, and Ellsworth Kelly; the weavers of many cultures who have labored more anonymously, above all those of the Navajo, the Asante, and the Bushong; and the beautiful places of the world, especially Point Reyes, the Sierra Nevada, the Rockies, the ancient rocks of the earth that care not a bit for the passing affairs of us mortals.

W. N. G.

The Author

W. Norton Grubb is a professor at the School of Education at the University of California, Berkeley, where he is part of the division of Policy, Organization, Measurement, and Evaluation. Prior to joining the Berkeley faculty in 1987, he taught at the LBJ School of Public Affairs at the University of Texas, Austin. He received both his B.A. (1969) and his Ph.D. (1975) degrees in economics from Harvard University.

Grubb was a founding member of the National Center for Research in Vocational Education at the University of California, Berkeley, which has supported a great deal of his recent research. He is one of the site directors for the Center, where his particular interests include the integration of academic and vocational education, postsecondary occupational education, and the nature of the "system" of occupational education and job training. Through the Center he has worked extensively with both secondary and postsecondary instructors and administrators on various reforms applicable to occupational education.

Grubb has published extensively on a variety of topics in the economics of education, public finance, educational issues, and social policy. Most recently, he edited a two-volume work on the integration of academic and vocational education titled *Education Through Occupations in American High Schools* (1995), and he authored a book on job training programs and their possible integration with education programs, titled *Learning to Work: The Case for Re-integrating Education and Job Training* (1996).

His current teaching and research interests include the economics of education, particularly the role of schooling and training in labor markets; the flow of students into and through postsecondary education; the nature of teaching and the effects of policy and other social forces on pedagogy; and social policy toward children and youth. He is currently at work on books about teaching in community colleges and about the relationship between employment and formal schooling.

Chapter One

Distinctive Characteristics of the Mid-Skilled Labor Market

Labor markets are critical because they shape the work opportunities available, but they are also abstractions that many individuals do not understand. Many of those who participate in the sub-baccalaureate labor market seem mystified by its operations. Employers, whose hiring practices help define this segment of the larger labor market, are bewildered by the variety of education and training providers; they have often complained about the quality of potential employees they consider. Many of the students seeking to enter employment are poorly informed. They face a greater variety of options, from short-term job training programs to community colleges and four-year colleges, but they generally lack the information about employment consequences necessary to sort through these options. For many students, the image of the well-informed consumer (so crucial to the efficiency of market mechanisms) is inconsistent with reality. And educational institutions, the crucial intermediaries between students and employers, often lack the information necessary to play this role well or to provide the kinds of skills that would improve the employment prospects of individuals and the productivity of the labor force. As we see in this chapter and in Chapter Six, many community colleges and technical institutes, and some of the faculty who teach in them, are uninformed about local labor market conditions and poorly connected to the local employer community.

In the resulting situation, information is inadequate for rational decisions by students, employers, educational institutions, and policy makers who can influence some (but not all) of these practices. The great need, therefore, is better information about how sub-baccalaureate labor markets operate. In this chapter, I first present evidence based on national statistics to clarify the dimensions of sub-baccalaureate employment. However, such statistics provide little sense of exactly *how* sub-baccalaureate education is used by employers, or *why* higher levels of schooling lead to higher earnings. For this kind of information, I rely on interviews with employers and education providers—qualitative evidence that provides better information about how jobs are organized in the sub-baccalaureate labor market, the skills that employers are looking for, and the use they make (or fail to make) of credentials from postsecondary institutions. The evidence from statistics and interviews combined gives a better sense of precisely how formal schooling leads to employment—and by extension, how educational providers could improve their programs to enhance the employability of their students.

The Importance of the Sub-Baccalaureate Labor Market

Why should anyone care about the sub-baccalaureate labor market? In the first place, the sub-baccalaureate labor market is a large and rapidly growing part of the labor force. Individuals with some college education but less than a baccalaureate degree represented 13.1 percent of the labor force in 1967 but 28.3 percent in 1992 (as summarized in Table 1.1). Those with high school diplomas alone constituted 34.2 percent of the labor force in 1992. Thus the sub-baccalaureate labor market as I define it—*those individuals who have at least a high school diploma but not a baccalaureate degree, individuals who may or may not have some college education*—includes about three-fifths of all workers. An increasing proportion of this group has "some college," either a sub-baccalaureate credential such as an associate degree or certificate, or postsecondary attendance without completing any credentials. In contrast, those with baccalaureate and graduate degrees increased from 11.6 percent of the labor force to 23.7 percent over this period. That is a higher rate of increase, but this group remains only a third the size of the sub-baccalaureate group, and smaller even than the group with "some college."

The occupations in the sub-baccalaureate labor market cover a wide variety of mid-skilled occupations. As the figures in Table 1.2

Table 1.1. Trends in the Labor Market, 1967–1992.

	1967	1972	1977	1982	1987	1990	1992
Percentage of the labor force:							
Less than high school	39.0	31.2	25.6	19.5	17.3	15.5	13.8
High school diploma	36.3	39.6	39.8	40.5	40.0	39.4	34.2
Some college	13.1	15.5	18.0	19.8	20.8	22.1	28.3
College graduate	11.6	13.7	16.6	20.2	21.8	23.0	23.7
Earnings ratios: males							
Baccalaureate/high school	1.439	1.472	1.476	1.577	1.630	1.717	1.713
Some college/high school	.972	.772	1.010	1.049	1.109	1.160	1.112
High school dropout/high school	.760	.735	.680	.656	.639	.619	.582
Earnings ratios: females							
Baccalaureate/high school	1.541	1.496	1.411	1.445	1.591	1.686	1.683
Some college/high school	.985	.971	1.039	1.076	1.163	1.156	1.131
High school dropout/high school	.694	.680	.651	.620	.590	.606	.583

Source: Current Population Survey data analyzed in Grubb and Wilson (1992), updated.

indicate, in 1990 about one-third of individuals with associate degrees, one-quarter of those with vocational certificates, and one-fifth of those with some college but no credential were managers and professionals. These are the middle- and lower-level managers, the administrative assistants, the claims adjusters and financial analysts of the business world; nurses with associate degrees, radiological technicians, and a variety of other medical and dental technicians; and child care workers, teachers' aides, and some social welfare workers. The sub-baccalaureate labor force includes the largest proportion of technicians—like electronics technicians, computer technicians, drafters and engineering technicians—as well as the mechanics and electricians whose jobs have been upgraded through computer technology, and the machinists who now work with numerically controlled cutting and forming equipment. A large fraction of the sub-baccalaureate labor force is in sales and clerical positions, embracing purchasing agents, accounting department supervisors, and higher-level administrative assistants, along with large numbers who are in more routine positions such as data entry clerks, secretaries, and bookkeepers.

Smaller numbers of sub-baccalaureate workers are in service occupations, for example, cosmetologists, bank tellers, and restaurant workers; such positions, along with machine operators, transportation workers like bus drivers, and laborers, are more likely to be held by high school drop-outs.

Of course, the boundaries of this labor market are somewhat fuzzy since some individuals with B.A. degrees can be found working alongside those with associate degrees and certificates, and others with considerable amounts of college can be found in unskilled positions otherwise filled by those not having high school diplomas. In the main, however, the occupations held by people with at least a high school diploma or differing amounts of college require a middling level of skill. In part by dint of numbers, in part by the nature of their work, they constitute the critical core of the economy, even if they do not direct it.

Furthermore, many occupations in the sub-baccalaureate labor market are projected to continue growing. The occupations with the highest growth rates between now and 2005 include health technicians; technicians and related support occupations; marketing and sales occupations; and some administrative support occupations, including computer operators. All of these typically

Table 1.2. Occupations and Employment by Levels of Education, 1990.

Occupation	Ph.D.	Prof.	M.A.	B.A.	Assoc.	Voc. Cert.	Some College	High School	H.S. Dropout
Managerial	15.2%	4.9%	19.3%	20.0%	16.0%	8.2%	12.9%	8.0%	2.8%
Professional	69.6	82.7	64.4	40.6	18.9	19.8	7.1	3.6	0.7
Technical	8.7	3.7	2.2	5.5	7.9	10.9	3.8	2.2	0.9
Sales/clerical	6.5	4.9	11.7	25.7	40.4	38.5	53.0	49.5	10.6
Service	0	3.7	1.9	5.9	12.0	16.7	16.3	20.9	40.5
Mechanic/repairer/ precision production	0	0	0.3	0.7	1.2	1.4	1.4	3.0	3.5
Machine operator	0	0	0.2	0.6	1.9	3.1	2.8	8.3	20.4
Other[a]	0	0	0	1.0	1.7	1.4	2.3	4.3	7.3

[a]The "other" category includes laborers; farm, forestry, and fishery workers; construction workers; and transportation workers.

Totals do not sum to 100 percent because of round-off error and omission of the armed forces.

Source: Survey of Income and Program Participation, 1990. The SIPP is conducted by the U.S. Bureau of the Census.

require some education beyond high school but less than a baccalaureate degree (Silvestri 1993, Tables 1 and 2).[1] Many of the recent commission reports concerned with the state of education in the United States have repeated this convention; for example, *America's Choice: High Skills or Low Wages!* stated that "more than 70 percent of the jobs in America will not require a [four-year] college education by the year 2000. These jobs are the backbone of our economy, and the productivity of our workers in these jobs will make or break our economic future" (Commission on the Skills of the American Workforce, CSAW, 1990, p. 3).

As part of the report's program to promote a high-skills economy, it went on to recommend a system of technical and professional certificates and associate degrees "for the majority of our students and adult workers who do not pursue a baccalaureate degree" (CSAW, 1990, p. 77). Even if occupational forecasting is a risky business, the educational level of the labor force is almost certain to continue increasing; much of the growth will take place at the sub-baccalaureate level.

Another way to see the importance of the mid-skilled group is to look at trends in relative wages, since in conventional economic analysis changes in relative wages signal patterns of demand. Among men, those with "some college" earned 3 percent *less* than men with a high school diploma in 1967, indicating that employers were then unwilling to pay any premium for whatever knowledge or skills these individuals had (see Table 1.1, row 6). By 1982, those with some college earned 4.9 percent more, a trivial difference but one that increased to 10.9 percent in 1987 and to 16 percent by 1990. Among women, those with "some college" also earned about the same as did high school graduates in the late 1960s and early 1970s; but by 1982, they earned 7.6 percent more, increasing during the 1980s to 16.3 percent in 1987. Similarly, the premium for completing high school has increased substantially, leaving high school dropouts further and further behind. In 1967 male dropouts earned 76 percent of what those with a high school diploma did, falling to 58 percent in 1992. The situation was also dismal among women high school dropouts, who earned 69 percent of high school graduates in 1967 but the same 58 percent in 1992. Evidently, the demand for the skills of individuals in the sub-baccalaureate labor market—both individuals with a high school

diploma, and those with some college but less than a baccalaureate degree—has been growing substantially over the past twenty-
five years, with employers increasingly willing to pay a premium for
the skills associated with more formal schooling.

By various measures, then, the sub-baccalaureate labor market
is large and growing. It is likely to continue growing, as part of the
process of upgrading the education and skill levels of the labor
force throughout this century, and as many of the jobs transformed
in the shift to a high-skills economy require some technical training past high school but less than a baccalaureate degree. The sub-
baccalaureate labor market may be large and varied, and for these
reasons difficult to understand; but for the same reasons it is crucial to analyze its implications for students, the providers of education and training, and public policy.

Studying Local Labor Markets

Despite the size and growth of the sub-baccalaureate labor market, there has been a surprising lack of attention to it. While the
benefits of college-going—almost always defined as attaining a
baccalaureate degree—are well known (for example, Leslie and
Brinkman, 1988; Pascarella and Terenzini, 1991), information
about the effects of sub-baccalaureate education has been sparse,
in part because the data used to analyze education and employment usually lumps the sub-baccalaureate education into the crude
category of "some college." The data presented in Chapter Three
helps remedy this lack of information.

Furthermore, there has been little investigation of how sub-
baccalaureate labor markets operate and what employers require
of their employees and their new hires. An older literature in labor
economics examined issues of this kind by interviewing employers
directly. As examples, Gordon and Thal-Larsen (1969) documented
the kinds of informal and subjective hiring standards among
employers in the San Francisco area that I report in this chapter,
and Diamond and Bedrosian (1970) came to many of the same conclusions for employers in New York and St. Louis. More recently,
Wial (1991) interviewed employees and determined that informal
neighborhood networks—and certainly not formal hiring procedures or school-linked programs—were crucial in gaining access to

primary-sector employment. But this kind of examination has fallen out of favor in economics, replaced by elegant theorizing and complex number crunching. Sociologists have continued to examine the nature of labor markets with interviews and case studies, but they have been largely concerned with the process of how occupations become professionalized and how skills are changing, not in the nature of the relationship between education and employers. Thus there is virtually no analysis of sub-baccalaureate labor markets comparable to that available for professionals and managers.

In the absence of reliable information, discussions about employment have relied on commission reports and rhetoric of uncertain reliability. For example, the report of the (federal labor) Secretary's Commission on Achieving Necessary Skills, *What Work Requires of Schools* (SCANS, 1991) captured the nation's imagination by posing a world in which companies reorganize themselves into more flexible production requiring not only basic academic skills (reading, writing, math, listening, and speaking) but also thinking skills (decision making, problem solving, knowing how to learn) as well as the personal qualities necessary at work (responsibility, sociability, self-management, integrity, and honesty). Similarly, *America's Choice: High Skills or Low Wages!* posed the choices starkly, with the Commission on the Skills of the American Workplace again spurring many to call for an educational upgrading of the labor force. Community college administrators have also repeated these perspectives, for example in the report of the Commission on the Future of Community Colleges, *Building Communities* (1988), and a joint report of community college and occupational educators, *Productive America* (1990). But none of these reports provided much evidence about the extent of transformation; for example the CSAW provided no evidence at all for its assertion that 5 percent of employment was in flexible work organizations. Although there proves to be considerably more employment affected by work reorganization than CSAW estimated, such changes do not necessarily affect the hiring from sub-baccalaureate institutions, as I clarify in this chapter. And the future of employment is much less certain and more varied than SCANS, or *America's Choice,* or any other popular manifesto recognizes, as I argue in Chapter Eight. As a result, there have been few reliable guides for students, educational institutions, or policy makers.

To learn more, my colleagues and I carried out interviews with employers and with community college administrators and instructors in four local labor markets, chosen to reflect variation in the kinds of jobs available:

- Fresno is a small city of about 350,000 people in a rich farming region; while agriculture services and processing form the core of its employment, it has been diversifying into services and light manufacturing.
- San Jose, a city of about 750,000 within an area (including Silicon Valley) of 1.5 million, has concentrated on computer and other high-tech development and manufacturing.
- Sacramento, a rapidly growing city within an area of almost 1.5 million, has diversified from government and services into high-tech and light manufacturing.
- Cincinnati, a city of about 350,000 within an area of 1.5 million people, has a substantial amount of manufacturing, although its diversification into such sectors as consumer goods helped it weather the recession of 1990–1992.

While each area has concentrated in certain sectors, all four include large numbers of the jobs that typify the sub-baccalaureate labor market: secretarial and other business support staff, technicians, various health occupations, wholesale and retail sales workers, and the like. The choice of any four communities is of course arbitrary, but the four we examined provide substantial variety and seem reasonably typical. Surely other local labor markets could vary considerably from the ones we studied; therefore *there is no substitute for educational institutions conducting their own surveys of hiring practices in their own labor markets.*

Within these four communities, we chose six specific groupings of occupations to examine:

Electronics technicians

Machinists

Drafters

Accountants

Computer-related occupations, including programmers

Business occupations

These six can be aligned in numerous groupings. They include several occupations that have been part of vocational education virtually from its inception (machinist, drafter, and business occupations) and several that are relatively new (electronics technician and computer-related occupations); several that predominate in manufacturing (electronics technician, drafter, and machinist), susceptible to the general decline in manufacturing in this country, and several that are not especially allied with manufacturing (accountant, business occupations, and computer-related occupations); several that are highly gender-segregated (electronics technician, drafter, machinist, and certain business occupations), and several that are more integrated (accountants and computer-related occupations). With the possible exception of business occupations, each area requires certain specialized knowledge and therefore is appropriately included in a study of mid-skilled labor markets.[2]

However, job titles at the sub-baccalaureate level may be quite ambiguous. Programs carrying the label *electronics* vary widely, with some short-term job training programs teaching soldering for assembly-line work while two-year associate programs prepare highly autonomous technicians. Some machinist programs teach the use of only one or two machines for repetitive assembly-line work and do not train skilled machinists or tool-and-die makers. Independent accountants and CPAs almost always have baccalaureate degrees, so community college programs often train clerical workers or data-entry clerks in working with accounting and spreadsheet programs (with the result that these workers are sometimes referred to as "para-accountants"). Similarly, most computer programmers now have baccalaureate degrees, so the extensive offerings in community colleges are usually for computer applications required in other positions; in this field (as in accounting), some instructors stress that transfer to a four-year college is necessary for professional-level employment. And while virtually every community college has extensive offerings in business, their relationship to the jobs available is unclear because it is commonly held that "business management is too general." As a personnel supervisor in Cincinnati commented in our interviews, "The PC has decimated the middle-management rank, whose sole purpose was to supervise ten or fifteen clerks. That job doesn't exist anymore. . . . So I don't know what someone with an associate's degree in business management would do with it."

Because of such ambiguity, community colleges often prepare individuals for lower-level occupations than students might imagine, or educate them for occupations where employers do not typically hire directly from educational institutions. The result is often a mismatch between the titles of educational programs and the realities of the sub-baccalaureate labor market.

In each of the four cities, we chose to interview a cross-section of employers having relatively large representations of the six occupations selected. We also interviewed administrators in local community colleges, technical institutes, and more specialized vocational training institutions; several instructors in the six occupational areas; and a very few individuals with a broad overview of the local labor market. In all, we interviewed seventy-five educators in nineteen institutions, 164 employers in 124 companies, and eleven general respondents.

The dearth of individuals with a broad overview of local economies highlights a problem with studying labor markets. Markets are, in many ways, abstractions. They result from the interactions of many demanders (employers, in this case) and many suppliers (educational institutions and their students), but each participant experiences only a small part of the market and can therefore reliably describe only a piece of it. Most employers and educators do not think of themselves as operating in markets; instead they describe their experiences as specific transactions— hiring an individual, finding a particular job, placing students with a specific company—isolated from other participants in the market. To describe an entire labor market, it is necessary to synthesize the responses of many participants, each with an incomplete picture of the market. Fortunately, given the volume of information from the employers and educators we interviewed, the results settled into fairly obvious patterns.

The Local Nature of Sub-Baccalaureate Labor Markets

The sub-baccalaureate labor market is almost entirely local. In their search for employees, firms generally advertise locally; if they establish relations with any educational providers, they do so with community colleges or area vocational schools within the same community. Two-year colleges target local employers as well, and deans and instructors report that their students search for employment almost exclusively within the local community. In contrast, employers routinely search regionally and nationally for their upper-level professional and managerial positions, and individuals with baccalaureate degrees are much more mobile (for job-related reasons) than are less well-educated individuals.[3]

We found only a few exceptions to the local pattern of sub-baccalaureate labor markets. One appeared in cases of highly specialized skills. For example, one company that produces lasers in the Silicon Valley area hires most of its workers from a community college in Iowa and from a technical institute in Texas, both of which provided virtually firm-specific instruction. In a very few cases (3 out of 124 employers, all 3 relatively large), employers have established good working relations with distant community colleges, each for idiosyncratic reasons. In addition, two employers hire consistently from particular proprietary institutions that have stable reputations and strong relationships with numerous employers. (Note that these were virtually the only two positive mentions of proprietary schools; other references to them by employers were generally negative, citing their short period of training and the lack of hands-on experience.)

Local educational decisions sometimes force employers to search further for their new hires. For example, when electronics programs in the Silicon Valley area closed because of the lack of demand during the recession, one employer searched in Sacramento for technicians. Employers also advertise more widely during periods of expansion and shortages of qualified workers, so the geographic span of sub-baccalaureate labor markets varies with the business cycle. However, these are clearly exceptions; for most occupations, most employers, and most educational providers, the sub-baccalaureate labor market is a local phenomenon.

One consequence is that shortages in specific occupations can persist because it is difficult for wage mechanisms to lure trained workers from other areas. For example, because of its agricultural base and relative dearth of manufacturing, Fresno lacks a substantial pool of production workers, including skilled machinists and repairmen; since it is difficult to induce such individuals to move from other areas and the intermittent employment in manufacturing provides little incentive for developing local programs, the shortage persists. More generally, in the transitions of the national economy—for example, as population has moved out of rural areas, as manufacturing in the Midwest and Northeast has given way to high-tech sectors in the west and south—spatial adjustments are slower because of the local nature of these markets, and local shortages and surpluses persist longer.

For my purpose, however, the most important consequence for students is that finding a job locally that is related to one's field of education is important to realizing the economic benefits from one's sub-baccalaureate education. An individual who does not find such a position locally is unlikely to look in other regions, and conversely employers are less likely to recognize credentials from distant community colleges. In turn, this places a premium on the mechanisms that connect local institutions to local employers. That is the subject of Chapter Six.

The Informality of Employment Policies

Employment practices for sub-baccalaureate positions are quite informal. Employment policies are rarely written down, and hiring procedures are quite casual. In most cases, these involve interviews, often by teams of production workers and particularly in companies that are self-consciously trying to make their production workers more responsible. This particular format is a way of determining the "entire profile of the individual," including communications skills, responsibility, and other aspects of personality; as a director of electronics technicians for a semiconductor firm remarked about the interview procedure, "We kind of have the department vote as to whether the person looks like they fit in." A few employers give informal or truncated performance tests, for example, reading mechanical drawings and assembling a few parts, or examining circuit boards with known defects, or requiring applicant electronics technicians to take a thirteen-item test on digital technology. But very few employers devise formal or complex hiring procedures for these sub-baccalaureate jobs. While small size may in some cases explain the lack of formal job tests, even relatively large companies lack formalized employment-related tests, partly because of fear (or simply ignorance) about the legality of such tests.[4]

Several aspects of these occupations contribute to this informality: cyclical variation in employment, the dominance of small employers in initial hiring, and changes in technology and organization. For students and educational institutions, the most important consequence is that the nature of jobs, careers, and the competencies necessary for employment and mobility are difficult to understand, contributing to the difficulties in moving from education to employment.

Cyclical Variation in Employment

Hiring in the sub-baccalaureate labor market is strongly cyclical, increasing during boom times but decreasing to the vanishing point during recessions. Employment is more cyclically sensitive than it is in the market for professionals and managers with advanced degrees, who have greater job security because of their control over production, their greater firm-specific skills,[5] their power over hiring and firing, and the like. A common pattern in the 1990–1992 recession was to lay off less-well-educated workers and substitute better-educated managers and technicians, since less-well-educated workers with less specific training could more easily be hired when economic conditions improve. In addition, many individuals from community colleges find their initial employment in small firms, the ones likely to go out of business during recessions.

The most obvious consequence is simply that intermittent employment increases the variation in earnings and reduces average earnings within the sub-baccalaureate labor market. Also, the incentives for individuals to invest substantially in skills over long periods of time are weaker. This is clearest in the case of machinists: there is a long history of complaints from employers about "shortages" of skilled machinists, and the employers in our sample were no exception. Many mentioned the long period of both formal and on-the-job training necessary to become a skilled machinist or repairman and bemoaned the apparent unwillingness of young people to invest the time necessary. At the same time, employers had laid off many of their machinists in the recent recession and had failed to hire for two or three years. There are, as a result, no economic incentives for individuals to spend long periods of time developing a broad range of machining skills. As the staff director for an employers' association commented, "One of the reasons [for shortages] is that we can't get employers focused that this is a long-range thing—that if you think you need three or four years to go through more sophisticated programs, you've got to have meaningful jobs downstream."

A more subtle consequence of intermittent employment is that hiring standards and procedures are less well codified: procedures developed during periods of hiring are abandoned during recessions and thus constantly being developed anew. Having done little hiring during the recent recession, many employers were vague about their employment standards and hiring procedures simply because there has been no need recently to have such procedures. The notion of a "hiring policy," something that prospective employees (including students in postsecondary institutions) and educational providers can count on, simply does not exist. Consequently there is greater uncertainty about what employers want.

The Dominance of Small Employers and "Small" Institutions

Another characteristic of the sub-baccalaureate labor market is that initial employment is dominated by smaller firms. Individuals leaving community colleges and those trying to find new positions generally find employment in smaller companies at first. Then, because there can be relatively little mobility within small companies, the path upward requires them to move to larger firms with greater opportunities for on-the-job training, specialization, supervisory positions, higher earnings and benefits, and more stable employment.[6] In part, this pattern emerges because larger firms, with their better earnings and working conditions, are able to attract the most applicants and then are able to demand substantial experience from the individuals they hire. As the director of placement for a well-regarded community college in the Silicon Valley area admitted, "I hate to say this, but a lot of the smaller employers like to find students with us and can find students through us because their salaries are not as competitive as, say, IBM's. And they know that we would have students who would be willing to get a job to get the experience at a lower salary."

Another consequence of the dominance by smaller firms is that, again, hiring procedures are highly informal. Small companies lack personnel departments and formalized hiring criteria; they rarely articulate specific requirements for hiring—a particular educational qualification, for example, other than the widespread requirement of a high school diploma—and instead use casual assessments of skill to make their choices. In addition, they hire too few individuals in any one occupation to develop well-established ties with particular providers of education such as local community colleges, or to accumulate information about the strengths and weaknesses of educational providers. Thus the employers who dominate hiring in the sub-baccalaureate labor market are relatively uninformed about the supply of educated labor.

The providers of education and training in the sub-baccalaureate market, too, are "small," but in a somewhat different sense. Even in a community college with substantial enrollment, many students take only a course or two, or take remedial education, English as a Second Language (ESL), or avocational courses. Many are "experimenters," unsure of their plans but using low-cost community colleges to explore various options (Manski, 1989), and even occupationally oriented students may take very few courses, or drop out before completing a program (Grubb, 1989b). Therefore the number of completers in any one occupational area is likely to be quite small, perhaps in the range of ten to twenty per year even for an institution with an enrollment of 25,000. Furthermore, there are typically many potential providers within any community: several community colleges within a reasonable distance, area vocational schools, perhaps some remaining high school programs, a few proprietary schools, and shorter-term job training programs. There is a widespread sense among employers that the job-related education and training system is chaotic and fragmented. A typical comment came from the director of an economic development program:

> It sometimes feels like there are a million different training programs in the area. . . . I've been in this business for seven years, and I still can't tell you who they all are. Between the junior colleges, private nonprofits, CBOs [community-based organizations], K–12 school systems which also operate separate adult schools, and there

seems to be two or three different tracks of vocational training . . .
it's hard to keep track of it. I think it would be difficult to plan what
to train for when it's hard to develop a comprehensive view of
what's out there. I can't keep track of them—and I have a vested
interest in it.

Therefore many employers are unable to assess the strengths and
weaknesses of various educational institutions.

The existence of many small companies and many small
providers of education and training may appear to match the textbook case of a market, with its multiple demanders and suppliers.
In practice, small size thwarts the development of the information
that is necessary for markets to operate efficiently. Each participant
is relatively uninformed about the others because the small size of
the institutions makes it difficult to accumulate information. In most
communities there are no organizations whose business it is to provide information about this labor market; community college placement offices are weak (as Chapter Six describes), and local labor
market information is quite imprecise. The result is a labor market
in which it is relatively difficult for individuals to find their way.

Long-Term Changes in Organization and Occupations

Several interrelated changes that are much discussed in the
debates over the direction of the American economy[7] were unmis-
takably present in the companies we examined, among them
changes in the organization of work and the slow introduction of
new technologies (especially those based on computer applications), with new and old production processes coexisting.

The dominant change in the organization of work has been
the trend toward flatter hierarchies with fewer supervisory layers;
as a consequence, individuals must perform a wider variety of tasks.
As the manager of a medium-sized manufacturer of vending
machines described, "We can't afford to have one person who just
does electronics and one who does all of the others [nonelectronic
machines]. We're a small company, and the whole drive is to be
more flexible. The more flexible you are, the more skills you have.
If you want to find a machinist who can also troubleshoot all the
equipment, it's very difficult."

As a result, older occupational divisions are no longer clear. For example, the distinction between *machinist* and *electronics technician* has begun to blur. With the advent of computer numerically controlled (CNC) machining, individuals who at one point were traditional machinists, skilled on various conventional metalworking equipment such as lathes and drills, now need to know some computer programming and electronics as well. The individuals who serve as repairmen and mechanics now require an ensemble of skills of machinists, electricians, and electronics technicians (to diagnose and repair computer-driven equipment). A personnel director for a glass manufacturer in Fresno commented, "It just seems to be getting much more complicated than just the two-year tech. And maybe they're getting left out because they don't have the other half. I don't see industry as being computer programmers over here and electronics people over there, and if there is an electrical problem or a hardware problem you call the electronics tech and if there is a software problem you call the programmer in. I guess I see those people becoming more and more one person."

An electronics instructor in Sacramento described the skills required of students in the future: "Metallurgy, pneumatics, hydraulics, mechanics, electronics—these are the kinds of things that I see coming together to give the student a broad-based, salable skill. And those are the ones we're going to have to address more. I don't see electronics as being the ultimate: I see it being a portion of everything."

Similarly, the boundaries among various business, accounting, and computer-related occupations have blurred as employees need to know spreadsheet and word processing applications, enough accounting to complete spreadsheets, and the business procedures that a specific firm uses. Furthermore, with greater responsibility, individuals in nontechnical positions (as in the accounting and business occupations) may need to know more about the technical side in order to identify and resolve problems. As the manager of accounting in a high-tech company explained, "As [the firm] changes jobs and we grow [employees] into varying areas, adding additional responsibility, they have to understand a lot more from the business aspect but also from the technical aspect, particularly on the accounting side."

For jobs whose boundaries are expanding, postsecondary vocational programs are often too narrowly defined, since they provide only a subset of the skills required:

> The problem we have is finding a two-year [electronics] tech person who wants to be a grease monkey as well. . . . We have a lot of people come in and want to do the electrical part, and they are these people that have a two-year degree, and they may have been doing electrical tech work at a company that has a little different structure from ours, and that's all they do. . . . But this guy doesn't want to take a motor out; he doesn't want to go to the top of the material elevator and pull a belt up that thing with three other guys and end up dusty from head to toe.

In this firm, the inability to find enough broadly trained individuals led to establishing a training program with a local private vocational school, customized to fit the company's requirements. A similar problem arose in the Sacramento area, where a human resource manager for a large computer manufacturer commented, "Most community colleges seem to train electronics techs for bench tech positions. But jobs [in this company] are very mechanical. A mechanical aptitude is necessary to do electronic work. A lack of mechanical training is a problem with community college training. . . . We also need communications and teamwork. The line techs are middlemen [between production-line workers and managers], and they have to work with production and engineering. They have to present ideas and reports to managers. [At the same time], this is a dirty job; it's not a suit and tie job."

The blurring of occupational boundaries seems especially prevalent in the sub-baccalaureate labor market, for at least two reasons:

1. While large employers can still afford a detailed division of labor, the small and mid-sized employers which dominate the sub-baccalaureate labor market cannot.
2. Small and medium-sized companies have introduced new technologies, especially computer-driven technologies, slowly. Thus production facilities include a hodgepodge of ancient and modern equipment, and many hybrids made by retrofitting traditional machinery with computerized elements.

As one foreman of a cable manufacturer described it, "People who come out of school who've been into the new technology—transistors, PLCs [programmable logic controllers], digitals—I take them over here next to a DC drive, which is one step above tubes, and they don't understand it. American businesses [have to] suffer with what we've got as long as we can make it run. You get out of school, you don't expect to see that because they don't teach you that."

Therefore many operatives and technicians have to be able to work on a range of traditional electromechanical machines and modern computer-based equipment. And they need both the skills of the traditional craftsman—including the ability to cobble together repairs to outmoded equipment with tricks and baling wire—at the same time that they can troubleshoot computerized machines.

The replacement of clearly defined jobs by positions with a wider range of responsibilities places a new premium on workers with numerous skills, including many competencies that are not well-taught in schools. But these changes also generate considerable uncertainty about jobs in the sub-baccalaureate labor market since neat categorization of occupations and clear delineation of skills has been replaced by greater flexibility at work and greater uncertainty about the best ways of preparing for these jobs.

The Skills Employers Want

There has been considerable discussion recently about "the skills employers want." The reports about changing employment and work requirements are numerous, but evidence is thin. Especially given the false alarms about technological change that have been raised in the past, it is appropriate to be skeptical of claims to know what employers want—particularly because small employers and those hiring for sub-baccalaureate positions may differ substantially in the skills they require.

Even so, the employers we interviewed were remarkably consistent in their claims. Although they varied in size, sophistication, and sector, they repeatedly stressed the importance of skills in four distinct areas:

- Job-specific skills
- Basic academic skills
- Motivation and interpersonal skills
- Certain more elusive skills, including aptitude and "common sense"

What is remarkable about this list, however, is that unlike the emphasis in the SCANS report on the ways in which formal schooling can prepare for the high-skilled workplace, most of the competencies required by employers in the sub-baccalaureate labor market *cannot* readily be taught in schools and colleges.

Job-Specific Skills

The dominant skill required by the majority of employers is variously characterized as facility on specific machines or with particular manufacturing processes, familiarity with procedures specific to a given job (for example, accounts receivable or cost accounting), or knowledge of a specific computer program. In other words, it is facility in highly job-specific skills. As an example, the head of a firm in Cincinnati that employs contract drafters described the specificity of different CAD (computer-assisted design) systems: "In any case, you do a certain amount of targeting. I mean, if they ask themselves, 'What do I want to draft?' and if the answer is 'I want to draft aircraft,' then they should see what the GE, the Pratt and Whitney, the Allison, and the McDonnell-Douglas systems are. On the other hand, if you say, 'Well, I want to live in Cincinnati and work on [consumer products],' there's only one answer: AUTOCAD. You've got to know AUTOCAD or you're out of the business. So they need to look and target."

The preparation that educational programs provide was consistently criticized as too general. A manager of electronics technicians for a semiconductor firm complained:

What we'd really like to have that we can never really find is things that are more focused on semiconductor processing. There is no hope of finding somebody out of school who has done anything in plasma processing, or knows what lithography is, or any of the basic diffusion. We actually would have a course for our own technicians where we say, "This is diffusion, impurities diffusion, sifting solids at different rates at different temperatures," and [we] start going through and teaching that; "Here is what plasma etch is, and here is how you create plasma, and here is how you set up electric fields to etch." All that stuff we have to teach on our own because I'm not aware of any college anywhere that we could get qualified students [from].

In some cases, employers acknowledged that school-based programs could not possibly meet their needs because the demands of the job are too idiosyncratic. As the manager in the Fresno cable manufacturing firm said, "Unless you've worked in plant maintenance in the past, it's really hard to come in here and start working. Plant maintenance is kind of strange. Industry is not standardized. Electronics technicians come in [from educational institutions] and see our technicians all greasy and funky from the equipment, and they don't know what to make of it—they don't want any part of it. There are just so many different variables. This plant needs a specific type of worker. To train for this specific type of worker—I don't know if you can actually do that."

This individual recommended more work-study programs as a way to combine general education and job-specific training, a solution similar to the co-op programs in Cincinnati. But in the absence of such a program, he stressed the value of experience in hiring decisions.

The overwhelming importance of highly specific job-related capacities helps explain many other employment practices in the sub-baccalaureate labor market, especially hiring decisions that rely on seeking similar work experience. Another is continuing education; when employers mentioned sending employees back to school, they did so to have them learn the particular computer systems or production technologies required on that specific job, not for general education.

Basic Academic Skills

A second area of skills cited as necessary in almost every employment situation is basic reading, writing, and arithmetic. The shift to flatter organizational hierarchies, where frontline workers are expected to cope with problems on their own, is partly responsible. Employers spoke frequently of the need for workers to read instruction and repair manuals, make appropriate calculations on their own, and learn by themselves instead of relying on supervisors to tell them how to work out some problem. The need to retrain workers, especially in computer-based technologies, is another change that makes certain academic skills crucial.

The employers we interviewed complained constantly about the lack of basic skills among their sub-baccalaureate employees, with emotions ranging from bitterness to bewilderment but always accompanied by some anger. "The education system is falling apart," said one personnel manager in the Sacramento area: "Local school systems are highly political and very disorganized, [and] the kids suffer." This particular company used to have internships— presumably, given the need for screening and experience, an ideal way to educate new workers—"but we have found out that it is not cost-effective for us: the students don't have the three Rs." Some blamed the process of "dumbing down" the curriculum for deficiencies in basic skills. A manager of a machining shop for a large Cincinnati employer—one that found it had to provide remedial math to many employees—described the process as follows: "What [vocational schools] tend to do is, students are there, they're not excelling in the academic classes, so they're obligated to give them something. And they lower the level of training to what the people in the class can accept. They lower [standards] down so that the people will not fail, but at the same time they really hurt the people."

In many other cases, employers complained that applicants have sufficient technical skills but lack basic cognitive skills for the job. They also say that basic skills are being neglected in occupational programs. As the director of personnel for a large machining company in Silicon Valley grumbled, "Kids coming out of these programs after one year want to be machinists. And it's just a longer process than that. And these programs, they try to feed so much into them in this 1,000–2,000 hours that they're doing, they try to run the gamut between some math, some blueprint reading, but they skip on those to get them onto the machines, and when they don't have those [basic] skills they become nothing more than just operators."

Two other employers in Cincinnati corroborated his point. With "a lot of the vocational schools," said the first, "when you look at their curriculums, in some cases they've dropped away some of the humanities and the verbal side of the training for the sake of concentrating on vocational or technical skills that they're trying to impart." Said the second: "That's absolutely one of my pet peeves: vocational schools will come to you and say, 'Well, what do you want as entry-level requirements?' and then they'll develop these entry-level requirements, and some of them are skill things, but the educational level of things [is] always less than the high school level. Well, I don't want that."

The most concrete manifestation of the necessity of basic skills is the ubiquitous requirement of a high school diploma. Without a diploma, no applicant will even be considered for the mid-skilled occupations we examined. Employers generally avoided job training programs—such as JTPA and JOBS—since they include many clients lacking in basic skills. Otherwise, however, employers appeared stumped about what to do to remedy deficient basic skills.

These employers have not generally instituted their own basic skills test, sometimes because they fear lawsuits. Only a few employers have sent their employees to remedial programs or invested in workplace literacy programs. In general, employers regard the secondary schools as responsible for instilling adequate basic skills, and they express considerable anger and amazement that education has failed with so many of their prospective employees.

Another skill requirement that has become nearly ubiquitous, and that can now be considered "basic," is familiarity with appropriate computer applications and programs. As a result, many employers look for some computer skills when they hire. Consistent with wanting preparation that is as job-specific as possible, they prefer to see applicants familiar with the specific applications and programs they use on the job. The rise of computer applications provides a role for formal schooling; as mentioned above, education providers have responded with a variety of computer courses in both their regular offerings and in contract education. However, many employers feel that they can teach relevant computer skills on the job or that individuals can learn such skills once at work. One manager reported requiring a baccalaureate degree for drafters but admitted to having on staff an excellent self-taught drafter; others reported taking experienced machinists and teaching them the programming required for CNC machines on the job. As a result, formal schooling is not necessarily a prerequisite for jobs requiring computer skills since the particular skills can be obtained in different ways.

Motivation and Interpersonal Skills

Employers commonly mentioned a number of motivation-related and interpersonal capacities: motivation, initiative, judgment, an appropriate attitude (especially in services and occupations dealing with the public), and communications skills. Indeed, while technical and job-specific skills are important, many employers rated certain "foundation" skills as even more important.[8] Topping the list is motivation. The manager of a custom machining company in Cincinnati described the importance of technical skills and motivation in the following way: "Skill is nice, but not . . . we have guys out there who are super-skilled, but you can't get anything out of them because they don't feel like working that day. You have other people who are adequate [in their technical skills] who work hard all day—you're going to get just as much out of them."

One crucial skill is initiative. Several employers expressed this capacity as the combination of initiative and responsibility; one described it as "ownership." The director of human resources of a sophisticated high-tech manufacturer in the Silicon Valley area reflected on that capacity: "It's the lack of willingness to take ownership [that causes people to leave], not being forward. If you see a problem, you own it, regardless of who you are and what level you are at. That's kind of a cultural thing here. Sometimes it's not well-received by people: 'I'm here to do my job and that's all. Just because there is a problem over here, it doesn't mean that I'm going to do anything about it.' I think that's where the majority [of problems with employees] come in."

Similarly, the manager of an accounting department complained about the difficulty in getting people who are "interdisciplinary": "There are many things within our organization that require coordination across departmental boundaries. Problems arise. What we're trying to do is train our people to respond to those problems and get an effective solution, as opposed to compounding those problems. That's one deficiency we've seen in people coming in the door."

Many employers tended to lump motivation with basic cognitive skills. They glide from complaints about academic deficiencies and blaming the schools into complaints about discipline. As the director of an employers' association in Fresno reported, "Employers are concerned that employees are coming to them and they don't have the basic skills, and they don't understand that [basic skills] are job-supportive. I mean, they come, they can't fill out an application form. They're sloppy; they don't come to work on a regular basis. What is going on out there? The work ethic isn't the same as it used to be."

Motivation and persistence—a "good work ethic"—is important in every kind of employment. But it becomes especially crucial in production facilities with flatter hierarchies where individuals have several responsibilities, because the absence of any one person or an individual's tendency to slack off is more likely to hold up other workers. Initiative and judgment are increasingly necessary in such workplaces simply because there is less supervision and a greater reliance on individuals. Similarly, communications skills become increasingly crucial as responsibilities expand, since one employee is more likely to have to communicate with fellow workers or with suppliers and customers in order to maintain the flow of production.[9] In several ways, then, the importance of these personal and "foundation" skills is linked to trends in employment.

Aptitude and Common Sense

Finally, employers mentioned a number of skills that are difficult to define but that play a crucial role in production—skills they definitely look for in hiring. For certain jobs, employers mention "aptitude," a facility they felt they could identify but which in their view cannot be readily taught. Aptitude describes a facility with a certain kind of task that speeds up production and minimizes errors, an enjoyment of the task that improves the elusive fit between individuals and their jobs. Those who are hiring machinists look for mechanical aptitude and sometimes "test" for it by asking applicants about their hobbies. Others mentioned the importance of visual aptitude in drafters, aptitude with numbers for accountants and others working with numbers, and aptitude with people for those individuals working directly with customers. Aptitude describes a facility with a certain kind of task that speeds up production and minimizes errors, an enjoyment of the task that improves the elusive fit between individuals and their jobs.

In some cases, of course, individuals lacking a necessary aptitude find their way into an occupation nonetheless, but it is not always possible for them to compensate for the lack of aptitude with other skills. The director of a company in Cincinnati that hires contract drafters described a change in drafting with the coming of CAD and the decline of certain visual capacities:

> You're seeing a subtle revolution in the drafting field. It used to be that your drafter . . . was probably a person who could visualize. . . . They have a real conceptual mind. Also what you had in the past were a lot of frustrated artists who got into drafting. "Well, I can't be a Van Gogh or Picasso, but I like to draw and I have this capability, so I can use my artistic talent and make money doing it." So you really had frustrated artists with [that concept] doing this. Today you've got computer people doing this. . . . You're dumping out your frustrated artists and really bringing in the computer hackers . . . because a CAD operator can make drawings without the skills and knowledge of manual drafters. They are not artists. But with a computer they can draw a picture of an airplane or a turbine engine as well as a manual drafter [can]. The only difference is the CAD operator cannot think conceptually and does not have design skills.

Another elusive capacity mentioned by several employers is "common sense." While its meaning is not always clear, common sense seems to refer to the judgment necessary in any work situation to avoid mistakes, to facilitate and speed up production. One of the clearest discussions of common sense came from an engineering manager in a Cincinnati semiconductor firm:

> We're looking for common sense, which is something that schools aren't real good at. There's nothing in the school system to test that. I've worked with a lot of book-smart people. I'm a mechanical engineer myself, and you get the guys that excel within the academic environment that—if it's in a textbook, textbooks tend to be black and white. There is *a* correct answer and if there's usually enough information provided, they do fine. They study well; they

test well. In the real world, you don't have the certainty. You don't necessarily even have the optimum-point-on-the-curve-type scenarios. You have to go in and you have to find something, understand what's wrong with it. It's dirty, it's messy, you have multiple conflicts for your time. It's a different environment, one that at least the academic environments I've been through don't mimic well. . . . Knowing something is only half the equation if you can't produce results with it.

In this description, common sense is the ability to apply knowledge—including the kind of job-specific skills learned in school—in production settings whose complexity precludes there being any simple, correct procedure or textbook solution. But such a facility, while it may be impossible to teach except in the work setting, is anything but "common." It requires both deep understanding of the production process and the capacity to weigh several competing goals in order to judge the appropriate steps to take. In a production setting where individual employers have greater responsibilities and less supervision to help them through problems, common sense becomes an increasingly important capacity.

Contradictions in What Employers Want

In employers' descriptions of what skills are necessary, one particular contradiction arises time and again. On the one hand, employers value highly job-specific skills, sometimes too specific to be taught in educational institutions and therefore to be learned on the job. They then look for experience in using those skills, or for educational programs that are as specific to their production processes as possible. They often criticize educational institutions for including too much "theory" and general education, and not enough hands-on or specific training. Yet employers also complain about the lack of general and "academic" capacities, including the abilities to read, write, and communicate in other ways, and the ability to understand and apply math in unfamiliar settings. Some employers therefore castigate occupational programs for concentrating on specific skills to the detriment of more general or academic capacities.

Which do they really want: job-specific skills or basic academic skills? Perhaps employers simply want their workers to have every

conceivable capacity. However, a different explanation of this conflict is more likely: the skills necessary for entry-level employment
are much more specific than those required for promotion and
positions of increasing responsibility. In our interviews, those individuals who stressed specific skills were more often production-level
supervisors, while those emphasizing the lack of more general
capacities—common sense, problem solving, and other higher-
order, less specific skills—were more frequently personnel managers and those who viewed the firm from the upper levels in its
hierarchy. (Similarly, the complaints in many national reports have
come from business representatives at high levels within their
firms, not from production-level supervisors.) The same division
also emerges among firms of various sizes: the small companies
that are more likely to hire individuals directly from community
colleges and some high school programs often stress specific skills,
while the larger firms who hire experienced workers for positions
of greater flexibility and responsibility emphasize more general
capacities.

The problem for students and educational providers is that the
skills necessary in the *short* run may obscure the skills necessary for
promotion and mobility in the *long* run. If employers press community colleges to provide highly specific skills, then instructors
may fail to teach those capacities which are crucial for promotion;
recall the employer quoted above who complained that colleges
developing entry-level skills neglect academic skills. What is even
worse is that the job-specific skills taught in occupational programs
may still not be specific enough. This is just what the overwhelming reliance on experience (documented in the next section) indicates. Students from occupational programs are left in the worst
of both worlds: lacking the specific skills necessary for entry-level
jobs and also without the more general competencies necessary for
promotion over the longer run.

In reviewing the skills that employers claim are the most crucial, we see one striking conclusion: how *unimportant* the kinds of
capacities usually learned in formal schooling are. Basic academic
competencies and some computer skills are the most obvious candidates for school-based learning, but other skills are not. For
instance, the technical skills required on the job tend to be more
specific than community colleges and area vocational schools can

offer, and many of them must be learned on the job. Certain capacities, notably aptitude and common sense, cannot be taught in schools and colleges, and the behavioral and interpersonal capacities (including interpersonal skills and motivation) included among so-called foundation skills are often viewed as innate characteristics. It is striking to see how many of the skills employers perceive as critical are not learned in school. It is also not surprising to find the role of formal schooling in hiring standards to be relatively weak.

Hiring Standards: The Roles of Experience and Education

The need for competencies that are not well taught in educational institutions means that virtually all employers in the sub-baccalaureate labor market look for experience when hiring, particularly experience in virtually the same kind of procedure or production facility. Much more than formal schooling, experience is an indicator of the presence of skills that employers value in sub-baccalaureate positions: mastery of specific machines, production processes, or office procedures; evidence of motivation and persistence; and the proven ability to work with others.[10] Requiring substantial experience is the best way to reduce the unavoidable uncertainty in a new hire.[11] Over and over again, employers in our four labor markets insisted on the primacy of experience over formal education—even for such relatively low-level positions as accounting clerks. As a compensation manager in Silicon Valley acknowledged, "It would be unlikely that anyone could come directly [from schooling] into this [position], although it's not exactly a high-level job; but we're even requiring several years of accounting experience before someone could be in that position."

It is usually crucial to have experience in work specifically related to the firm's production process. For example, the director of machining for a company that makes castings reported that he looks for experienced machinists, but only "if I can find [experience] related to castings. You have to know what to select as a cutter, how to use the cutter, but there's a lot of technique with machining castings, you don't just throw it in the machine and hit the button. . . Basically what I'll see [and hire] is a person who's been a machinist for four or five years, and they'll have smatterings of machine castings; two or three times in their career they've learned castings."

Similarly, the manager of a company manufacturing precision metal-working machinery seeks "experience, and [other] skills, depending on what we're looking for at that time. We usually have a specific need. We need an engine lathe filled, or we need a CNC grinder filled. So we're looking for someone who can run that type of machine."

In some cases experience is required because of technological sophistication; the human resource manager of a semiconductor firm in Silicon Valley said, "The demands of the factory are so sophisticated it takes someone with quite a bit of experience to understand and appreciate the environment they're going to be working in. What we don't want to do is turn a beginner loose on a $4 million machine. So therefore what we're looking for is experienced people."

In other cases, experience is an indicator of personal skills necessary for the job. For example, a payroll processing company that stresses personal service to their customers looks for experience in any personal service capacity: "We feel that we can give technical and payroll training, but we can't change anyone's personality; we can't force them to be nice on the phone. So we basically go by service experience. Have they worked in a service industry and given quality service?"

Given the ubiquitous demand for experience, formal schooling is generally insufficient for hiring. The human resource manager for a moderate-sized tool and die company described their hiring:

> When people come out of [the local community college and area vocational schools] they still truly have [only] the basics. Now, granted, they have a lot stronger basics than what we would normally find if we were just hiring somebody off the street. But we still consider that to be without previous shop experience. We would consider that to be entry-level. We would have a window between $6.00 and $7.50 an hour. That is what we would normally pay someone that was just coming out of a vocational school or out of [the local community college] with little or no experience. Because truly, in those areas, the experience is really the key. You can't . . . learn everything there is to know in the classroom in order to excel

and climb up the ladder. They're not going to go to a school and come in here at the top. It will not happen.

Furthermore, it is difficult for individuals to compensate for a lack of experience with sub-baccalaureate credentials. An individual without experience would not find a position simply by accumulating community college credits or degrees. For example, the human resource manager for a large computer networking firm in the Silicon Valley area said the following about hiring individuals for business management: "It would depend upon what work experience they've had as to whether we'd be interested. For example, we hired someone in our department, in employment, who was working as a temporary in an employment department [in a different firm] in a clerical position. She did have an A.A. degree, I think it was in general business, but it was really the work experience that did it. . . . An A.A. business degree by itself wouldn't buy a whole lot."

In part, the ambivalence toward formal education is linked to the need for highly specific skills which are too narrow to find in any educational institution. For example, the personnel manager of a firm that produces box-forming and cartoning machines reported:

> I have specifically told [the engineering manager] that I do not
> want anyone any longer whom we have to train. I want someone
> with either a college education, even if it's [the local community
> college], or junior college education, but I want somebody who has
> some background and work experience if possible. . . . You can have
> a super education, [but] if they don't have anything in our line of
> products, it's worthless. It's start from square one. . . . There is,
> only, I think, one college in the United States that really has a pro-
> gram that trains for our industry, and I think it's . . . in the Midwest.
> . . . I think it [the skill required] is just too specific [for colleges to
> offer programs].

In practice, then, experience is the only way to break into such an industry, despite whatever general value schooling might have.

In a few cases, employers did acknowledge that a combination of formal schooling and experience would be ideal, or that education made progress on the job easier. As a personnel manager for a Silicon Valley credit union mentioned, "I have personally noticed that those individuals who were hired because they had a two-year or a four-year degree, in comparison to others who have worked their way up, tend to know their job and take less time in training to learn their job than those who have worked their way up and are cross-trained. The level of what they can do on the job is far more advanced because they have the technical background to do it. . . . You can only do so much cross-training and then you really need [formal schooling]."

However, this employer requires experience for virtually all its employees and they do not compel employees to have postsecondary education. So their practice contradicts the statement about the superiority of better-educated workers.

The only exception to the general pattern of requiring experience among new hires came in a few companies working with such advanced technologies that a pool of experienced workers does not yet exist. For example, a Silicon Valley manufacturer of lasers could not find local individuals experienced in laser production because the technology is too new, and so it hired its employees from an Iowa community college and a proprietary school that have established programs carefully tailored to the firm's needs. But this example does not challenge the general pattern of preferring experience over formal schooling; it simply reflects a rarefied case where experienced workers do not yet exist.

The Value of Sub-Baccalaureate Education

Because of the dominance of experience, informal job tests, and probationary periods in hiring, we found little role for subbaccalaureate credentials in the occupations we examined. A crucial exception is the high school diploma, which is required for virtually every position. The certificates and associate degrees awarded by community colleges and technical institutes, the shorter programs available in area vocational schools, and the short programs that students put together by taking a few courses in a community college were rarely mentioned as hiring *requirements*. This generates a serious problem for new entrants: if every employer requires experience, it becomes difficult to enter the sub-baccalaureate labor market and accumulate this experience. As one employer acknowledged, "My feeling is that entry level is tough: they really don't have any place to go unless there's a tremendous shortage."

The dominance of experience generates a real puzzle. If formal schooling above the high school diploma is not required or rewarded in hiring, then what could explain the economic benefits of sub-baccalaureate education (which will be more carefully documented in Chapter Three)? There prove to be a number of answers to this puzzle. But they differ from occupation to occupation, which helps explain why the economic benefits to sub-baccalaureate education are so varied.

Technical Training

One important exception to the general pattern of requiring experience over formal schooling appeared in technical fields. Several high-tech manufacturers in the Silicon Valley area require associate degrees for their electronics technicians, particularly an international firm whose employment standards are set by the national headquarters in New York. Many of the companies we examined in Sacramento require associate degrees for electronics technicians, and several firms in Cincinnati require associate degrees in electronics or electromechanical engineering for their technicians. Of the six occupational groups we examined, such requirements occur almost exclusively in electronics and related technical fields, and not for other occupations. For example, the computer networking firm in Silicon Valley whose human resource manager declared that "an A.A. business degree by itself wouldn't buy a whole lot" requires an associate degree for its electronics technicians. A phone company whose personnel director acknowledged that "a two-year degree really does not make someone a better candidate" does prefer that electronics technicians have at least a two-year degree. These technical fields are exceptions, then, to the general indifference toward sub-baccalaureate credentials.

Varied Sources of Training

A second use of formal schooling appears in situations where employers require a certain amount of training regardless of the source, rather than requiring a sub-baccalaureate credential. For example, one high-tech company in Silicon Valley looks for two years of training, but without differentiating whether it comes from formal schooling, the military, or on-the-job training elsewhere.[12] The same phone-company director of personnel stated: "For our general clerical jobs . . . those with the educational background aren't really rated higher than those with just clerical experience. . . . A two-year degree really does not make someone a better candidate than someone who has a work history and no college. We give most of our applicants general aptitude tests; we also give tests in skills such as typing and keying. They just have to meet all the basics. So a two-year degree doesn't really give anyone a higher rating."

In light of employers' focus on competencies rather than the source of training, a number of educators acknowledged that subbaccalaureate credentials do not have any special value. As the dean of vocational education in a community college near Sacramento acknowledged:

> [Students] get a certificate so they have something to show to the welding [employers], where they really don't care. The industry could care less [about credentials], just so they can do the job. And in the mechanical trades, they don't really care. The manufacturers allow them to have A.A. degrees, but they just want them to have the skills. It's just depending on which particular areas you're talking about. And the reason [the demand for credentials] is high in electronics is because to get the position of technician it is required by the industry to have an A.A. degree. Now [as] we move into more of the service [occupations], they won't care.

In firms that look for certain competencies regardless of their source, there may be a trade-off between experience and schooling. In one such case, the personnel director of a high-tech manufacturing firm in Silicon Valley asserted: "The rule of thumb is two years' experience for every year of education. If [applicants] have been doing test technician work for four years, again the rule of thumb would be the equivalent of an A.A. degree—if they were paying attention [in college], and it doesn't always hold true."

The other example came in a revenue accounting department of a Cincinnati employer, where a manager claimed that an associate degree was the equivalent of two or three years of experience.

In all these cases, formal schooling is *one* of the ways to acquire the requisite training. Individuals with community college education will find themselves working alongside individuals without post-secondary education but who learned their skills elsewhere, for example, but they do gain access to these sub-baccalaureate positions through their education. In the process, postsecondary education gives some individuals an advantage over high school graduates who have not obtained the required skills in other ways.[13]

Preferences for Community College Education

A third role for postsecondary education is that some employers express a *preference* for sub-baccalaureate credentials; that is, an individual with postsecondary education will be hired over an applicant with similar experience without such education—though some experience is still commonly necessary. For example, the Silicon Valley credit union manager said about their management and accounting positions, "We'd prefer a two-year degree at least. We have made exceptions if they have previous experience. We will occasionally find someone who is an incredible individual, who has no college background and possibly no experience in the financial industry, but has, say, wonderful interpersonal skills. . . . But we usually don't hire someone with absolutely no experience at all."

Similarly, a human resource manager for a large Sacramento computer manufacturer who claimed to recruit from two-year colleges stated that "community college degrees are desirable, but we look for experience most of all." Similarly, a recruiter for a temporary agency for drafters and other technical workers in the Sacramento area said, "We do hire those people [from community colleges]. The more education, the better; the more experience, the better. We don't hire for education alone; job experience is more significant."

In these cases it is clear that experience is the basic requirement and community college education an additional benefit, rather than the other way around. However, the preference for community college education means that individuals with such credentials will fare better in the labor market than those with similar experience and training but less formal schooling.

Because employers give some preference to applicants with community college credentials, such individuals can often make their way into mid-skilled positions by working their way up from relatively unskilled positions—a process we might call (as many instructors do) the "foot in the door" method of gaining access, or "working up the hard way." As an architecture instructor described it,

> [A company] will hire someone at a two-year level as the go-fer. It's a good opportunity. They see how the business operates and sometimes get to do some drawing. . . . They get some good experience. If they show some aptitude toward drafting, they might get put on the boards. . . . In fact, I've run across a small number of people who have worked up through the architectural ranks over the years, where you can actually become an architectural engineer by putting in an amount of time—eight years for an architect—which qualifies you to take a test, and if you pass that then you can take the licensing test and go on to become an architectural engineer. That's what we typically call working up the hard way.

In this case, initial positions directly after completing a community college program are unskilled; only with "aptitude," experience, and mobility over time do individuals move into mid-skilled positions.

Among those employers who express some preference for postsecondary education in deciding whom to hire, none of them provides a wage differential simply for additional schooling.[14] Therefore, individuals with sub-baccalaureate education increase their earnings by gaining access to higher-skilled and better-paid positions. Their postsecondary education may make them more productive on the job, which will earn them promotion over time. But their postsecondary education will not itself move them higher up the salary scale. As a manager in a high-tech firm remarked about postsecondary education in general: "It comes to the reward that you will get from attending these classes or education. And the answer is zero. You do not get a financial reward for attending any class. You do not get any financial reward for showing proficiency through attendance at educational universities. You do get financially rewarded for performance, which perhaps is enhanced by having a better education. You do get financially rewarded for results, which again may be enhanced by having a broader knowledge of the subject."

Cyclical Variation in Hiring Practices

Another role for formal schooling arises from the cyclical variation in hiring practices. Several employers mentioned that they hired more individuals from sub-baccalaureate institutions during the mid-1980s, when unemployment rates were lower. Similarly, an employer in Cincinnati described how hiring standards varied during periods of surplus and shortage:

> [In the mid-1980s] we got [1,800 manufacturing] people from a lot of these companies that had gone down. So we raised the bar [i.e., hiring standards] at that point in time based solely on experience, not on education. Now we've got 1,000 people laid off, so it's '80 and '84 people [who] are going away, and all of a sudden we're going to be down to '79s. [The numbers refer to the year hired in a seniority-based layoff system.] If we ever hire again, and someday we will, I keep preaching that the fertile ground won't be there for these skilled people because by the mid-'90s they will have passed through the system, been retreaded . . . and then we're going to have to take people with training as opposed to people with experience.

That is, during periods when a surplus of labor in any particular occupation develops, employers base hiring primarily on experience; but when unemployment goes down and experienced workers are in short supply, employers begin to hire individuals with formal schooling rather than experience.

Licensing and "Organized" Occupations

A final role for sub-baccalaureate education is one of the most powerful. In a few occupations, most of which are in the health sector, occupations are subject to public regulation through state licensing requirements. These requirements specify the educational requirements for particular occupations, including the duration of programs, the skills that must be taught, and the related academic content that must be included. In health occupations, such requirements are binding on both employers and educational providers since employers must hire licensed health care workers and providers must meet licensing requirements if their students are ever to get jobs. This in turn means that various sub-baccalaureate credentials are *required* for entry in health occupations, providing an obvious explanation of their role in gaining entry to sub-baccalaureate jobs. Of course, these licensing mechanisms may also restrict entry into these occupations, much as professional licensing in other areas is thought to restrict entry as a way of driving up salaries. In turn, this may explain why the economic benefits of certificates and associate degrees in health occupations are greater than in other occupational areas (as Chapter Three documents).

The existence of licensing provisions specifying the educational requirements for particular health occupations creates a clear relationship between schooling and employment. The contrast is striking between these *organized* occupations, in which required skills have been carefully codified by committees of employers and providers, and markets for other occupations where required skills vary substantially and are not codified at all. In the *unorganized* labor markets typical of sub-baccalaureate occupations, there is much more variation in the skills required among different types of jobs that are identically labeled (as the next section clarifies) and much less consistency in what employers expect from their employees and what educational institutions provide. In contrast to health occupations, where the occupations and their requirements are well known and the requirements in educational programs to enter occupations are unambiguous, students are on their own with little guidance about job prospects and the best ways of qualifying for them.

The Heterogeneity of Qualifications

The responses from our employers clarify that formal schooling affects hiring decisions in very different ways. Furthermore, formal schooling is only one of the many ways workers get the training necessary for sub-baccalaureate occupations. The varied role of formal schooling in this labor market is corroborated by other evidence. Surveys of employees undertaken by the Department of Labor in 1983 and 1991 asked them about the qualifications necessary for their jobs (Eck, 1993; U.S. Department of Labor, 1992; Bowers and Swain, 1994). As Table 1.3 clarifies, individuals with baccalaureate degrees are overwhelmingly in jobs requiring some kind of education or training, since only 16.2 percent reported that they needed no training. Of those who required some kind of training, the vast majority needed formal schooling rather than other types of preparation such as formal company training or on-the-job training.[15] At the other end of the spectrum, relatively few high school dropouts (only 27.8 percent) are in jobs requiring any kind of training at all, and the majority of them require nonschool preparation, largely on-the-job training; only 4.1 percent report that they are in jobs requiring some kind of formal schooling. In these two segments of the labor market, then, there is not much variation in the types of preparation required: most of those with baccalaureate degrees are in jobs requiring formal schooling, and most of those without a high school diploma require no schooling whatsoever.

However, in the middle there is much greater variety in the kinds of training required. Among those with some college, 35.7 percent reported that their job needed some formal schooling, 27.4 percent required some other kind of preparation—again, largely informal on-the-job training—and 36.9 percent said that no special training was necessary. For high school graduates, slightly over half (53.8 percent) required no preparation at all, while two-thirds of the remainder needed informal training rather than formal schooling. Within the sub-baccalaureate labor market, then, the ways of training for occupations vary substantially, and the balance of formal schooling and less formal training (including experience or on-the-job training) is approximately equal, though of course the necessary balance may vary substantially from occupation to occupation.

Another way to examine the heterogeneity of training in the sub-baccalaureate labor market is to see what proportion of individuals in particular occupations receive formal schooling. For jobs that require a four-year college education, virtually everyone in these occupations has a baccalaureate degree: 95–100 percent of high school teachers, 92 percent of speech therapists, 87 percent of dentists, 82 percent of chemists, and the like. However, of the occupations that most commonly use preparation in community colleges and technical institutes, much lower proportions receive this kind of formal schooling: 47 percent of inhalation therapists,

Table 1.3. Education and Training Required for Employment, 1991.

	Percent of the Labor Force	Percent Needing		Percent Needing[a]									
		No Training	Formal Schooling	Other Training Only	High School Vocational Training	Post High School Vocational Training	Community College/ Technical Institute	4-yr. College	Formal Company Training	Informal On-the-job Training	Armed Forces Training	Correspondence Course	Friends, Relatives, Others
All workers, 16 and older	100.0	43.3	32.1	24.6	3.9	2.7	7.7	18.8	12.1	27.2	2.1	1.1	7.4
High school dropouts	13.5	72.2	4.1	23.7	1.6	1.1	1.1	0.2	4.6	18.1	0.4	0.4	5.9
High school graduates	39.5	53.8	15.0	31.2	6.0	3.2	5.3	1.1	11.6	26.4	2.1	1.0	7.2
Some college	22.1	36.9	35.7	27.4	4.5	4.1	19.5	10.8	15.9	32.1	3.1	1.5	8.0
College graduates	24.7	16.2	71.7	12.1	1.2	1.5	4.6	64.7	13.7	29.0	2.1	1.2	7.9

[a]Proportions may not sum to 100 percent because of multiple sources of training.

Source: Eck (1993), Table 6.

45 percent of dental hygienists, 43 percent of funeral directors, 34 percent of drafting occupations, 30 percent of registered nurses, 25 percent of stationary engineers, and 21 percent of electronic repairers, for example (U.S. Department of Labor, 1992, Tables 23 and 25). For those occupations for which a baccalaureate or graduate degree is most common, then, there are usually no other routes into the occupation; but for occupations where sub-baccalaureate education is most common, one-half to four-fifths of workers receive their training in other ways. There are, then, multiple routes into the mid-skilled occupations of the sub-baccalaureate labor market, and formal schooling must compete with many other forms of preparation.

Promotion Practices and Advancement

Virtually unanimously, employers report that positions above entry-level jobs are filled through internal promotion. Almost universally, internal promotion is based on job performance assessed informally by supervisors. As in the case of hiring standards, promotion practices are only rarely codified in personnel policies; the small and medium-sized firms are particularly informal. Typically, firms post notices of opportunities for advancement, and employees bid for these opportunities. Supervisors then rank those who have bid for an opening and then choose the "best" applicants based on their job records and the match between their skills and those required in the promotion opportunity.

One change from past practice is that seniority rarely counts in promotion decisions. The human resource manager in a mid-sized tool and die manufacturer in Cincinnati contrasted the current promotion policy as follows: "[Seniority] was [a factor in promotion] in the past, isn't as much anymore. . . The good-old-boy network is not going to happen here because we are now in a global marketplace, and from a corporate standpoint we are trying to broaden our horizons and diversify our business."

What emerges consistently, in promotion as in initial hiring, is a world in which competition is squeezing everyone to hire and promote only the most productive individuals, a world in which there is renewed emphasis on job performance that might have been missing in a world of lesser competition or institutionalized promotion practices (such as those associated with unions).

The dominance of internal promotion and of promotion based on job performance means that the capacities employers cite as necessary on the job—motivation, cooperation, initiative, adaptability, communications skills, the ability to learn new tasks, and other foundation skills—are crucial for long-term success. Employers consistently cite these capacities as more important than job-specific skills such as command of machining techniques or knowledge of accounting principles. This also means that certain capacities that may not be particularly important for entry-level jobs become crucial when individuals are considered for promotion. As the manager of the accounting department of a Sacramento firm explained,

> One of the things you do more than anything as you rise up in general is that communications becomes the thing that separates people more than anything else, that it becomes the most important skill that you have—maybe even beyond what your technical skills can be. You can be very good technically, but if you can't communicate, that's going to hold you back. So I think that's much more critical than most people understand when you're coming up through school. English is never fun. You think, "I don't need that. I'm going to be a rocket scientist; I don't need to know those other things." But really you do.

This reinforces the notion that employers differ on which are the most important skills because entry-level competencies—technical and job-specific—vary from the higher-order competencies necessary for advancement. Needing different capacities as individuals are promoted creates certain difficulties, for educational institutions and for students alike. The capacities most necessary for higher-level positions may not be visible, and the rationales for taking academic subjects that are "never fun" are unclear. Then, too, individuals in entry-level positions in sub-baccalaureate labor markets may lack the skills required for mobility into more advanced positions.

This in turn creates a constant need for upgrade training. By all accounts, the amount of upgrade training supported by employers has increased substantially over the past several decades.[16] Firms vary in how they accomplish upgrade training: some place the burden for upgrading on the employee, while others assume responsibility for directing certain individuals to improve their skills. In some cases, on-the-job training takes care of the problem, as when employees are rotated around different machines or procedures. In other cases, firms send selected employees to vendors, that is, suppliers of new machines or of new computer applications, to learn new skills. The use of contract education, often from community colleges or local four-year colleges, is also widespread (Lynch, Palmer, and Grubb, 1991; Doucette, 1993). Finally, some employers encourage their employees to attend formal schooling—very often with firm-paid tuition subsidies—as a way of upgrading their skills, particularly in cases where technology is advancing rapidly and requires computer applications.

Because promotion policies are informal and because promotion depends on what opportunities become available, job ladders in most companies are not clearly defined.[17] That is, when individuals within a company bid on promotion opportunities, the path that they follow typically depends on what jobs become available, what range of skills they have acquired, and what competition they have from fellow employees at any specific time. So the path taken up through a range of jobs of increasing responsibility and pay varies from person to person. There are a few exceptions among the firms we interviewed: the accounting department in Cincinnati had a particularly rigid pattern of progression for accounting clerks, and several companies were governed by union contracts. But the norm among the employers we interviewed is for job ladders to be much more flexible and loosely defined.

Of course, opportunities for promotion vary. Large firms have more opportunities than do smaller ones. There are fewer opportunities as well among those that have moved to flatter job hierarchies, those that have cross-trained their workforce so that individuals can perform a variety of jobs, and those that have made greater use of temporary employees for entry-level work. For some individuals, mobility can come only by moving once they have accumulated experience within a smaller or less advanced firm, but mobility among companies is difficult because of the tendency for all companies to hire from their existing pool of employees. Consequently, opportunities for upward mobility and growth in earnings depend crucially on how an individual gains entry into the sub-baccalaureate labor market.

Conclusions: Navigating in the Sub-Baccalaureate Labor Market

Several characteristics of the sub-baccalaureate labor market make it difficult for individuals to learn about it and then make their way into it. The fact that most hiring is local may facilitate information about job availability and job requirements. However, the lack of formal hiring criteria, the dominance of relatively small employers without clear personnel practices, the cyclical variation in hiring hindering the development of well-known hiring practices, and the dominance of promotion through a post-and-bid system without clear job ladders all make it difficult to see what kinds of careers are available. The conventional notion of a "career"—which we may define by a clear progression of jobs, from a modestly skilled entry-level position to those of greater skill, responsibility, and earnings—has been replaced (if it ever existed[18]) with careers that individuals have to shape for themselves, that they must construct by moving among positions and among employers. The domination in hiring of experience over formal educational credentials also makes it difficult for individuals to know what the value of formal educational credentials is: while sub-baccalaureate education does provide a number of different routes into employment, and does lead to higher earnings, it does so in different and shifting ways (as Chapter Three clarifies). All in all, the characteristics of the sub-baccalaureate labor market make it more difficult to know how to prepare for entry into many of these occupations, how to find initial employment, or what avenues of upward mobility are likely to materialize.

These characteristics also help explain why the economic returns from sub-baccalaureate education are so uneven. Associate degrees and certificates are much less likely than are baccalaureate degrees to be absolute prerequisites for employment. With the exception of health occupations, and a few community college programs (such as those in electronics) that have established close working relations with employers, there are few occupations for which community college credentials are absolutely necessary. In addition, the overwhelming preference for experience over formal schooling, because of its greater value in signaling the specific skills and the personal competencies that employers stress, means that education by itself is rarely sufficient. To be sure, employers often express *preferences* for some postsecondary education, particularly in combination with experience, and the foot-in-the-door method of getting into entry-level positions gives some advantages to individuals with community college education. But formal schooling is only one of several factors that influence hiring, and individuals without experience, or without the personal characteristics that employers are searching for, find it difficult to compensate with formal schooling alone.

The characteristics of sub-baccalaureate work also clarify why it is so important to find employment related to one's field of study (as the statistical work in Chapter Three verifies). The strong employer preferences for highly specific skills, particularly for entry-level jobs, means that training in another area is not generally valued. Furthermore, the general competencies that an individual might learn in another subject area—academic skills, problem-solving abilities, and other SCANS skills, personal competencies such as discipline and initiative—are not likely to be considered, at least not until an individual is ready for advancement above entry-level work. Thus to find individuals employment in the field of their education, placement efforts are crucial to the economic benefits of community colleges. I return to this conclusion in Chapter Six.

In general, then, the informal and unorganized nature of sub-baccalaureate labor markets helps explain the difficulties students have in navigating through educational institutions and into employment.[19] There are, however, some clear exceptions to this general pattern. One involves health occupations, where licensing enforces uniform practices on educational providers and employers alike, as well as generating "organized" or codified markets from the informal practices that dominate elsewhere. Another exception comes in cases like the electronics programs in Sacramento, where community colleges have established programs in close conjunction with local employers who then provide a ready source of employment as well as advice on the content of education. A third exception, closely related in spirit, involves the co-op programs in Cincinnati (which I examine in greater detail in Chapter Six). These efforts, combining school-based learning in two-year colleges and work-based learning in companies, establish clear routes from educational institutions into employment, consistent with the smooth transition from school to work envisioned in the current School-to-Work Opportunities Act. By providing on-the-job experience as well as formal schooling, these efforts also provide students with the experience that is so necessary for hiring in the sub-baccalaureate labor market.

There are, then, several ways in which the informal practices and the inattention to formal schooling typical of the sub-baccalaureate labor market can be changed. I return to these proposals in Chapter Seven, on the public policies that might influence employment in the sub-baccalaureate labor market. But there are also ways in which postsecondary institutions can do a better job of recognizing the characteristics of the labor market they serve, and modifying their practices accordingly—both their teaching practices (examined in Chapter Five) and how they are linked to employers (in Chapter Six). In both cases, it is crucial for both policy makers and educators to understand that the practices of employers constrain whatever education and training programs can do. Comprehending employers' practices is therefore necessary to improve the prospects for all students seeking advancement through postsecondary education.

Chapter Two

Educational Pathways into the Mid-Skilled Labor Market

Over the past thirty years, the sub-baccalaureate labor market has been shaped not only by the nature of employment, but also by shifts in the supply side: the educational institutions contributing to this segment of the labor force. During this period, postsecondary education grew substantially, particularly with the expansion of public colleges and universities devoted more to teaching than to research and with the explosion of enrollments in low-cost community colleges and technical institutes. Area vocational schools developed, first as ways of providing richer vocational programs to secondary students and then through adding postsecondary programs. Private proprietary schools have also expanded during this period (although data on their enrollments is hard to come by). Finally, a variety of job training programs have expanded as well, starting with the Manpower Development Act of 1963; while they are generally viewed as forms of short-term *training* outside the ambit of schools and colleges rather than *education,* they overlap to some extent with the purposes of educational institutions.

The expansion of postsecondary education and training programs has meant that high school graduates contemplating their futures face a greater variety of options. If students are well informed, then the proliferation of education and training options is a cause for celebration; but if the consequences of different routes through postsecondary education are unclear, then the likelihood of students making rational choices is dim. For students, therefore, the expansion of options in the sub-baccalaureate labor market is both a blessing and a curse, making our understanding of the sub-baccalaureate labor market and the routes into it all the more important. The variety of routes into mid-skilled occupations and the proliferation of programs has also been a source of confusion to employers (as documented in the previous chapter) and to students, as well as policy makers seeking to impose some coherence on the entire "system."

For reasons I clarify in the first section of this chapter, two-year colleges, including both comprehensive community colleges and their occupational relatives, technical institutes, have become the dominant institutions explicitly preparing students for the sub-baccalaureate labor market. Therefore improving the preparation of the sub-baccalaureate labor force requires first understanding what community colleges and technical institutes do, and then seeing where improvements are possible. However, to begin with it is necessary to confront the charge of numerous critics that these institutions primarily "cool out" individuals by tracking them away from the higher rewards associated with four-year colleges (for example, Zwerling 1976; Pincus 1980; Brint and Karabel 1989). Settling this debate is important because improving these institutions might be a waste of energy, at least from the students' vantage, if they tend to depress educational attainment. In the second section of this chapter I address this question, providing evidence that educational advancement—the use of community colleges by students who might not otherwise attend postsecondary education at all—seems to dominate cooling out. This finding strengthens the case for two-year institutions as mechanisms of access to postsecondary education and to the mid-skilled jobs of the sub-baccalaureate labor market.

But once students get into two-year institutions, what do they do? Many of those with postsecondary education but less than a bachelor's degree appear to be dropouts: they have started postsecondary education, often with the stated intention of completing degrees, but have not done so. Furthermore, the incidence of dropping out appears to have increased during the 1970s and 1980s, in both two- and four-year institutions, a phenomenon that is of concern not only because it suggests that increasing numbers of students are unable to realize their dreams but also because the economic benefits of postsecondary education for noncompleters are substantially lower than for those who have completed credentials (as Chapter Three shows). Whether noncompleters are in fact dropouts or whether they have completed what they intended to do has been a subject of considerable debate, one that I answer in several different ways. But in addressing this question, more direct information about the intentions of students is helpful. So I present the results of interviews with community college students, to help illuminate their purposes. Based on their responses, a striking result emerges: many students are there because they are unsure of their options, and the community college is the lowest-cost way of discovering the alternatives and testing their abilities. The community college may not be optimally set up for these experimenters, but it is virtually the only alternative they have.

The intentions of community college students clarify the essentially vocational purpose of these institutions. Overall, 59.4 percent of students in community colleges and all those in technical institutes say they are there for occupational purposes.[1] But many of those who are "academic" students, who say that they want to transfer to four-year colleges and complete baccalaureate degrees, are also there to "get into the world," as one community college student memorably expressed it: to find some way into jobs that are well-paid, stable, and with prospects for advancement. Like the high school, and indeed like most four-year colleges and universities, the community college is an inescapably occupational institution; improvement of occupational preparation should therefore be high on its agenda.

In this chapter I have tried consistently to rely on an empirical rather than theoretical or ideological approach. Unfortunately, this has generated a problem that I have not completely solved. The variety of community colleges in this country is so great that almost every generalization must be wrong for a few institutions. For example, I argue later in this chapter that community colleges are not in general mechanisms of cooling out students who might otherwise go to four-year colleges; nevertheless, this may happen in a few communities, particularly where relatively unselective four-year colleges coexist with two-year colleges. The proportion of students who are undecided about their purposes is likely to be much higher in community colleges with low tuition and flexible schedules than in colleges with higher costs, or in technical institutes that require entering students to have made a preliminary career choice. The economic benefits substantiated in Chapter Three rely on national data, and some institutions surely have much lower benefits, while others may have substantially higher returns. The sub-baccalaureate labor market practices described in Chapter One may be quite different in a few localities. I have tried to qualify my generalizations about community colleges, and to say that "most" or "many" behave in particular ways. The only real solution to the problem of variation will come when there is more analysis describing both the nature and the sources of variation among community colleges and local labor markets.

The Varied Routes into the Sub-Baccalaureate Labor Market: The Importance of Community Colleges

There are several approaches to examining the paths into the sub-baccalaureate labor force. As the figures in Table 1.1 clarified, 62.5 percent of the labor force in 1992 had either a high school diploma or some college. A slight majority of these (about 55 percent) had high school diplomas only. This fraction has been decreasing steadily, as more and more individuals enroll in postsecondary education and find their way into mid-skilled jobs with some amounts of college.

Increasingly, entrance into postsecondary education comes through community colleges and technical institutes. As Table 2.1 shows, 17.6 percent of all enrollments in postsecondary education in 1965 were in two-year institutions, increasing to 37.8 by 1992. Because two-year college students are more likely to be part-time, their fraction of full-time equivalent enrollments (29.8 percent in 1992) is somewhat lower. However, postsecondary institutions include juniors, seniors, and graduate students, who by definition do not attend two-year institutions; for students attending college for the first time, two-year colleges increased their proportion of such students from 19.7 percent in 1960 to a high of 51.1 percent in 1975, dropping somewhat to 45.2 percent by 1992. Thus almost half of students entering postsecondary education do so through community colleges and technical institutes. Furthermore, the importance of these institutions is much greater for minority students: in fall 1992 27.3 percent of all white students were in two-year institutions, compared to 40.6 percent of black students and 55.2 percent of Hispanic students. Two-year colleges are therefore the mechanism of upward mobility for a disproportionate number of minority students.

Once individuals have enrolled in postsecondary education, there are many ways for them to enter the sub-baccalaureate labor force. While many community college students plan to transfer to four-year colleges and earn baccalaureate degrees, a small and declining number manage to do so. Overall, the proportion of students entering community colleges and transferring within four years fell from 28.7 percent among members of the high school class of 1972 to 20.2 percent in the class of 1980.[2] In addition, a majority of students in community colleges (about 60 percent, according to 1992–93 figures) and all those in technical institutes (representing only 3.3 percent of students in public two-year institutions, and 1.4 percent of postsecondary students overall) are occupational students, intending to enter the labor market directly after earning a certificate or associate degree (Tuma, 1993, Table 2.1). In addition, an increasing fraction of students enrolling in four-year colleges fails to complete baccalaureate degrees (Grubb, 1989b). This adds a quite different group to the sub-baccalaureate labor market. Nontraditional attendance has become increasingly popular, with more and more students in both two- and four-year colleges attending part-time and stopping out with plans to resume their education later; but many of these individuals never manage to find their way back to resume their education, and they end with some postsecondary education but without a credential.

The information in Table 2.2 summarizes the results of these different routes through postsecondary education, based on data describing the high school class of 1982 ten years later, when they were about twenty-eight years old. In these results, 5.7 percent of the group had dropped out of high school, 70.5 percent were in the sub-baccalaureate labor force as I have defined it (including 27.6 percent with a high school diploma only), and 23.8 percent had a baccalaureate degree or more.[3] About half the students initially entering a four-year college (51.6 percent) had completed a baccalaureate degree, and another 10.9 percent had earned a postgraduate degree. But almost 10 percent had shifted to a community college or other institution and completed an associate degree

Table 2.1. Proportion of Postsecondary Enrollments in Public Two-Year Colleges.

	1960	1965	1970	1975	1980	1985	1990	1992
Total fall enrollments	N.A.	17.6%	25.6%	34.3%	35.8%	34.9%	36.2%	37.8%
Total full-time equivalent fall enrollment	N.A.	N.A.	22.0	29.1	28.2	27.1	28.2	29.8
First-time freshmen fall enrollment	19.7	24.1	41.4	51.1	50.8	46.2	46.1	45.2

Source: Adapted from NCES (1994), Tables 170, 177, and 196.

Table 2.2. Educational Attainment, by Type of Postsecondary Enrollment, High School Class of 1982 as of 1992.

					Educational Attainment				
	Less than High School	High School	Some College	Certificate	Associate	B.A./B.S.	M.A./M.S.	Professional	Doctorate
Initial Enrollment									
Four-year colleges	0	0	27.4%	4.3%	5.2%	51.6%	8.0%	2.8%	0.06%
Two-year public	1.1	0	51.2	14.2	16.8	15.4	1.1	.02	0
Other postsecondary	0.1	0	24.1	48.3	16.7	8.7	0.1	.03	.01
No postsecondary enrollment	16.1	83.9	0	0	0	0	0	0	0
Total	5.7	27.6	23.9	11.1	7.9	20.0	2.7	1.1	.02

Source: High School and Beyond data, sophomore cohort, in Tuma and Geis (1995), Table 2.4A, with supplementary calculations.

or certificate, and one quarter (27.4 percent) had not completed any credential at all. Of those entering two-year colleges, fully half (51.2 percent) had not completed any credential; 31 percent had earned a sub-baccalaureate credential, while another 16.5 percent had managed to transfer to four-year colleges and complete baccalaureate and post-graduate degrees. The "other" institutions of postsecondary education—largely proprietary schools and area vocational schools, with a very few private junior colleges—clearly "specialize" in certificates, since nearly half of these students earned certificates while a quarter (24.1 percent) left without any credential. Thus there are several routes to earning sub-baccalaureate credentials, and the group with some college but no credential is similarly varied.

Looking at these results in another way, we see in Table 2.3 a description of the composition of the sub-baccalaureate group in the high school class of 1982, ten years after they left high school. Two-fifths (39 percent) had a high school diploma only, while another 28 percent had either an associate degree or an occupational certificate.[4] Of those in the elusive category with "some college," 18.1 percent started in two-year colleges, 11.3 percent started in four-year colleges, and 4.5 percent started in another type of institution (largely proprietary schools). Based on these results, therefore, we can see that while the plurality of individuals in the mid-skilled labor market have a high school diploma only, the second-largest group includes individuals who started their postsecondary education in community colleges but failed to complete credentials, while a substantial but somewhat smaller group started in four-year colleges and subsequently dropped out. Among sub-baccalaureate credentials, associate degrees are dominated by students entering and graduating from community colleges, whereas certificates tend to be earned by students in community colleges and technical institutes and in private proprietary schools.

Thus an emphasis on community colleges and technical institutes is justified because of the sheer numbers involved. These are the institutions that are the most important source of employees in the sub-baccalaureate labor market. In addition, two-year colleges *intend* to prepare students for sub-baccalaureate employment, and they have developed large numbers of occupational programs that are explicitly aimed at sub-baccalaureate occupations, in such fields

**Table 2.3.   Composition of the Sub-Baccalaureate Group,
High School Class of 1982 as of 1992.**

Sub-Baccalaureate Group (70.4% of the HS&B cohort)		
With a high school diploma only	39.1%	
With a certificate:	15.8%	
started in a two-year college		5.0%
started in a four-year college		1.8%
started in another institution		9.0%
With an associate degree:	11.2%	
started in a two-year college		6.0%
started in a four-year college		2.1%
started in another institution		3.1%
Some college, no credential:	33.9%	
started in a two-year college		18.1%
started in a four-year college		11.3%
started in another institution		4.5%

Source: High School and Beyond data, sophomore cohort, in Tuma and Geis (1995), Table 2.4A, with supplementary calculations.

as business, health occupations, computer applications, electronics and related technical fields, drafting and graphic arts, hospitality-related fields, and the traditional crafts. To be sure, there may be an equally important story to tell about dropouts from four-year colleges, particularly since their numbers appear to be increasing (see Table 2.4); these are students who are likely to be especially disappointed in their aspirations, and they may be completely unprepared for the mid-skilled labor market. However, with their exclusive emphasis on the baccalaureate degree, four-year colleges do not aspire to prepare students for the mid-skilled labor market. So while it is important to reduce their dropout rates (see, for example, Tinto, 1987), they are not otherwise appropriate targets for efforts to improve the preparation of the sub-baccalaureate labor force.

Aside from the short-term job training programs that are the subject of Chapter Four, the other institutions and programs providing access to mid-skilled occupations are either much smaller, or in some other way peripheral:

Table 2.4. Proportion of Students Leaving Postsecondary Education Without Credentials, Within Four Years of Graduating from High School.

	Students Entering Community Colleges		Students Entering Technical Institutes		Students Entering Private Vocational Schools		Students Entering Four-Year Colleges	
	Class of 1972	Class of 1980	Class of 1972	Class of 1980	Class of 1972	Class of 1980	Class of 1972	Class of 1980
All students	36.0%	49.6%	38.5%	50.1%	44.9%	51.9%	25.1%	28.8%
White	35.3	48.8	39.5	50.3	43.9	50.3	24.2	26.5
Black	41.8	59.7	36.5	62.5	57.3	65.6	33.3	42.1
Hispanic	42.1	49.5	N.A.	25.2	N.A.	46.7	32.6	41.6
Low SES	41.1	58.4	47.2	58.8	41.8	54.5	32.5	45.1
High SES	30.8	42.6	34.2	31.8	51.8	46.1	19.6	24.1
Low test scores	42.1	58.9	46.6	67.0	48.4	67.4	46.5	53.2
High test scores	30.6	37.1	34.5	55.7	32.6	44.3	18.1	20.3

Source: Grubb (1989a), Tables 2 and 5; Grubb (1989b), Table 6.

N.A. = not available because of small sample size.

• Proprietary schools, or private vocational schools, represent about 8.5 percent of all students enrolled in postsecondary education. About 9 percent of a typical cohort enter postsecondary education through these institutions. Based on the results in Table 2.3, perhaps 10–12 percent of individuals in the sub-baccalaureate labor market started in private proprietary schools.[5] Proprietary schools sometimes develop special niches within the sub-baccalaureate labor market; some employers develop relatively firm-specific training through proprietary schools, as the previous chapter documented. And there are well-known proprietary schools in certain fields like the culinary arts and technical subjects; they provide a kind of flexibility to the education and training system, expanding and contracting with demand. But they are also notable for the large amounts of student aid they consume: in 1986–87 they enrolled 5.4 percent of all students and 7.7 percent of low-income students but accounted for 24.9 percent of student aid (Grubb and Tuma, 1991). They also have high default rates among their students. Contrary to the claims of advocates, who like to argue that only a few "rotten apples" spoil the reputation of proprietary schools, these institutions are much less effective in increasing the earnings of their students than are community colleges and technical institutes (Grubb, 1993c; 1994). They have also been largely beyond public control, since efforts to regulate their quality and reduce default rates have been largely ineffective. And the faith in market mechanisms necessary to believe in proprietary schools is unwarranted, as the results about student uncertainty and lack of information presented later in this chapter illustrate. By and large, these are not promising institutions for improving the preparation of the sub-baccalaureate labor force.

• Area vocational schools, instituted during the late 1960s and 1970s to provide secondary vocational education, have often developed short-term programs for adults. However, their enrollments are typically quite small, and the programs they offer are often so short—for example, fifteen-week programs with half-day sessions, or about forty-five hours of instruction—that they are more equivalent to the job training programs examined in Chapter Four.

• Firms provide a great deal of their own training, as Table 1.3 clarified. Some of this is provided through their own training facilities, and some through private vendors of training services including community colleges and technical institutes. Much of the privately provided training is beyond the influence of public policy; indeed, those who feel that there is insufficient training in this country have not yet devised ways of enhancing firm-based training through government action (Lynch, 1994). And while contract training for specific firms has been a growing business for two-year colleges, it is still a relatively small enterprise, disconnected from the regular occupational programs of these institutions, and with relatively little accountability (Lynch, Palmer and Grubb, 1991; Doucette, 1993).

Thus it is appropriate to concentrate on community colleges because of their size, their centrality to sub-baccalaureate labor markets, and their stature as public institutions. While policy at the state and federal levels has often neglected these institutions, as I point out in Chapter Seven, the possibilities for improvement are still substantial.

Do Students Benefit from Community Colleges? Dropping Out, Cooling Out, and the Purposes of Students

Since community colleges are crucial points of access to the sub-baccalaureate labor market, it is important to know what happens to the increasing numbers of individuals who are enrolling in them. The results in Table 2.2 indicate that while about one-third of these students earn sub-baccalaureate credentials, about half leave without completing any credentials. Unfortunately, rates of noncompletion seem to be going up. In comparing the postsecondary experiences of the high school class of 1972 and the class of 1980, the rates at which students left postsecondary education without credentials increased for all types of institutions. For example, from the first row of Table 2.4, 36 percent of students from the class of 1972 entering community colleges had left postsecondary education four years later, increasing to 49.6 percent of the class of 1980; the increase in noncompletion was similar for those entering public technical institutes and private proprietary schools. By comparison, noncompletion among students entering four-year colleges increased from 25.1 percent to 28.8 percent, a much smaller increase.[6] Not surprisingly, these dropout rates are higher, and the *increases* in dropout rates have been greater, for minority students compared to white students (and especially for black students), for students of lower socioeconomic status, and for students with lower high school grades—precisely the "nontraditional students" that community colleges pride themselves on serving. Thus the overall trend of increasing dropout rates has affected different groups of students disproportionately, in ways that undermine the equity claims of two-year institutions.

Among those students who fail to complete credentials, the number of credits earned varies widely.[7] About a quarter of students (23 percent) initially entering community colleges but leaving without credentials earn six credits or fewer; about one-third (35.3 percent) earns seven to eighteen credits, while 44 percent earn over eighteen credits. These credits tend to be spread out over a variety of different fields rather than concentrated in one academic or vocational area, evidence of "milling around" or experimentation. (Not surprisingly, the number of credits earned by students leaving four-year institutions is substantially higher, and many fewer earn very small numbers of credits.) Furthermore, it appears that those who leave these institutions without credentials are spending shorter periods of time in postsecondary education: the average credits earned by community college dropouts fell from 27.5 in the class of 1972 to 22.8 in the class of 1980. I conclude, reluctantly, that noncompletion from two-year institutions is high by any standard, probably increasing, and leaves many students with very small amounts of postsecondary coursework accomplished. Because these patterns are more pronounced for minority and lower-income students, they undermine the claims to equity and to serving nontraditional students that these institutions frequently make.

One possibility is that the supposed dropouts are really completers—that they have accomplished what they intended, to complete a few courses necessary for advancement, or to master a particular skill necessary at their existing job, as community college administrators and instructors sometimes claim. For example, Cohen and Brawer's (1989, pp. 56–57) statement that students who are apparently dropouts "prove often to be those who seek only a few courses now and then to satisfy their personal interests or to learn the skills they need for job entry or promotion" is representative of these claims. There are certainly many such students who use community colleges for short-term occupational purposes, as well as many others who enroll for essentially avocational purposes—to take Lamaze classes, or art or Spanish or photography classes, for example.

However, several kinds of evidence suggest that this argument has been overblown, and that many noncompleters had planned to complete credentials. One is evidence about student intentions. Of the students enrolled in two-year colleges in 1990, for example—a group encompassing all ages, including the older students that community colleges attract—only 6 percent intended to complete a program of less than two years. Another 17 percent aspired to an associate degree, and the overwhelming majority aspired to more than that: 39 percent expected to receive a baccalaureate, and 38 percent expected a postgraduate degree of some kind (Tuma, 1993, Figure 2.2).[8] If we ask students in these relatively simple ways what they intend, we find that the proportion who are there for short-term vocational purposes is very low.

A second kind of evidence about whether dropouts are really completers is based upon earnings patterns. If noncompleters have taken a few courses to improve their prospects for advancement, or to improve a skill necessary in their existing jobs, then we could expect some economic benefit, such as higher earnings among those who are promoted, or at least stable earnings among those who might be demoted or fired if they fail to keep up with skill requirements. However, as the results in Chapter Three reveal, the economic benefits of small amounts of postsecondary education (less than one year) are virtually nonexistent for both men and women, and even more substantial amounts (one or two years) are virtually worthless for women in particular. Furthermore, those with small amounts of postsecondary education are substantially less likely than individuals with associate degrees and certificates to be in occupations related to their area of training (see Table 3.4), whereas the argument that they are really completers suggests that their field of study and occupational area should be highly related. While some dropouts may have attained what they intended to, this explanation cannot account for the large fraction of students entering two-year institutions who fail to complete any credential.

The third and most powerful form of evidence comes from the comments of community college students themselves. From the interviews presented later in this chapter, it is clear than many students simply do not know what they want to do. They are searching for some way to get into the world, to find a stable job, well-paid, with the prospects for advancement and sense of purpose that we associate with careers. But many of them have no idea what kinds of careers suit them, or how to get into such careers; they take courses in community colleges as low-cost forms of exploration, not with specific goals in mind. If pressed, they may say that they intend to complete a transfer program and to get a baccalaureate degree, but this response seems to reflect the conventional wisdom about the value of the baccalaureate rather than any conviction about its relationship to a student's enduring interests. The certainty about purposes that is held by those who assert that dropouts are really completers—a certainty that would be confirmed by clear statements of how a program is related to current or intended employment—is true of only a small minority of students we interviewed.

Many students in community colleges, then, are experimenters (Manski, 1989): individuals unsure of what they want to do, who have no way to find out except by experimenting with different programs in low-cost institutions. Those who decide that postsecondary education is not for them appear to be dropouts, although they could be considered successes in the sense that they have gotten the information necessary to make informed decisions. Others find a program, whether occupational or academic, that fits their interests and proclivities, and they may complete their programs. Still others never discover what they are looking for and find little in either the coursework or the support services in community colleges to help them; they drift through postsecondary education looking for a career that might fit them while they support themselves in a series of unrewarding jobs. They too show up as noncompleters, but they are quite different from those who have made more principled decisions to leave postsecondary education. Any simple statement about this group—either the statement that they are all dropouts, or the contrary claim that they are all completers—is therefore inaccurate.

The implications for the sub-baccalaureate labor market are, once again, that the students entering this segment of employment are extremely varied. Some have completed associate degrees or certificate programs of real sophistication, in technical subjects of great demand. A very few have almost completed a baccalaureate degree, and may be almost the equivalent of college graduates for employment purposes. The large fraction (about one-third) of the sub-baccalaureate labor force who are noncompleters are themselves different: some of them have completed coursework which makes sense for their employment while others have been milling around, sampling courses in different subjects without finding any purpose. As the previous chapter clarified, employers treat these groups of students very differently, contributing to the variability in economic benefits.

There is another reason for dismay at high dropout rates, related to a long-running debate about community colleges: if students are diverted from four-year colleges (with relatively low rates of noncompletion) into two-year colleges with much higher rates of dropping out, then entering a two-year institution may be detrimental to their success. Therefore the expansion of two-year institutions may have contributed to *lowering* educational attainments, rather than raising them, and to exacerbating the barriers to advancement through schooling of nontraditional students, including low-income and minority students. Before I continue to argue for the improvement of practices in community colleges and technical institutes, it is necessary to examine this debate lest I wind up offering marginal improvements to what might be a damaging and inegalitarian institution.

When Burton Clark (1960) first introduced the idea that community colleges engage in "cooling out" students whose aspirations are loftier than their abilities, he described a process in which students slowly lower their expectations to be more "realistic"—more consistent with their abilities—and as a result shift from transfer programs into occupational programs. Students might do this on their own, as a result of their academic performance, but Clark also described a crucial role for counselors in this process, urging students to see the difficulty of achieving their aspirations and giving them other alternatives, particularly terminal occupational programs. This process helps resolve a problem endemic to our economic system: the fact that students often have high educational and occupational aspirations, within an inegalitarian economic system where there are relatively few high-level positions.

Subsequent discussions of cooling out shifted the emphasis from a process operating for individual students, within institutions, to one in which institutions as a whole (such as the community college) are responsible for cooling out large numbers of students. One well-established fact, consistent with the higher dropout rates for students in community college versus four-year colleges and with relatively low transfer rates from two-year to four-year institutions, is that students entering community college are much less likely to complete baccalaureate degrees than are their peers entering four-year colleges, with peers defined by equivalent family backgrounds, race, high school performance and ability, and the like (for example, Alba and Lavin, 1981; Anderson, 1981; Dougherty, 1987; Velez, 1985; see Dougherty, 1987, for a review). If some students (including many nontraditional students) are diverted by lower cost and proximity into attending a two-year college rather than a four-year college, their educational attainments are likely to be lower. Thus the critics of community colleges have consistently accused it of cooling out large numbers of students, rather than being the egalitarian institution it claims to be.

But there are at least three problems with this perspective. The first of them turns on an empirical point. The cooling-out view assumes that most community college students would otherwise go to four-year colleges; critics have therefore cited evidence that educational attainments are lower among those individuals who attended two-year colleges rather than four-year colleges and have compared the economic benefits of an associate degree to those of a baccalaureate degree. But they have often failed to notice that cooling out may co-exist with "heating up," or educational advancement, whereby students who would otherwise have ended their schooling at high school continue on to community colleges because of their lower cost, proximity, and accessibility. The possibility that both cooling out and educational advancement take place simultaneously is consistent with the relatively large rate of increase in two-year college enrollments (see Table 2.1) and with the reduced variation in educational attainment generally (Hauser and Featherman, 1976). Furthermore, if both take place, then one's judgment about whether the community college is egalitarian or inegalitarian turns on how important each process is.

One way to examine this issue is to analyze enrollment patterns. If cooling out takes place, then we would expect that the likelihood of enrolling in four-year colleges should be lower in states with larger two-year college systems. But this is not the case: even after considering the effects of a large number of variables that influence postsecondary enrollment, the likelihood of a high school graduate enrolling in a four-year college is if anything *higher* in states that have large two-year college systems.[9] The likelihood of enrolling in a two-year college rather than not enrolling in post-secondary education at all is, of course, higher in states with large two-year sectors; that is, the expansion of two-year colleges increases the postsecondary enrollments of individuals who would otherwise stop their education after high school. I conclude, therefore, that the establishment of two-year institutions has increased postsecondary attendance among those who might not otherwise go to college at all, without reducing the likelihood of enrolling in four-year colleges (see also Cohen and Brawer, 1989, p. 47). On the whole, educational advancement dominates cooling out.

Furthermore, if community colleges have shifted to more vocational programs as a way of attracting higher enrollments among those students who were persuaded that they are not "baccalaureate material" (e.g., Brint and Karabel, 1989), then one would expect the likelihood of four-year college enrollments to be lower in states whose two-year colleges have higher proportions of enrollments in vocational rather than academic (or transfer) programs. However, this proves not to be true: if anything, states with a vocational emphasis in their two-year institutions have *higher* enrollments in four-year colleges.[10] This may be a reflection of the fact that transfer rates from occupational programs such as engineering and business are now higher than from conventional academic programs (Grubb, 1991; Palmer, 1988). States with a vocational emphasis in their two-year colleges do have higher enrollments in these two-year institutions among men, although not among women. So the "vocationalizing project" of community colleges has increased the attractiveness of these institutions among men, but not at the expense of enrollments in four-year institutions.

A second problem with the conventional view of the community college as an institution of cooling out involves the specific mechanisms by which aspirations are reduced. Clark's original work stressed the role of the normal academic processes of testing, assigning students to remedial education, and grading, but he also emphasized the role of counselors. However, this was based on interviews with administrators and counselors and on a review of official documents, not on interviews with students, or observation of classes or counseling activities. Ever since then, critics of community colleges have repeated his views about the role of counselors without collecting any new information about their influences on students, or suggesting what other mechanisms might be to blame. In our interviews, however, the most indecisive and least motivated students did not make much use of counselors; even those students who found supportive services unhelpful tended to view counselors as useless rather than detrimental. Finally, counseling resources in many community colleges are sparse. It seems absurd to place the burden for cooling out on counselors; they simply do not have power or influence enough to accomplish all that they have been blamed for.

The final problem with the cooling out view of community college is normative: the mechanisms associated with cooling out are probably more equitable and more supportive than any of the alternatives. As Clark (1980) himself has argued, any relatively inegalitarian society that promotes high aspirations among its young people must eventually reconcile the two. If it cannot create more places at the top—and this country has been notably resistant to reducing inequality directly—then it must either reduce aspirations in the "soft" ways associated with cooling out, providing second-best alternatives to students that seem more attainable and realistic, or it must reduce them in the "hard" ways used in many other countries, for example by using high-stakes exams that deny individuals places in postsecondary programs once and for all. The hard approach may be more efficient, and in some sense more direct and honest, but it is also more brutal, more rigid, more inegalitarian, and more hostile to an ethic of continuous self-improvement. A society with cooling out may not be the best world we can imagine (a paradise where everyone can realize their highest ambitions would be infinitely preferable) but it is certainly better than the alternatives.

In sum, the hostility toward community colleges as institutions of cooling out has been misplaced. There is, based on the little empirical evidence, much less cooling out than educational advancement; the mechanisms of cooling out are probably more complex than those suggested by many critics; and cooling out is preferable to the alternatives. The problem is to be more precise about those factors that cause rates of completion in community colleges and technical institutes to be so low, causing so many students to mill around aimlessly and to leave before completing coherent programs.

Students in Community Colleges: The Challenges of "Getting into the World"

In examining the experience of students in community colleges— in deciding, for example, whether community colleges cool out or enhance educational opportunities, and in interpreting the high rates of noncompletion—it seems appropriate to hear what students themselves say. In one sense, students have the dominant voice. They vote with their feet, and their decisions to enroll or not, or to enroll in certain courses, reflect preferences to which educational institutions respond. Instructors in community colleges, too, are in constant contact with students and know well the variety of purposes, the nature of the dreams, and the conflicting pressures that students bring to community colleges. But in another sense students are relatively voiceless: most information about students in community colleges has been collected through impersonal surveys, rather than by talking with them,[11] and the results of these surveys are sometimes misleading—particularly, as we shall see, in distinguishing so-called academic or transfer students from occupational students.

To remedy this gap, my colleagues and I interviewed at length forty-one community college students selected randomly from four community college districts encompassing twelve distinct campuses in California.[12] The results cannot be considered representative, of course; forty-one students cannot possibly represent the enormous diversity of the seven million community college students across the country, and our results would be infinitely richer were we able to talk with students from a greater variety of institutions. Confining the sample to California (for obvious financial reasons) skews the results in certain ways; in particular the extremely low tuition and the large numbers of community colleges in California compared to other states probably increases the number of students who are undecided about their future, because experimenting through community college attendance is so easy. But these interviews are still illustrative of issues that come up again and again in thinking about how best to prepare students for the sub-baccalaureate labor market.

The most striking aspect of students in community colleges is that they come for an amazing variety of reasons. A surprisingly low fraction, under 10 percent of those in our sample,[13] were essentially avocational students, attending for language or art courses. Another small fraction—again, roughly 10 percent—were using the community college as a supplement to some other program. One was taking courses that might help him get into a nationally prominent culinary arts academy; another was taking remedial courses as an adjunct to her private vocational rehabilitation program. Another was taking ESL, and one was accumulating credits that would count toward her degree at a state college. A couple of students attended the community college as high school students, taking more advanced courses than were available in their local high school.

But the majority of students, at least three-quarters, were in the community college for essentially vocational purposes: to prepare for a specific career, or to discover a career worth pursuing. Some, of course, were traditional-age students, recently out of high school; nationally, 48 percent of community college students (but 70 percent of all full-time students) are in this conventional age range, eighteen to twenty-three. These students recognize that some kind of postsecondary education is necessary, even if they aren't sure why. In the words of one: "When I first came here I had no idea what I wanted to study. I knew I wanted . . . because I know the only way to have a good life is to get a degree. I didn't really have much idea of what I wanted to do. I knew I needed to go to school, though." Another clarified that the community college was to be his way into the world of adult jobs: "It's really the only way to get into the world—you can just be yourself and just go to college and then get out of college and do your own thing."

Overwhelmingly, they cited low cost and convenience, meaning proximity to home, as reasons for choosing a two-year college. In addition, these younger students often acknowledge their lack of direction as the reason for choosing a low-cost institution; in explaining why he chose a community college, one student replied:

"Realistically, it's economics. I don't want to spend all of my parents' money going to a four-year school when I don't really know what I want to do yet. So I figure, go to a community college and then find out what I want to do."

Similarly, one younger student likened community college to an audition: "I think it's a good basis to decide whether or not you want to go to school, and I think it's ridiculous to spend $3,000 a year and then decide that you're not cut out for that—and not everybody is— when you can get away with $55 or whatever. . . . If I'm a musician, I audition musicians before I hire them. I don't just hire somebody cold and say, 'OK, do the job.' This is a good audition."

A second large group, of course, includes older students: nationwide, 15 percent of community students are between twenty-five and twenty-nine, and 37 percent are over thirty.[14] In our sample a very few of these older students were "upgrade" students, attending community college in order to further a well-established career. One was a line cook attending a culinary arts program in order to move up to more independent and well-paid jobs in cooking, and another was a real estate agent who needed to pass a licensing exam. Some community colleges assert that most of their older students are job upgraders; this may be the case in certain labor markets or in community colleges that have structured their programs to serve individuals upgrading their skills. But the vast majority of older students we interviewed were individuals who had spent enough time in a series of low-paid, low-status, or dead-end jobs and were looking for *another* career, rather than upgrading their position in their current occupation. One individual who had decided, based on his part-time work as a teacher's aide, to become a physical education teacher described his intentions in enrolling: "Mainly it was just to knock down some kind of career goals and to, you know, get started on that type of path. And also, with the type of work I was doing at that time, I wasn't really earning a good deal of money, so it was really mainly just to work up to a career job . . . I was working in special ed, as a special ed assistant. And then I was a parking lot attendant. That's what I was doing."

Others, without any particular goal in mind, entered on the assumption that something would turn up with more promise than their current jobs: "Well, it'll be nine years this August that I've been licensed [as a manicurist], which is the longest I've ever done anything, and I really do enjoy it. But I feel like there's . . . you can only go so far, and I would just like to have an opportunity someday to do something else. I just don't happen to know what it is right now."

These older students have found themselves for a variety of reasons needing a new line of work: "career jobs" with real prospects for higher wages, greater stability, and some advancement. Some had not taken high school seriously, or had attended lousy high schools, or had come from family backgrounds where college attendance was unknown or financially impossible, and so had found themselves drifting around a series of unskilled jobs for a number of years. Others had managed to find satisfying careers but were bumped out of them by the sale of a company, by the decline of a particular sector (such as defense and aerospace, in California), by the owner of a small company displacing them from management jobs, or by any of the serendipitous and unforeseeable changes that occur in a fluctuating economy. Still others were in stable careers but wanted the chance for independence, including the American dream of owning their own businesses; an executive secretary, for example, had functioned as the legal coordinator of a corporation but wanted the independence and flexibility of starting her own business. And some were women who had always planned to spend their lives as homemakers but now needed to find employment because of divorce. For all these older students, the community college is truly a second-chance institution, allowing them another opportunity to get into a career.

For these older individuals, as for traditional-age students, the low cost and proximity of the community college are crucial to their decisions to enroll. However, for many of these individuals, the use of a community college is not really a choice, at least not in the sense of a well-informed decision among several alternatives based on reasonably accurate information about the consequences. Instead, these individuals typically consider only one institution, the local community college, and decide to go to it without considering any alternatives. As one student reported: "I didn't look around. They sent me a City College catalogue and they had all these courses listed there. City College here downtown was the only one that was giving out those books, so that's how I picked that. I wasn't being particular about any college. It was just where could I get those courses and which was the nearest, and that was the one. I don't feel like any school is different from another. If the courses are there, they're there. I don't feel there's any difference at all."

In some cases, of course, the choice is affected by factors that don't usually enter the model of rational decision making; as one student who had moved several hundred miles to attend a particular community college claimed: "They [friends] just said it was like right next to the beach, and I thought, 'Oh, cool!'"

The decision to go to a community college is typically based on casual recommendations, often from siblings or friends but sometimes from total strangers. One individual decided to attend based on conversations with her regular bus driver. Another said: "I heard about [the community college] at the carnival, and in downtown [city] there are [information] stands. I was looking for a college and somebody told me, 'You can go to college here.' And one time I saw this person at the college and I talked to them and asked many questions and they told me. Then I decided that this was a good place to come. I looked at the catalogue and decided."

Finally, the decisions to attend are based largely on the conditions of attending: cost, proximity, the safety of the campus, the nature of parking, the appeal of the courses. They are, evidently, rarely based on knowledge about outcomes except as stated in the most casual terms. Students do report hearing good things about programs, but these recommendations usually come from friends and other students who are in no position to know the long-term outcomes of particular programs.

To be sure, there are exceptions to the practice of casual decision making. One graduate of a four-year college who decided to go into the culinary field reported researching all the culinary arts programs in northern California. Another, also with considerable experience in four-year colleges, had learned about every prominent film school in the country. Still another, an older student who had suffered from poor counseling, took an exceptionally self-reliant attitude toward information from others: "Students can be very misleading because advice is given not knowing the full situation, and some people can have degrees that are very similar to yours, but they're not *exactly* the same thing. So you go to the advising department or whatever and it's in writing and you follow that and you get the catalogue and you follow that and you're safe. And then your friends, you ask them where the washroom is."

But these exceptions are strikingly few, and they contrast sharply with the much larger number of decisions in which no alternatives at all were considered and where the reliability of information was unclear at best.

When they enter the community college, the small number of individuals who are upgrading their careers know what they plan to study; for them, the community college may be quite a specialized institution. As the individual enrolled in the culinary program mentioned, "I don't really feel this is a college. For me, it's just a culinary arts program—the program here is, like, so different from any other part of the college."

Several of the "reverse transfer" students—those who had already earned baccalaureate degrees—were clear about their career goals, like the individual with a B.A. in psychology and Slavic literature who had researched culinary arts programs thoroughly before enrolling. A few others have decided on a career path because of some recent experience; for example, one woman planned to transfer and get a baccalaureate in business as a way of helping her family business. Another individual had spent a year in the Caribbean scuba diving and then enrolled in a marine technology program to become an instructor for recreational scuba diving.

But the majority of students by far were using their initial enrollment to find out what they might do, taking courses as a way of trying out different careers, seeing what the academic requirements are like, and assessing their own strengths and weaknesses. In the process, some of them find a career path and begin to take the classes necessary for that goal. Other students declare they have made a decision about a major, but their description of what they are doing suggests that their plans are quite insubstantial. For example, one young student who admitted that "when I first came here, I had no idea what I wanted to study," declared that he had decided to become a "technical engineer" "because one of my friends . . . well, my older friend who got me started riding motorcycles . . . he's an engineer, and he makes a lot of money. I mean, that's why I'm going to school, so when I get out I'll have a good job that's making a lot of money." However, he was taking general education courses, rather than any technical courses; he expressed a desire to get into computer programming, and graphics, and the business program as well as to become a "technical engineer." His description of what a "technical engineer" does was quite vague: "Well, just little things that engineers want, like . . . it's just a specific person . . . it's still an engineer, but he goes and does other things that . . . just little specific things . . . I'm not too sure how to explain it, but they do technical little things that are more difficult for the . . . just the regular engineer."

Another student declared that, after taking several courses in the transfer program, "I know what I want to do now": to go into the radiology technician program. But when asked how she had chosen this field, she replied, "You know, I don't know . . . well, I guess . . . a couple of years ago, my sister-in-law had a brain hemorrhage, and I started thinking . . . I always thought about the medical field, and I don't really know though, I just thought it would be . . . I looked at the pay scale, and it's really good, and it's a good work schedule."

In addition, she was unclear about the conditions for getting into the program (which, like those for most health occupations in community colleges, is highly competitive): "It's a two-year program, but you have to have, like, your biology, and you need recommendations from . . . well, it will help you get into the program—they have to select you, is what I understand, from so many people. And they told me that doing volunteer work would help; then I could get recommendations from people."

Both these individuals, and many others like them, can identify a career choice when asked, and they certainly will fill in the appropriate blank if given a forced-choice questionnaire of the type that educational institutions conventionally give their students. But the reasons for their choices seem insubstantial and unstable; their knowledge about their "chosen" occupations is limited; and they have not begun to take the courses necessary to move into these occupations. It seems all too likely that they will change their minds, or give up at the first sign of difficulty.

Still other students readily admit that they have taken substantial numbers of courses but still not found what they are looking for. As the manicurist aspiring to something better said: "And since then [since starting the community college seven years earlier] I haven't been able to find the one thing that I want to do for the

rest of my life. I thought I had it figured out with the physical therapy, and then that didn't work out, and I believe there's a good reason why it didn't work out . . . I don't know what it is right now, but
I know that there is something else I'm supposed to be doing, and
I just haven't figured it out."

A large number of the individuals hoping to find a career are
enrolled in the "general education" or transfer program, probably
because in the absence of any clear direction on their part, the
transfer program is at least a well-established route to a future (the
baccalaureate degree) whose value is substantial. As one woman
responded to a question about whether she had clear career plans:
"Not really. At the time, I was just concentrating on getting my
prerequisites [for transfer] and taking care of my daughter. I
really didn't know what I wanted to do, and life was too hectic
to really think about it. I knew I was mainly interested in art, health
and fitness, business, and advertising, and I was thinking I might
take a major in one of those four, and another of them would be
a minor, but I wasn't really sure which one."

Some colleges counsel students who are undecided about their
futures to enroll in transfer courses, simply as a way to keep them
moving toward some type of future:

> I think the bottom line is that it [the community college] was
> affordable, and I didn't know what I wanted to do, and I thought
> that . . . My first class, I think was a career planning class, which
> didn't help me. And I think I was advised to just plug along, just
> keep going, and get all the general stuff [transfer courses] out of
> the way, which is what I'm still doing, like I'm going at a very slow
> pace, and that's why I just keep going. It's interesting; I like it. It's
> a nice break in my work week. It's nice to learn things; there's so
> much to learn. I really enjoy that.

Although these students say they are in the transfer program,
they are still very much experimenters, taking a variety of courses
in the hopes of "getting a life."

It's important to recognize that many students find being in
school rewarding. Even if they have not yet made a decision, the
mere fact of attending college is active and participatory, and will
potentially lead somewhere. As one student who had not made up

her mind about any direction declared, "When I moved out here six years ago, I wasn't anybody—to myself. I didn't feel I was a person. You know, I wasn't whole, I didn't have . . . But now, through the job, through going to school, I've started feeling good about me again. I'm doing something for me, for my life. And it's been really great."

Another, a perpetual student who had taken many different courses in many different institutions, used more pungent terms to describe the value of enrolling: "I couldn't stand not being in school, it's like wallowing in your own shit. . . . I learned how to wait tables and bartend, and it's all like nightlife kind of shit and I was like 'God, I need to get back in school.' I thought my brain was becoming mush. . . . I love school."

However, for some students the process of taking courses in the hopes of finding a career direction is quite frustrating. As one student, who had finally decided to go into a nursing program, declared:

> [I enrolled in] general courses because I had no clue of what I wanted to be, what to major in or anything. . . . I finally decided that the classes that I took before, that was just general courses to help you find a career, how to study. I don't know, all these classes, I've been thinking back. These semesters that I've been here and taken all of these classes, what was I doing? Spending money, going around with—I don't have any goal, I was just like—that's the way I felt. At the time it was just like "I don't care, just put me in class." I feel now that, I just feel like I've wasted my time. What did I do?

Another student commented on this pattern, typical of large numbers of community college students:

> I know lots and lots of people out of high school who go to community college because they have nothing else to do, and have no idea what they want to do. And for some people that's fine—they go and they take their classes and eventually, a couple years down the road, they'll pick a major, and then they end up getting their bachelor's. But just as many don't. They just, you know . . . "What am I doing here? I have no idea why I'm taking these classes. I don't enjoy it. I have to be here to learn." That's the situation that I found myself in, and a lot of my friends.

There are, of course, other resources within the community college aside from random course taking to help students make career-related decisions. Several students mentioned guidance from particular instructors, but the most important institutional resource is the counseling staff. Indeed, a substantial number of students, roughly one third of those we interviewed, had found counselors helpful in providing them alternatives to consider, in clarifying the courses they would need to take, and in setting up schedules so that they could complete transfer requirements. The matriculation program in California, a process where new students are tested to see whether they need remediation and are provided initial counseling about their plans, was clearly helpful to some. Said one student: "The counseling that's available here, it's good counseling—they seem to think you can handle this, you can handle more, but you really have to use a little common sense. But they . . . drew up a little ed plan for us to follow, and scheduled my classes according to what I could handle. . . . So it helps that way to know someone to keep you from going through all of the runaround."

The most supportive environments were reported by a dyslexic student who was greatly helped by the disabled student office, and by an individual in a special program for Hispanic students: "The environment here is like a family. We get along well with everyone, and anytime we need help we can go and ask the counselors or our advisors or our mentors and they're always there to help."

However, the majority of students (roughly two-thirds) either did not use counselors or reported disappointing experiences, disappointing in the sense that counselors failed to provide them any clear direction. The role that counselors play is complex, however. The students with the clearest career goals (including the few students upgrading their jobs) report not going to see counselors because they do not need to. But the students with the greatest trouble making decisions about their futures also report not going to counselors. To some extent this may be caused by limited resources in counseling, inappropriate schedules, and the weak reputation of counseling at some institutions (and the weak reputation of counseling generally, often a legacy of bad high school experiences). But students also acknowledged that they were partly to blame, as one student wound up admitting in explaining why she had not been to see a counselor: "I don't know, though—it's so hard to get appointments there for the counselors. There are only specific times, and each counselor, too, that you see—it seems like they tell you a different thing. . . . Well, it's sort of hard for someone to give you direction if you don't have one." Another declared, "In order for someone to help you out at the college, you have to look for help."

And a few—the most passive students, with the least initiative and drive—seemed to be asking the institution to make every decision for them, rather than helping them with the decision-making process. For example, one student who wanted both to get a baccalaureate degree and to take word-processing courses to get a secretarial position said, "I figured, when I wanted to do this, that they should have sat me down and said, 'These are the computer classes you need to take, and these are your basic English classes, or whatever, and your technology classes, and these are the labs you need to take.' Nobody did that for me."

Another admitted: "It seems like it should be easier . . . getting registration, getting all the classes you want, I mean, getting to the point that you need to go and get everything straight. It seems like I need somebody to hold my hand and tell me that I need to do this, I need to do this, and get it all straightened out, so I know exactly what I'm doing."

A kind of triage seems to be taking place. The students with the clearest career plans do not need counselors, and rarely use them (except perhaps for scheduling problems). The students who are the least decisive, with the least initiative—the students who in many ways need counseling the most—also fail to avail themselves of these services. In the middle, a number of students do use counselors to help them sort through options, establish goals, set up reasonable schedules, and the like.

This apparent triage may be appropriate, if precisely the kinds of students who can most benefit from counseling make use of these resources. But the large number of uninformed and indecisive students suggests that more could be done to help those who are attempting to improve their lives through education and training. There could, no doubt, be some improvements in guidance and counseling. Resources could be increased, schedules made more flexible, and counselors educated to be more knowledgeable about the problems students face and the alternatives they consider. But the deeper problem is that the process of counseling and guidance is inherently limited, especially with students who enter without firm plans, with unclear (or even misleading) information from family and friends, and with a variety of pressures that prevent them from considering very carefully the alternatives open to them. The more active forms of considering career alternatives, particularly the work-based programs such as cooperative education or the work-related seminars developed at LaGuardia Community College (reviewed in Chapter Five), may be more effective ways of helping indecisive students.

The process of getting through a community college is bedeviled by one more crucial issue. Most students have no resources in reserve, and no parents who can help them financially, so they must earn their own way; the burdens of earning a living *and* attending school are often deadening. As the student who was afraid of her "brain becoming mush" described her resulting ambivalence about schooling: "I don't want to go back to school right now. I hate it right now. I mean I love school, I just hate the pressures I have, of like having to work and go to school and pay my bills and feed myself and all this shit. And now they're telling me that I'm not going to get any more financial aid and stuff and it's like I don't want the hassle anymore."

As a result, many students must attend part-time, so they accumulate credits at an excruciatingly slow pace. The period of time to completing a degree therefore stretches on and on, sometimes seeming to recede in the distance. As one student, who had started a community college in 1986 and was still working on his degree in 1993, put it, "I think I need about two semesters of work. I'm fifteen to twenty credits away . . Oh yeah, I can really see, you know . . . it's right there. I don't feel like it's far off or anything. The only thing that makes it seem kinda distant is the fact that right now I'm pretty well engaged in just keeping the financial end of things going."

Over so long a period of time various things can happen, including changes in family circumstances, geographical moves, or just exhaustion of resolve. In these cases students often stop attending, or decide to take a semester or two off but fail to return. In these cases the "decision" to drop out, like the decision to enroll, is not necessarily a well-considered choice. As one student commented on his leaving the community college: "It was not even a decision. I just didn't go. Sometimes you decide on certain things. It was not a decision at all. Just like you go home, tired from work, you don't decide about 'Oh, I'm just going to go to sleep now.' You just doze off and go to sleep. It wasn't a plan. That's the way [dropping] the class was: it wasn't a plan."

Such students are dropouts in the conventional sense. They have plans to complete a program that are unrealized, and they certainly have not left because they completed the coursework necessary for a particular job or promotion. But their plans are often not particularly robust, their decisions to enroll in the first place are sometimes serendipitous, and, given the hardships of attending while making a living, dropping out is simply the most sensible course even if it is not a well-considered decision.

From these students and their perspectives on the community college, a number of conclusions emerge. One is that there are few indications that community colleges operate to cool out these students. There are few signs of regret for attending a community college, for example no complaints of time wasted that could have been better spent in a four-year college, and there are no indications that counselors have misdirected them. Instead, many students indicate reasons for attending community colleges (low cost, proximity, the smaller scale, the more supportive environment) that suggest attending a four-year college was not a reasonable option, particularly among older students trying to find a career after some years of casting about.

A second conclusion is that many students entering community college do not know what they want to do. They use the college to figure that out, by taking a roster of courses (often transfer courses) in the hopes of finding something they like to do. The assertion that most of them are well-informed—that they are there for job upgrading, or to pursue specific careers—or the equivalent assumption on the part of policy makers that voucherlike mechanisms are appropriate because students are well informed is simply wrong. Instead, many students (indeed, the majority of students in our California sample) are really experimenters trying to figure out what they might do in life. For this very reason, some of the information about community college students is misleading. A large number of students are enrolled in transfer courses or call themselves transfer students, but they are still occupational students because they too are likely to be casting about for a career.

The remaining question is whether the community college is an effective place for those trying to get into the world. Clearly, some students do find a career direction from shopping among courses; others find instructors and counselors helpful in guiding them or helping put together realistic course schedules. But it is troubling to find substantial numbers of students who seem to be helped neither by course taking nor by counseling services, which they fail to use. Whether it is within the power of educational institutions to help these individuals make decisions and find careers is unclear; for these students the problem of dropping out may be impossible for the college itself to solve.

The Implications for Institutions and Policy

One obvious implication of looking more closely at the individuals in the sub-baccalaureate labor force is that this group is highly varied. The amount of formal schooling they have accumulated ranges substantially, from the slight majority who have completed only a high school diploma (but who may have other job-related training), to those with associate degrees and vocational certificates, to dropouts from four-year colleges and from community colleges and technical institutes, some of whom have accumulated very few credits while others have considerably more.

The picture is even more complicated when we recognize that many of the dropouts from community colleges are really experimenters unsure of their interests and abilities, who have attended to learn more about occupational alternatives and schooling requirements. Some leave upon determining that postsecondary education is inappropriate for them, and we would not expect them to derive much economic benefit from their short stay in postsecondary education and their mixed program of courses. Others are forced out by dislike of course taking, lack of support services, the exigencies of finances, the pressures of family, or any of the myriad other reasons beyond the control of educational institutions. Still others discover what they want to do, complete programs, and move successfully into the sub-baccalaureate labor force. But identifying the numbers who belong to each of these disparate categories is difficult, and in practice, as the interviews in this chapter reveal, even students themselves cannot always artic- ulate the mix of motives that propel them to drop out or continue, to follow one path rather than another.

With the help of these interviews, we can now see that a com- plex of factors affects these outcomes:

- Many students entering community colleges—between 25 percent and 50 percent in most states, and perhaps as high as 78 percent (Grubb and Kalman, 1994)—are below college standards in reading, writing, math, science, and other basic academic skills. Many then find themselves in remedial programs, whose task— to bring up to some appropriate level individuals who have not learned fundamental academic skills despite twelve years of con- ventional schooling—is self-evidently difficult. But given the mag- nitude of the task, most institutions have done little to experiment with alternative approaches, to evaluate their own efforts, or to raise remedial or developmental education from its marginal sta- tus in the institution.

- The nontraditional students attending community colleges, who by definition have not done especially well in conventional aca- demic settings, find themselves in institutions where didactic and teacher-centered instruction is still the norm. Very few institutions grapple with the pedagogical challenges of nontraditional students, even though many individual instructors have tried to do so.

- There remain financial problems for students in community colleges, despite the relatively low costs and the availability of stu- dent aid. Some causes—for example, the low rate of using finan- cial aid (Grubb and Tuma, 1991)—could be rectified by more active institutional practices; others are probably beyond the scope of any policy.

- The emphasis on access rather than completion that is preva- lent throughout higher education policy has sometimes been detri- mental. The rhetoric about a student's "right to fail," for example, has suggested that students rather than institutions are responsi- ble for completion. The correlative emphasis on providing classes rather than support services, and the funding mechanisms that emphasize enrollments but not outcomes, are other signs of insti- tutions that measure their success by size rather than effectiveness.

• Students who are highly unsure of their direction may need more than a menu of classes to take. The most indecisive students in particular are not likely to be helped by the most common approach to counseling, the provision of information. More active and experiential approaches, as mentioned in Chapters Four and Six, may be necessary.

Our interviews also reveal that community colleges are vocational institutions—not necessarily in the specific sense that all students think of themselves as occupational students (although about 60 percent of them do), but in the deeper sense that most students are there to find their way into the labor market. The large numbers of students who declare themselves to be transfer students may do so because they recognize the substantial economic benefits to the baccalaureate degree. But because of their uncertainty about their own futures, many of them may simply be repeating a conventional aspiration, or following the most obvious path through a community college. The statements that surveys collect from individuals about their educational goals cannot be trusted; for students unsure of their futures and unaware of their options, these statements are uninformed guesses rather than concrete plans.

Unfortunately, most educational institutions—and certainly many community colleges, which have relatively few resources devoted to supportive services including guidance and counseling—are poorly constituted to help students make decisions about getting into the world. The process of taking a variety of courses may help somewhat, but course taking provides information about *schooling*, not about *occupational futures*. In many institutions there are insufficient resources in guidance and counseling; but more resources may not be the solution if students fail to use such services, or if counseling is conceived as passive information transfer. The more active forms of career exploration—for example, the experimentation with different work settings possible in some co-op programs, or the co-op seminar operated by LaGuardia Community College for students to examine their work experience—provide more direct information about occupations, as well as about the relationship between schooling and future work. But they have been adopted in only a few institutions.

One implication for community colleges, then, is that they need to take their broadly defined occupational purposes more seriously than some of them do. They are not academic institutions—particularly not in the pejorative sense of institutions distant from the real world of employment—even when many of their students hope to transfer to four-year colleges. Because this is so, simply providing courses does not meet all the needs of their students. If their mission is to provide access to nontraditional students, those who have historically been unable to attend postsecondary education, then they need to take nontraditional approaches, an important aspect of which is providing greater resources and more active approaches to helping their students get into the world.

A corollary for both federal and state policy makers is that many postsecondary students are not well informed—not about their own preferences and certainly not about the labor market alternatives they face. Therefore policies that *assume* good information (such as voucherlike mechanisms for student aid, the perennial proposals to "voucherize" support for postsecondary vocational education and job training, and heavy reliance on proprietary schools) are completely inappropriate *unless* public policy also takes steps to inform students better. The mechanisms for doing so include better information about labor market opportunities, support for student follow-up mechanisms that can provide information about economic benefits (reviewed in the next chapter), support for co-op programs and other forms of work-based learning (described in Chapter Six), and a greater emphasis on support services including counseling and guidance. Such improvements must recognize the underlying problem of students' being unsure of their futures and must adopt a conception of educational institutions that addresses all the needs of students, not simply their course requirements.

In subsequent chapters, these points come up again and again. In the next chapter, for example, I show that many individuals who complete some college without receiving credentials, women in particular, do not benefit substantially. These results would be puzzling if such individuals had attended for specific purposes related to their employment. But they are quite consistent with the understanding that many noncompleters have taken incoherent programs in an effort to find a career direction. The emphasis among employers on selecting those who have completed associate degrees may, as some have claimed, reflect an unquestioned faith in the credentials as signals of persistence. But it is also consistent with the finding in this chapter that experimenters with small amounts of community college education have not learned enough in any one occupational area to be prepared for most mid-skilled occupations. And the teaching innovations outlined in Chapter Five are in part efforts to address the causes of dropping out, particularly when students searching for career direction find themselves in arid academic and remedial courses with no apparent occupational purpose. The motives of students are crucial to all these findings, and anything educational institutions can do to help students attain direction for themselves will help the preparation of the sub-baccalaureate labor force.

Chapter Three

Economic Perspectives on Educational Preparation

Despite the intellectual and political purposes of formal schooling, its economic value has come to be paramount, at least in a society in which education provides the most important routes into the economic system. In postsecondary education, most students recognize that occupational purposes are critical: in fall 1993 a record proportion of college freshmen (75.1 percent) cited vocational reasons for attending college, up from 49.9 percent in 1971; and 82.1 percent cited its value in getting a better job (Higher Education Research Institute, 1994). In debates over the community college, arguments about its economic value have been unending. It is therefore crucial to get the issue of economic benefits right, particularly because, as I have suggested in the previous chapter, the debates about opportunities open to students following different postsecondary courses and about the appropriate role of two-year colleges depend on such results.

Unfortunately, the data about the economic benefits of sub-baccalaureate education have not been especially reliable in the past. Most data have lumped together large numbers into the category of having "some college" without a baccalaureate degree, failing to distinguish among the kinds of schooling within this group. In the absence of definitive evidence, the debate over postsecondary education, and particularly over the economic value of the community college, has often taken a decidedly adversarial tone. The critics of community colleges have often argued as if there are no benefits whatsoever to community college education. For example, Fred Pincus (1980) criticized the "false promises" of community colleges, and of postsecondary vocational programs in particular. But the data he amassed were flawed in a number of ways, and he generally compared the employment of community college students with students from four-year colleges (as if they would otherwise have attended four-year colleges) rather than high school graduates.[1] Brint and Karabel (1989) similarly rejected the "vocationalizing project" of the community colleges as limiting rather than expanding opportunities for students. But they too relied on a number of articles with serious technical flaws and stressed repeatedly the same wrong comparison, between the economic benefits from community colleges and those from four-year colleges.[2] The defenders of community colleges have rarely offered any contrary evidence, although they have often insisted that students use these institutions to improve the skills necessary in their current employment—an argument that is quite overstated, as the evidence in the previous chapter clarifies. Both positions have logical as well as empirical flaws, and each neglects the complexity of sub-baccalaureate education, with its enormous variation in educational attainment, in the fields of study available to students, and in subsequent labor market experiences.

Fortunately, better information about the effects of sub-baccalaureate education is now available. In this chapter, I summarize the results of this information, relying especially on one particular data set (the Survey of Income and Program Participation, or SIPP) and drawing on several other studies whose results are summarized elsewhere.[3] While these results describe *national* studies, I also present complementary results based on *local* studies relying on Unemployment Insurance data, a highly promising approach local colleges can readily use. This kind of empirical work indicates how unhelpful the debate between critics and advocates of community college have been, ignoring on the one hand evidence of how such programs can *under the right conditions* provide students with substantial benefits, while clarifying that other students (particularly those completing very little postsecondary education, enrolling in low-paid fields, or unable to find employment in the fields for which they have been trained) may benefit not at all. In the process, these results clarify what happens in employment to the students described in Chapter Two and how their efforts to get into the world have been rewarded.

The Average Economic Effects of Postsecondary Education

While virtually nothing (save perhaps a substantial inheritance) can guarantee prosperity in our society, education remains one of the best bets. Formal schooling provides several distinct types of benefits. One of these, described earlier in Table 1.2, is that it enables individuals to move into occupations with higher status, with better working conditions and prospects for advancement— "careers" rather than "jobs." While managerial and professional jobs are dominated by those with baccalaureate and graduate degrees, earning an associate degree doubles the chances of becoming a professional or manager, compared to the chances for someone with a high school diploma. But even more importantly, an associate degree or certificate increases the chances of having a technical position; it substantially reduces the likelihood of being a laborer, or a farm worker, or having some other unskilled position. Thus sub-baccalaureate credentials, as well as postsecondary coursework without credentials, help individuals move from the bottom levels of the labor force into mid-skilled positions.

Employment benefits are usually summarized in annual earnings. Table 3.1 presents information from the SIPP about annual earnings for men and women who have completed different levels of education. These results suggest that the conventional wisdom about the value of formal schooling is just about right, since with only a few exceptions those with more formal schooling earn more. For our purposes, what is particularly important is that both men and women with associate degrees and certificates earn more than high school graduates, and, not surprisingly, less than those with baccalaureate degrees. In addition, the groups that have enrolled in postsecondary education but failed to complete any postsecondary credentials also earn more than high school graduates. These results suggest substantial benefits, even for those who might be considered dropouts.

However, there are many differences among these groups aside from the education they have completed. Individuals who have enrolled in postsecondary education tend to have higher grades in high school (as well as higher test scores), and to have been in academic rather than general or vocational tracks. They are more

Table 3.1. Mean Annual Earnings, by Levels of Education: Individuals 25–64.

	Males			Females		
	1984	1987	1990	1984	1987	1990
Ph.D.	$38,438	$36,883	$49,911	$14,710	$25,891	$28,614
Professional degree	44,205	46,272	57,030	23,782	24,737	27,695
Masters	26,355	31,238	35,967	15,001	18,994	22,811
B.A./B.S.	24,939	27,601	31,697	11,016	18,260	16,954
Associate degree	20,030	23,904	25,080	9,916	11,005	13,589
Vocational certificate	21,775	20,584	21,664	9,318	10,841	13,568
Some college, no degree:						
Four years	20,066	22,237	27,338	9,835	9,148	15,718
Three years	20,230	22,620	25,086	9,400	9,850	10,537
Two years	18,121	19,922	21,798	7,402	8,713	12,548
One year	18,574	21,541	22,139	8,063	8,965	10,702
< One year	18,396	18,837	22,404	8,070	8,995	10,496
High school diploma	16,815	18,233	19,811	7,322	7,916	9,890
9–11 years' schooling	12,647	12,457	13,907	5,573	5,566	6,486
≤ Eight years' schooling	10,265	11,661	12,609	4,827	4,430	5,225
n	7,983	5,452	10,601	6,561	4,952	9,940

Source: Survey of Income and Program Participation, various years.

likely to have parents who attended college and who can provide them information and support both during their postsecondary years and afterwards, in the complex transition from education to employment. And their families are likely to have higher incomes, thus enhancing their chances in other ways. Therefore it is necessary to account for the effects of these other potential influences on earnings through statistical techniques that can isolate the contribution of education to earnings apart from the influence of these other variables.

Table 3.2 presents the effects of education on annual earnings while removing the effects of the other variables just mentioned.[4] These results compare individuals to those with a high school education, so that they give the benefit of postsecondary education compared to what an individual would have earned with a high school diploma only. The figures in this and subsequent tables can be interpreted *approximately* as the percentage increase in earnings; for example, the figure in the upper left corner indicates that men with a Ph.D. in 1984 earned about 75 percent more than those with a high school education. Finally, some of these figures are positive, but because of uncertainties associated with sampling methods they might be positive only because the data collection wound up with an odd sample; those figures that are high enough and certain enough to be considered nonzero (or are significantly different from zero in a statistical sense) are denoted with asterisks.

In general, these results suggest a uniformly increasing effect of education, as one might expect.[5] Those with professional degrees, including medical and law degrees, enjoy the highest premium over high school graduates, followed by Ph.D.'s, master's degrees, and baccalaureates. Associate degrees have significant returns for both men and women, although not surprisingly they are lower than the returns to baccalaureate degrees; the returns to vocational certificates are smaller still. The results for 1987 are representative: men with baccalaureates earned about 39.4 percent more than high school graduates, those with associate degrees earned 21.5 percent more, and those with vocational certificates earned 14.6 percent more. For women the benefits of a baccalaureate degree—31.8 percent—are somewhat smaller than they were for men, but the benefits of associate degrees and certificates, 23.4 percent and 16.4 percent respectively, are slightly

Table 3.2.   Effects of Postsecondary Education on Annual Earnings: Individuals 25–64.

	1984 Earnings		1987 Earnings		1990 Earnings	
	Men	Women	Men	Women	Men	Women
Ph.D.	.750*	.659*	.676*	.828*	.800*	.881*
Professional degree	.953*	1.37*	.806*	1.03*	1.01*	.931*
M.A./M.S.	.435*	.500*	.442*	.646*	.500*	.576*
B.A./B.S.	.415*	.355*	.394*	.318*	.437*	.428*
Associate	.184*	.311*	.215*	.234*	.166*	.205*
Vocational certificate	.219*	.164*	.146*	.164*	.063	.219*
Some college, no credential:						
Four years	.298*	.378*	.256*	−.023	.327*	.409*
Three years	.215*	.249*	.237*	.240*	.197*	.083
Two years	.135*	.015	.123*	.062	.069*	.200*
One year	.123*	.100*	.161*	.090	.093*	.059
< One year	.120*	.030	.041	.063	.072	.030
Grade 9–11	−.218*	−.175*	−.265*	−.236*	−.224*	−.220*
< Grade Eight	−.353*	−.358*	−.275*	−.226*	−.276*	−.300*
n	7,982	6,557	5,452	4,952	10,600	9,939
R^2	.327	.282	.384	.359	.408	.383

Note: Asterisks denote significance at 5 percent, conventional two-tailed t-test.

Source: Survey of Income and Program Participation.

higher. High school dropouts earn about one quarter less than those who have completed high school.

For the group with some college but no credentials, the results are somewhat less clear. For women, the effects are generally insignificant, although larger amounts of postsecondary education (three or four years) tend to increase earnings. I therefore conclude that entering postsecondary education but failing to complete a credential does not improve earnings reliably, unless perhaps a woman has three or four years of college. In turn, this implies that the high rates of dropping out reviewed in Chapter Two (in Table 2.4, for example) are especially detrimental to women: these individuals may have benefited by learning that postsecondary education did not suit them, but they did not get any employment advantages as a result.

For men, the results are somewhat more positive. Moderate amounts of postsecondary education (one or two years) have benefits similar to certificates, while more substantial amounts (three or four years) provide benefits about equal to those of associate degrees. However, small amounts of postsecondary education (less than one year) had no effects in 1987 or 1990.[6] Therefore some men benefit from postsecondary education, even if they fail to earn credentials. But small amounts of postsecondary education (for example, what individuals accumulate when they take a few courses for a semester or two) are unlikely to benefit either men or women.

Other data sets tend to corroborate these results (Grubb, 1995h). Most published studies find a significant economic benefit for the associate degree in the range of 20–30 percent, generally higher for women compared to men. The benefits of vocational certificates, less widely examined, are more varied and lower, ranging between zero and 20 percent. The results also suggest, as do those in Table 3.2, that some individuals do benefit from small amounts of postsecondary coursework even if they fail to complete credentials. But these benefits are typically quite small, usually in the range of 5–10 percent, and are certainly less than those from a certificate or associate degree. In addition, in some results the benefits depend on whether the credits are academic or vocational; by extension, I suspect that if we had better information about fields of study we would find benefits to small amounts of coursework in some areas but not in others. Under conditions of such uncertainty and generally low returns, students would be best advised to complete programs, and not to think that any kind of postsecondary education will generate benefits.

Another question that these results can answer is whether there are benefits from completing credentials, above and beyond the benefits of completing the equivalent years of schooling. There are different ways of interpreting such effects. A somewhat negative view might label these "sheepskin" or "credential" effects, suggesting that the benefits of completing a credential have little to do with how much an individual learns because employers give undue emphasis to the diploma or sheepskin. I prefer to label these "program effects," because the courses of study leading to associate degrees and certificates typically constitute relatively coherent programs, with vocational courses of increasing complexity and related academic coursework. In contrast, the coursework of individuals who have not completed such programs is more likely to consist of unrelated courses, as students search around for subjects they find interesting and compatible with their abilities.

The results in Table 3.2 suggest that completing credentials does yield positive program effects. One way to see this is to compare the benefits of a baccalaureate degree with four years of "some college," the benefits of an associate degree with two years of some college, and of a certificate with one year of some college. Of all these comparisons, the benefits of credentials are higher than the equivalent years of college without credentials in all but three cases. For example, for men in 1987 the return to a bachelor's degree is .394, compared to .256 for those reporting four years of college without a credential; the return to an associate degree is .215, compared to .123 for those with two years of college. For women, the differences are even more powerful: the return to an associate degree is .234 and to a certificate is .164, while the benefits of one or two years of postsecondary education without a credential cannot be considered different from zero. Within the limits of the self-reported SIPP data, then, there appear to be program effects associated with completing postsecondary credentials.

Finally, the benefits of postsecondary education are roughly consistent during this period of time since there are few obvious trends in the coefficients from 1984 to 1990. It is possible that the vocational certificate is losing its value for men, since the premium over a high school education was 21.9 percent in 1984, falling to 14.6 percent in 1987 and essentially to zero in 1990; in addition, the benefits associated with two years or less of postsecondary education also seem to be falling. However, in general the trends across these three years are not particularly pronounced. Thus I conclude that the benefits of postsecondary education in general, and of sub-baccalaureate education in particular, are reasonably stable.

These results refute the views of both the critics of community colleges and their staunchest supporters. Clearly, there are substantial benefits to completing associate degrees and vocational certificates, for both men and women—not, to be sure, benefits as high as those associated with the baccalaureate degree, but substantial nonetheless. At the same time, not everyone benefits from postsecondary education: women entering postsecondary education but failing to complete credentials tend to earn no more than high school graduates, and small amounts of postsecondary education are similarly worthless for men. And those who have completed credentials earn more than individuals who have completed roughly the same amount of postsecondary education but without earning credentials, signifying, in my interpretation, program effects due to the greater coherence of credential programs.

The Effects of Credentials by Field of Study

The results in Table 3.2 are informative, but they describe *average* effects for individuals enrolled in very different kinds of programs. For students contemplating postsecondary programs, average effects are irrelevant; they need to know which particular fields or occupational areas are likely to afford them an economic advantage. There are likely to be substantial differences among fields of study, parallel to the variation among occupations for baccalaureate degrees (Leslie and Brinkman, 1988; Rumberger and Thomas, 1993; Grubb 1992a, 1995e).

Table 3.3 presents the returns to certificates, associate degrees, and baccalaureate degree by field of study. Despite problems with small samples in certain occupational areas, some clear patterns emerge. The modest average return to vocational certificates for men in 1987 of about 15 percent (in Table 3.2) is probably due to the effects of engineering, computer, and health-related certificates (although small sample sizes preclude much certainty). The insignificant coefficient for 1990 appears to be an average of higher returns for business and engineering/computers, balanced by lower and possibly negative returns in other fields. For women, health-related certificates (and business and vocational/technical fields in 1990) have significant returns but other fields do not, including the relatively common fields of business and vocational/technical subjects.

The effects of associate degrees are somewhat clearer because sample sizes are larger. For men, the returns to associate degrees are highest in engineering and computer fields; public service (fire fighters, police, some social service workers and legal aides) and vocational/technical fields (including trades and construction crafts) have significant returns in 1987 but not 1990, while business is significant in 1990 but not 1987. For women, business and health-related occupations have consistently positive returns, while others do not; indeed, in vocational/technical fields (which include low-paid cosmetology programs) and in education (which is largely child care) the coefficients are negative though insignificant. Evidently, because of the substantial gender segregation in occupations at this level of the labor market and in the corresponding vocational programs, the results are substantially different for men and women except in business. This finding also suggests that efforts to move women into nontraditional occupations need not only persuade women to enroll in the appropriate educational programs but also must change the employment patterns that deny women the economic returns equivalent to those of men.[7]

For associate degrees in academic subjects, the coefficients are generally insignificant or erratic from year to year. This finding suggests that the academic associate degree, which was historically the path for transferring to four-year colleges, is not necessarily a good investment for those who fail to transfer. Also, because transfer rates from occupational subjects (especially business, computers, and technical fields like electronics) are as high as they are for academic subjects (Grubb, 1991), the academic associate degree has lost its special role as a route to transfer.

Finally, the results for baccalaureate degrees replicate familiar results: the highest returns come in business, engineering/computers, health, and math/science. Returns are lower in social sciences

Table 3.3. Effects of Postsecondary Credentials, by Field of Study: 1987 and 1990.

	1987		1990	
	Men	Women	Men	Women
Certificates:				
Business	.071	.139	.141	.276*
Education	—	.621	.055	−.084
Engineering/computers	.384	−.974	.217	−.070
Health	.307	.286*	−.287	.288*
Public service	.270	−.907	−1.57*	.455
Vocational/technical	.101	.074	.087	.174*
Other	.187	.133	.038	−.003
Associate degrees:				
Business	.113	.375*	.195*	.181*
Education	.286	−.225	.115	−.149
Engineering/computers	.359*	.299	.309*	.202
Health	.093	.369*	.139	.355*
Public service	.444*	.829	.030	.474
Vocational/technical	.211*	−.335	.085	.146
Other vocational	.355	.462	−.066	.199
Math/science	−.047	.352	.294*	.009
Humanities	.117	.005	.132	.235*
Social sciences	.326	−.103	.186	.377*
Other	.232	.373*	.107	−.075
Baccalaureate degrees:				
Business	.503*	.509*	.044*	.622*
Education	.126	.153*	.184*	.316*
Engineering/computers	.652*	.838*	.633*	.630*
Health	.308*	.445*	.436*	.518*
Public service	.247	−.314	.371*	.664*
Vocational/technical	.411	−.126	.214	−.122
Other vocational	.343*	.136	.392	.199
Math/science	.314*	.572*	.475*	.567*
Humanities	.166*	.226*	.262*	.332*
Social sciences	.320*	.513*	.433*	.413*
Other	.276*	.141	.450*	.429*
n	5,452	4,952	10,600	9,939
R^2	.391	.367	.409	.385

Note: Asterisks denote statistical significance at 5 percent.

(at least for men) and the humanities, and lower still in education. The category of "other vocational" includes such fields as journalism, communications, and library science; it proves significant for men but not for women. In general, however, these results are more consistent between men and women than are the results for associate degrees, because patterns of gender segregation are more powerful in sub-baccalaureate occupations than they are in occupations for which a baccalaureate degree is common.[8]

Evidently, at the sub-baccalaureate level it matters a great deal what field of study an individual enters. Some programs prepare their students for such poorly paid occupations that there is no real advantage to attending a community college or technical institute. Others, particularly in technical fields and business for men and business and health for women, have more consistent and substantial returns. Some relatively common fields of study at the sub-baccalaureate level (education, that is, child care for women, and certain trades and crafts at the certificate level) provide very little if any increase in earnings over those of high school graduates. Finally, the returns to academic associate degrees for those who fail to transfer to four-year colleges are often low or uncertain.

What remains unclear is whether students are well informed about these patterns, so that they can make well-informed choices among the occupational alternatives. Of course, earnings are only one factor influencing occupational choice. Desirable working conditions influence these decisions, particularly in some low-paid fields like child care and horticulture, and some students are precluded from well-paid technical fields by their lack of appropriate math and science. Still, given numerous complaints about the lack of guidance and counseling in both high schools and community colleges, it seems likely that many students are making poorly informed choices and entering programs where economic returns are insubstantial.

The Effects of Finding Related Employment

In the case of vocational and professional programs, the economic benefits of postsecondary education may depend on whether an individual finds employment related to his or her education. Because vocational programs are relatively job-specific, with technical and manipulative skills that are useful in only a subset of jobs, the economic returns may be low or even zero if an individual does not find related employment. Therefore the average effects of post-secondary education reflected in Table 3.2, for example, may represent averages of higher returns for individuals who have found related employment with lower returns for those with unrelated employment. While there have been only a few studies examining the effects of related and unrelated employment, they tend to confirm that the economic benefits where employment is related are higher (Rumberger and Daymont, 1984; Grubb, 1992a).

How common is it for individuals to have employment linked to their postsecondary education? Table 3.4 presents information about the extent of related and unrelated employment, using a relatively simple procedure linking fields of study with occupations.[9] For individuals with baccalaureate degrees, roughly 60 percent of individuals in occupational areas have related employment. For those with associate degrees, the proportion of related employment is lower for men but higher for women; in examining the extent of matches by occupation, this proves to be due to especially high rates of related employment in business and health occupations, which tend to be dominated by women. The extent of relatedness among individuals with certificates hovers around 55 percent. Among individuals with some college but without a credential, the patterns for men suggest that those with more years of postsecondary education are also more likely to find related employment; but the patterns for women are erratic. Overall, individuals with credentials have higher rates of related employment than do those with small amounts of college, and so part of the higher economic benefits of completing coherent programs is due to the advantage provided by finding employment related to one's field of study. However, it remains unclear whether these figures are "high" or "low," since there is no obvious benchmark to establish what appropriate levels might be.[10]

Table 3.5 presents the effects of postsecondary education on annual earnings, differentiated by whether an individual had employment related to his or her field of study, unrelated employment, or an academic field of study for which there was no attempt to match employment. Consistently, the returns to related employment are higher than the returns to unrelated employment, both

Table 3.4.   Proportion of Individuals in Vocational Areas
with Related Employment.

	1984		1987		1990	
	Males	Females	Males	Females	Males	Females
B.A./B.S.	63.8%	64.2%	61.0%	56.3%	61.9%	61.2%
Associate	56.7	70.4	47.9	63.9	47.2	63.0
Certificate	59.5	68.6	50.5	54.3	55.3	55.3
Some college, no credential:						
Four years	50.0	34.5	32.1	47.6	39.4	52.6
Three years	53.0	55.4	50.7	44.2	44.1	43.2
Two years	42.4	53.8	40.6	44.6	45.4	44.9
One year	43.4	56.0	43.7	52.1	35.2	50.2
< One year	32.8	51.2	40.6	47.8	33.5	44.1

Note: Individuals with unknown relatednes of employment and with academic credentials are not included in these calculations.

Source: Survey of Income and Program Participation.

for individuals with credits and for those with some college without credentials. These results confirm the hypothesis that the job-specific nature of vocational education reduces its value in unrelated jobs. In a few cases, for example, the baccalaureate and associate degrees for men, the value of even an unrelated occupational degree is positive and significant (even though substantially lower than the value of a related degree). This implies that these occupational degrees do have some general components that enhance productivity and earnings even in occupations unrelated to the field of the credential. However, in the majority of cases, and particularly for women, the coefficient for unrelated employment is not significant. These results imply that completing coursework is necessary but not sufficient: placement in a related occupation is absolutely crucial to realizing the potential benefits of occupational education. While community colleges do have mechanisms to link their programs to employers, thus enhancing the prospects for students to find related employment, in many cases these linking mechanisms are quite weak (as I review in Chapter Six).

Table 3.5. Effects of Postsecondary Education on Annual Earnings, for Related and Unrelated Employment: Males, 1990.

	Males			Females		
	Related Employment	Unrelated Employment	Academic Field	Related Employment	Unrelated Employment	Academic Field
B.A./B.S.	.524*	.365*	.388*	.594*	.231*	.396*
Associate	.248*	.105*	.174*	.387*	−.034	.231*
Certificate	.039	.113	—	.348*	.083	—
Some college, no credential:						
Four years	.642*	.256*	.240*	.522*	.322	.334
Three years	.305*	.139*	.153	.190	.179	−.177
Two years	.201*	−.022	.064	.342*	.084	.212*
One year	.228*	.069	.056	.118*	−.044	.063
< One year	.150	.033	.085	.166	−.170*	.138
	$n = 10,601, R^2 = .412$			$n = 9,940, R^2 = .394$		

Note: Asterisks denote significant at 5 percent, conventional two-tailed *t*-test.

Source: Survey of Income and Program Participation.

From these results, I conclude that the best course for a student is to complete an occupational credential and find related employment. An academic degree is second-best, both at the baccalaureate level and the associate level, where the returns to academic associate degree are substantial but less than those to related occupational credentials. The least beneficial course is to complete an occupational degree but then fail to find related employment. These patterns are roughly the same for individuals with postsecondary education who fail to complete credentials: related postsecondary schooling provides some advantages but unrelated schooling does not, and the benefits of uncompleted academic programs are highly variable.

Overall, these results confirm the importance of finding related rather than unrelated employment. In part, this finding helps explain the variation in returns to different fields of study, since some fields—business and health occupations, for example—have higher rates of related employment than do others; the higher returns associated with completing credentials rather than coursework without credentials is also partly due to this effect. For educational institutions and policy makers, these results confirm the value of efforts to link programs to employers and to help students find jobs related to their programs of study.

Local Evaluations of Economic Effects

As difficult as it has been to determine the benefits of sub-baccalaureate education, the results presented so far are in a sense still inadequate. They reflect *national* estimates of the value of postsecondary education. But students contemplating what education to complete, as well as institutions and policy makers deciding what improvements are necessary, need *local* information about the employment effects. (This is particularly true because, as the results in Chapter Four show, sub-baccalaureate labor markets are generally quite local, with both employers and potential employees searching locally.) In addition, it seems reasonable that the economic benefits of sub-baccalaureate education should vary with local economic conditions; for example, labor markets with high unemployment rates might have lower returns to postsecondary education of all kinds than those with strong employment, and periods of recession are likely to reduce the employment of community college students as employers cut back on hiring. The ideal results, therefore, would provide information about the employment effects of *local* programs, and in particular occupational areas.

In the past, institutions have sometimes sent questionnaires to their graduates to find out about their employment rates and earnings. Unfortunately, several unavoidable methodological problems with such studies often make the results nearly useless.[11] A somewhat more promising approach to local studies has developed over the past few years. This method involves obtaining information from the Unemployment Insurance (UI) system about the employment and earnings of individuals who have enrolled in postsecondary institutions (Baj, Trott, and Stevens, 1991; Levesque and Alt, 1994). Such data are regularly collected from those in most forms of employment; there is no need to send out a special-purpose questionnaire and risk low response rates. Furthermore, such data are collected over an individual's entire employment history, potentially allowing an institution to see whether employment and earnings rise over time. They are, of course, available for students in different occupational areas, allowing comparisons among fields of study (as in Table 3.3). Finally, by linking an individual's earnings history to his or her school records, it is possible to control for at least some of the variation in earnings that might be due to higher achievement levels while in postsecondary education, race and ethnicity, gender, family background (including income), and possibly other personal characteristics.

The results of using UI data so far have been promising, and consistent with the national results. For example, earnings and employment results using UI data have been calculated for Santa Barbara and Grossmont Community Colleges (California); the analysis was able to obtain wage-record data for 93 percent of all students (Friedlander, 1993). The results in Table 3.6 indicate that three years after leaving college, those with associate degrees earn more than certificate holders, who in turn earn slightly more than those who left with at least twelve credits but without any credential. (Those with fewer than twelve units were eliminated from the analysis on the grounds that they hadn't completed enough coursework to make any difference.) Furthermore, while those students who had been poor ("economically disadvantaged") earned less

Table 3.6. Employment and Earnings, Santa Barbara and Grossmont Community Colleges.

	Earnings, Year Prior to Leaving College	First Year After College		Third Year After College	
		% Working Four Quarters	Earnings	% Working Four Quarters	Earnings
Educational Attainment					
Associate degree	$8,545	63%	$18,443	71%	$26,078
Certificate	6,426	69	18,914	76	21,729
12+ units, no credential	8,479	62	16,080	67	20,519
Degree completers:					
Economically disadvantaged	7,055	67	21,802	73	27,645
Not disadvantaged	12,023	76	25,026	78	29,182
12+ units, no degree:					
Economically disadvantaged	8,357	54	17,989	56	22,554
Not disadvantaged	16,634	67	21,942	73	25,599

Source: Adapted from Friedlander (1993).

than those who were not, as one would expect from the considerable literature on the effects of family background, obtaining credentials increased the earnings of both poor and nonpoor students and narrowed the gap substantially from what it was prior to leaving college.

Table 3.7 presents the results for different majors. Clearly, technical fields (drafting, electronics, computer science) and medical occupations (nursing and radiology) have the highest returns, as one might expect. Less technical fields, such as restaurant management, graphic arts, business, and office and information systems (OIS), have the lowest returns, with differences sharper three years after leaving college than one year out.

Of course, it is not difficult for a hard-nosed statistician to critique these results. They may reflect variation in motivation, ability, or labor market experience; the substantial differences between the experiences of men and women are not reflected in these numbers (although they could easily have been differentiated); and patterns evident after three years may vanish in subsequent years. Still, the data on earnings in the year prior to leaving college suggest that there was not substantial variation in earnings capacity among groups with different credentials, and the consistency of the results and their comparability to national figures give them additional credence. They are certainly more useful to students in the Santa Barbara area than any national results could be, and they appear powerful enough to reinforce warnings about weak programs.

The results of national studies, using more complete data sets, and local studies, with data more pertinent to students but less comprehensive, will always be somewhat inconsistent with one another. However, improvements in the methods used in local studies can enhance their usefulness over time. The process of comparing national studies and local studies, as by trying to test results from national studies (for example, the results in Table 3.5 about the effects of finding related employment) with local data sets, or trying to use national data to resolve puzzles and ambiguities uncovered in local studies, can over time lead to a convergence of results. That should generate better information for students deciding what postsecondary education to complete, and for educational institutions trying to identify and then improve their weakest programs. All these developments help to make community

Table 3.7. Employment and Earnings by Major Field, Santa Barbara and Grossmont Community Colleges.

	First Year Out		Third Year Out	
	Worked Four Quarters	Earnings	Worked Four quarters	Earnings
Major field				
Admin. of justice	80%	$17,941	86%	$26,505
Business	65	20,674	73	25,823
Computer science	72	22,591	77	28,271
Drafting/CAD	100	24,796	67	28,360
Electronics	69	29,131	75	31,990
Graphic arts	60	14,145	67	24,969
Marine technology	55	22,618	70	24,595
Nursing	87	30,564	86	33,760
Official Information Studies	88	20,700	82	24,311
Radiology	84	28,313	78	31,065
Restaurant management (two-year certificate)	68	18,356	71	22,479

Source: Adapted from Friedlander (1993).

colleges and technical institutes more outcome-oriented, a consequence that in the long run will lead to improvements for students, employers, and taxpayers alike.

Conclusions and Policy Implications

The results in this chapter provide some clear answers to questions about the value of sub-baccalaureate education, about which information has been sparse. First and foremost, it is clear that the critics of community colleges and other two-year institutions who claim that they provide no economic benefits are incorrect. Both occupational certificates and associate degrees increase the earnings of those who receive them—not, of course, by as much as baccalaureate degrees that require between two and four times as many credits, but still by substantial and statistically significant amounts. Some fields of study, especially business and health occupations for women and business and technical subjects for men, have especially high returns; and individuals in jobs related to their fields of study while in college enjoy especially high benefits.

However, it is equally clear that some kinds of postsecondary education provide no economic advantage at all. Most obviously, short periods of time in postsecondary education have uncertain effects, particularly for women. Low-earning fields of study such as child care, agriculture and horticulture, and many academic fields, have low or uncertain returns, and those who have failed to find related employment often do not benefit from their postsecondary education. As a result, simple recommendations for individuals to continue their education in community colleges and technical institutes under any and all circumstances are unwarranted.

What are the implications of these findings for policy? In the first place, it is unclear that prospective students, facing an array of postsecondary education options, have sufficient knowledge to make rational decisions. The benefits of a baccalaureate degree are well known, and the lower returns to certain fields such as education, agriculture, and social welfare are also well known; it is hard to argue that students elect these fields unaware of their economic consequences. But the large proportion of new entrants to postsecondary education through community colleges and other two-year institutions, many of whom plan to transfer to four-year colleges and earn baccalaureate degrees, may not realize how few students manage to transfer and complete baccalaureate degrees, or what the consequences are of completing sub-baccalaureate credentials, or of failing to complete any credentials at all. A very different group of students coming to community college is older; many have found themselves unemployed as a result of changes in the economy. As we saw in Chapter Two, many community college students, both of traditional college age and older, are casting about for careers, unsure of their own proclivities or of the options open to them. The career counseling available to them is usually inadequate, and information about local labor market alternatives is usually either nonexistent or unreliable. Given the variation in the benefits of different postsecondary programs, one obvious recommendation is that information about the effects of various programs be made more widely available to students than is now the case.

In addition, state policy has often paid inadequate attention to the outcomes of these institutions. States are only now beginning to experiment with the kinds of local follow-up studies described in Tables 3.6 and 3.7, which are powerful ways of identifying the local benefits of occupational programs. Most state funding mechanisms provide incentives for higher *enrollments,* rather than *completion,* since they provide funding on the basis of enrollment or attendance. Similarly, with only a few exceptions states provide equivalent funding to all programs; this in turn means that low-cost programs in fields of study with lagging demand are funded the same as high-cost programs in such high-demand areas as health, electronics, and other technical fields. An obvious implication of these results, however, is that states should be more concerned about the *results* of various sub-baccalaureate programs. For example, Florida requires vocational programs to have rates of placement in related employment of 70 percent and eliminates programs which consistently fall below this level. Idaho can terminate programs if they fall below 75 percent placement for two years; Tennessee reserves 5 percent of funding as incentive bonuses for institutions with high placement rates (Hoachlander, Choy, and Brown, 1989). A number of states provide differential funding for programs with different costs, either by formula or through negotiated funding (McDonnell and Zellman, 1993, Table 3.5), partially eliminating the bias against high-cost programs.

Finally, like state policy, federal policy has been more concerned about providing access to postsecondary education, particularly through grants and loans, than with the quality of postsecondary programs, including their content or coherence, completion rates, or effects on employment. Because student aid has dominated federal postsecondary spending, default rates have tended to drive revisions in postsecondary education policy. But this has tended to focus attention more on proprietary schools than on other sub-baccalaureate institutions such as community colleges, which have lower default rates and much lower amounts of student aid. But default rates are not necessarily the best guides to policy, particularly for institutions like community colleges and technical institutes where tuition and student loans are low. The other instrument of federal policy in this arena, federal grants for vocational education through the Carl Perkins Act, has generally been dominated by secondary concerns and had little influence on postsecondary vocational programs. Overall, then, federal policy has had little influence on the quality of postsecondary vocational programs; the potential for greater influence has always been present but unrealized.[12]

These three strands of concern—with the well-being of students, with state policy, and with potential federal influences on the quality of postsecondary education programs—converge in a set of recommendations that have started to be implemented. Setting standards for outcomes, operationalizing them in performance standards, and then using the resulting information to provide better advice to students about career options and better information for state and federal policy makers are obvious remedies for the information problems that now exist. The 1990 Amendments to the Carl Perkins Act have begun this process by requiring all vocational programs to develop performance measures, with most states developing at least some postsecondary standards reflecting labor market outcomes (Rahn, Hoachlander, and Levesque, 1992). While these may be retained in some form in the consolidated legislation now being considered by Congress, the current performance measures do not affect the funding of programs and therefore have no necessary influence on institutional behavior.

In many ways, the increasing concerns with outcomes reflect both the expansion and the maturing of the sub-baccalaureate labor market. As the number of individuals with "some college" has grown, the question of what happens to them has become more important. During the same period, expansion has caused post-secondary occupational programs to mature and become better institutionalized. But the effectiveness of these programs has not always been carefully considered, as the weak ties of many institutions with local employers and the emphasis of state and federal policy on enrollment and access rather than outcomes illustrate. Appropriate policies can correct these causes of uneven economic returns, in the process helping ensure that the promise of the sub-baccalaureate labor market is realized.

Chapter Four

Creating a Unified "System" of Workforce Preparation

Americans are great system builders. Throughout the nineteenth century and into the twentieth, reformers tried to develop systemic approaches to social and economic policy, creating transportation systems (canals, railroads, and highways), a justice system, a social security system for the elderly, a comprehensive approach to imports and tariffs, and a tax system.

So too in education: the nineteenth and early twentieth centuries were periods of building an education system, creating a smooth progression from kindergarten, through a sequence of grades with each a prerequisite for the next, and on to higher education through the mechanism of college entrance examinations, even to publicly supported Ph.D. and M.D. degrees. The creation and expansion of new institutions, of the community college itself, for example, or the downward extension to prekindergarten and early childhood education, have also been part of this process of system building. The result is a series of institutions, as in elementary schools, middle schools, high schools, colleges, and postgraduate institutions of various kinds, each with definitive characteristics that are relatively well-articulated. It is a system where the requirements for progression are so regularized that many observers speak of the "pipeline" of education.

A different set of job-related preparation programs has been developing since the early 1960s, one constructed apart from the schooling system. This process began with manpower programs during the 1960s, which were then consolidated in the Comprehensive Employment and Training Act (CETA) during the 1970s and reformed in the Job Training Partnership Act (JTPA) during the 1980s. Job training programs are also provided through the welfare system, especially the Job Opportunities and Basic Skills (JOBS) program of the Family Support Act of 1988, which supports job training specifically for welfare recipients. Other special-purpose efforts have proliferated, including those for dislocated workers who become unemployed as a result of economic changes beyond their control, as in the decline of defense industries or competition from foreign producers. According to the General Accounting Office, the accumulation of programs at the federal level has generated 163 distinct programs supporting education and job training, spending $20.4 billion (U.S. General Accounting Office, 1995). Many states have initiated their own economic development programs to provide yet other training resources, often intended to lure employment from other areas, facilitate local expansion of employment, or prevent employers from leaving the area.

The establishment of job training programs manifests one of the most generous American impulses: to provide economic opportunities for as many people as possible, in this case through second-chance programs for individuals who have not managed to find stable employment through the "first chance" institutions of the educational system. The ambitions of job training programs are not very different from those of occupational education: to move individuals from chronic unemployment, welfare, or wages too low to permit escape from poverty, into jobs that are stable and well-paid and have some future prospects. By and large, this now requires access to the mid-skilled jobs of the sub-baccalaureate labor market.

However, the creation of job training programs has led to special difficulties. One of the most obvious is that, in generating other ways of preparing for the mid-skilled positions of the sub-baccalaureate labor market, job training seems to overlap with existing high school and community college programs. This has led to turf battles as well as concerns with waste and duplication. In addition, the proliferation of job training programs itself creates confusion about what services are available, among employers (as we saw in Chapter One) as well as among potential clients. As *America's Choice: High Skills or Lower Wages!* described the problem, "The network of public training activities in the country has thus been created as a result of unrelated education, social, and economic development goals rather than from any overall vision of human resource development. . . . The result is a crazy quilt of competing and overlapping policies and programs, with no coherent system of standardization or information exchange service on which various providers and agencies can rely . . . a maze of subsystems that are often incomprehensible to those who seek to use them at a local labor market level" (CSAW, 1990, pp. 53-54).

Above all, on the whole job training programs have been quite ineffective despite thirty years of experimentation with new approaches. While many of them increase employment and earnings for those who have enrolled in them, the increases are so small—in the range of $200–500 per year on the average—that they cannot hope to lift individuals out of poverty, or allow them to leave welfare; even these modest benefits tend to disappear after four or five years. As a second-chance route into the sub-baccalaureate labor market, the job training "system" is inadequate.

In this chapter, I first present a diagnosis of the problems in the current job training system so-called, based on extensive investigation of job training programs around the country.[1] I then offer a vision of an alternative system with programs arrayed in a progression or "ladder" of increasing sophistication and skill, in which existing job training efforts would be linked to the education system, with two-year colleges as the crucial linchpin between the two. This is another way in which two-year colleges can "work in the middle," since they would be responsible for connecting the current job training system with the education system. Fortunately, this vision can build on principles that have already been articulated in federal legislation, in the School-to-Work Opportunities Act of 1994. The final section of this chapter clarifies the elements and the services that are necessary to realize a unified education and job training system.

Diagnosing the Problem: The Fragmentation of the Job Training "System"

In the development of job training programs independent of schools and colleges, a distinction has emerged between *education* and *job training*. While the difference is not always clear, job training programs are generally much shorter than educational programs, perhaps ten to fifteen weeks long. Second, they are open only to those who are eligible, for example, to the long-term unemployed or dislocated workers in JTPA, or to welfare recipients in welfare-to-work programs. The consequences of restricted eligibility are two-edged. On the one hand, job training programs concentrate on individuals who would typically not find their way into community colleges or other education institutions. As Table 4.1 shows, job training programs are most common among high school dropouts; relatively few individuals with postsecondary education have been in public job training. To view these results another way, 61 percent of all those in JTPA held a high school diploma or less. But the dark side of providing an alternative entry into employment is that job training programs concentrate on individuals who by definition have had problems getting into employment.

In contrast to the provision of education in familiar institutions—high schools, community colleges and four-year colleges—job training services are offered in a bewildering variety of educational institutions, community-based organizations (CBOs), firms, unions, and proprietary schools, making it difficult to determine how services are organized and provided. While the services provided in education programs are relatively standard and include classroom instruction in both academic subjects and vocational courses, job training programs offer a much greater variety of services. They include classroom instruction in both basic (or remedial) academic subjects like reading, writing, and math; vocational skill training; on-the-job training, where individuals are placed in work sites; work experience, where individuals work for short periods of time; job search assistance, in which clients are given some training in looking for work, writing resumes, making applications, interviewing for jobs, and the like; and job clubs, in which clients are required to spend a certain amount of time looking and applying for jobs. Job training programs also support placement efforts somewhat more often than educational institutions do, reflecting another division between education and job training: those in educational institutions are more likely to declare that they are responsible for "education, not employment," while those in job training are more likely to accept that they have a responsibility for placing individuals as well as training them appropriately. Finally, the goals of education programs generally encompass political, moral, and

Table 4.1. Participation in Job Training Programs by Education Level, 1990.

				Education Level			
	Baccalaureate	Associate	Certificate	Some College	High School	High School Dropouts
Proportion with						
JTPA training	2.6	5.1	8.8	6.7	6.6	12.0
Other public job training	2.3	6.3	4.3	4.3	6.4	13.6
Training at						
Private vocational school	15.6	23.0	28.1	22.7	33.3	25.8
Community college	9.1	19.8	16.0	13.6	8.5	7.0
Four-year college	20.0	6.1	5.2	4.7	1.7	0.5
On-the-job training	37.3	43.0	39.8	41.6	37.8	38.6
Formal training at work	45.8	38.0	37.0	38.3	28.8	28.6

Source: Survey of Income and Program Participation (SIPP), May 1990.

intellectual purposes as well as occupational ends; but job training programs focus exclusively on preparing individuals to become employed.

By construction, then, the emerging system of job training—really a nonsystem of disparate programs that have built up over the years—has been independent of the better-developed system of education. However, the creation of a separate system has been unfortunate in several respects. One is that the existence of separate job training and vocational education programs, and the continued proliferation of separate job training programs, has created the sense of having too many programs all doing the same thing. The dominant complaint among policy makers has been that the proliferation of separate programs leads to overlap and duplication of services, that is, to waste and inefficiency, because any programs are providing essentially the same services to the same clients. The response has been to create a series of coordination policies, mandating programs to inform one another about their plans, requiring governing boards to include representatives of other programs, and otherwise requiring collaborative planning (Trutko, Bailis, and Barnow, 1989).

Contrary to this conventional wisdom, there are remarkably few cases of outright duplication in vocational education and job training.[2] One reason is that programs vary in their services, with vocational programs concentrating on longer-term certificate and associate programs while JTPA and welfare programs emphasize short-term training and other services. Programs also vary in the individuals they serve, with JTPA and JOBS serving more disadvantaged individuals than community colleges. An overall shortage of resources means that there is generally more demand than existing programs can supply. Since the major employment-related federal programs have diverse goals (with the Perkins Act providing marginal resources to improve vocational education otherwise funded by states and localities, JTPA providing the entire funding for shorter-term job training and related services, the JOBS programs supporting programs only for welfare recipients, and the Adult Education Act emphasizing remediation only), the duplication among federal efforts has been slight.

Again contrary to conventional wisdom that more coordination is necessary, at the local level there is substantial coordination.

In most communities there is a system in the sense that administrators of every program are familiar with all others, and extensive referral and contracting among programs takes place (Grubb and McDonnell, 1991, 1996). In the most typical pattern, for example, secondary and postsecondary vocational programs are linked by articulation agreements and two-plus-two plans; JTPA and welfare-to-work programs subcontract with community colleges to provide some (though not all) of their training and remediation, with adult schools usually providing the lion's share of remediation; and community colleges provide customized training with their own resources as well as funds from state economic development efforts. There are other variants on this "standard model" of coordination, of course. In some communities education programs are reasonably well coordinated, and job training and welfare-to-work programs collaborate, but the education system and the job training system interact very little—often because of differences in purposes, clients, and politics. In some cases a local community college provides virtually all education and job training services, effectively becoming the kind of one-stop education and training center that other states have tried. At the other extreme, some communities have a series of autonomous institutions without much interaction. But such examples are relatively rare; coordination is far more common than the simple rhetoric about waste and inefficiency would lead one to believe.

Because of the lack of duplication and the presence of at least some coordination, the conventional diagnosis of waste and inefficiency and the need for coordination is misplaced. Instead, the real problem with job training is the effectiveness of existing programs. To be sure, most job training programs do increase employment and earnings, and they reduce the amount of welfare benefits individuals receive; except for the least effective programs, the benefits of job training usually exceed the costs, so they are "worth doing" in this sense.[3] However, the benefits are too small to change the lives of individuals who have enrolled in them. A good example of job training effects can be seen in Table 4.2, which presents the results of evaluating JTPA, the major job training program. To be sure, the program did increase earnings by about $1,000 a year, for both adult men and women, and the benefits outweighed the costs of the program. But job training left

Table 4.2. Impacts of JTPA on Total Thirty-Month Earnings: Assignees and Enrollees, by Target Group.

	Mean Earnings		Impact per Assignee		Impact per Enrollee in Dollars
	Treatment Group (1)	Control Group (2)	In Dollars (3)	% of (2)	
Adult women	$13,417	$12,241	$1,176***	9.6%	$1,837***
Adult men	19,474	18,496	978*	5.3	1,599*
Female youths	10,241	10,106	135	1.3	210
Male youth nonarrestees	15,786	16,375	–589	–3.6	–868
Male youth arrestees					
Using survey data	14,633	18,842	–4,209**	–22.3	1,804**
Using scaled UI data	14,148	14,152	–4	0.0	–6

Statistical significance: *** = 1 percent, ** = 5 percent, * = 10 percent.

Source: Adapted from Bloom et al. (1994), Exhibit 5.

their earnings so low—$13,400 among women, and $19,500 among men—that they would still be among the "working poor." Even these results may be generous: a meta-analysis of job training found earnings increases of between $200 and $540 (Fischer and Cordray, 1996).

Furthermore, while these benefits may be present for two or three years after enrolling in a job training program, they begin to decline in year four, and five years after enrollment there is typically no difference between those who have enrolled in job training and individuals who have not (Friedlander and Burtless, 1995). Evidently these short-term programs have not been successful in giving welfare recipients the skills necessary for long-run success in the sub-baccalaureate labor market. Even in JTPA, which is conventionally thought to be outcome-oriented because of its performance standards and governance by business-dominated PICs (Private Industry Councils), local programs tend to be *performance-driven* but not *outcome-oriented:* they "play to the indicators," concerned with meeting specific performance targets, but ignorant about other dimensions of success such as long-term employment prospects or the difference in effectiveness among local providers. The result is that the official performance indicators are completely uncorrelated with the actual effects on earnings (Doolittle and others, 1993, p. 10).

As a way into the mid-skilled jobs of the sub-baccalaureate labor market, or a long-run solution to the problems of underemployment, poverty, and welfare dependence, the second chance programs of the job training system are unreliable. While there are many reasons for the weak results of job training programs, a dominant one is simply that small programs have small effects. The individuals enrolled in job training often have multiple problems and several barriers to employment. They often lack job-specific skills, general academic skills, and the kinds of values (including motivation, punctuality, persistence, and the ability to work with others) necessary to find and keep employment. Some of them have more serious problems like drug and alcohol abuse, physical handicaps and health problems, depression, and mental health problems that may be more biological than experiential. But most job training programs are "small" in the sense that they last a very short period of time, rarely more than twenty weeks. Also, they often provide a single kind of service rather than a variety of complementary services for individuals with multiple needs; and they cost much less—in the vicinity of $2,200 per person—than do community college programs, whose cost per person averaged $5,700 in 1993 (Grubb, 1996, chapter six). Job training administrators often take pride in this aspect of their programs, saying for example that they offer "Chevrolet" programs compared to the "Cadillac" programs of educational institutions. By this they mean that they can get to the same destination at much lower cost; they often scorn education programs for being too "academic" and unconcerned with immediate employment. But this attitude masks the profound disjunction between the needs of those who have not found stable employment and the small size of job training programs, for which reason the trivial effects on employment should not be surprising.

Given the multiple barriers to employment of many individuals, a related problem is that job training programs typically provide "one shot" efforts, with any particular program not linked to others, either programs with complementary services (such as remediation) or those with more advanced training. There are very few mechanisms for following individuals through the system, helping them make transitions among programs, providing them assistance if they falter, or giving them information about the alternatives available. As a result, referral among programs—for example, from JTPA to adult education, or from a JOBS program to a community college—is likely to result in individuals becoming "lost," rather than being an effective method of cooperation, even in welfare-to-work programs where caseworkers are responsible for tracking individuals. One JOBS administrator lamented sending clients to "the black hole of adult basic education," since the lack of tracking mechanisms meant that the program (like most others) never knew whether the individual arrived at the remedial program, completed the program, made it back into job skills training, completed training, and finally managed to find stable employment. In a few communities the dominance of the community college (or, less often, a particular adult school) has consolidated all services in one institution, facilitating tracking and referral among services. Some states (notably Wisconsin) have experimented with one-stop education and training centers. But such efforts are rare; in most communities, what could be a well articulated system with a continuum of remedial and job-specific education is experienced as a patchwork of disconnected pieces.

Several other problems with job training programs have been caused by the separation of training from education. One is the basic assumption underlying most job training programs, which have stressed moving individuals into employment quickly on the assumption that once an individual gets a job he or she will remain employed. This tactic assumes that *job finding* rather than *job keeping* is the basic problem,[4] and that there are plenty of jobs available to those who want to work. Contrary to education programs, there has been much less attention paid to the problem of enhancing the basic competencies—cognitive, vocational, and personal—of job trainees, except in a limited number of intensive and experimental programs. Given the lack of attention to fundamental abilities, it should not be surprising that the long-run effects of job training are so paltry. At best they can urge individuals to be employed more, but they do not prepare them for more skilled and better-paid occupations.

In addition, most job training programs are completely ignorant about issues of good teaching. Job training programs almost universally use conventional pedagogical techniques based on "skills and drills," with instructors breaking complex competencies into tiny subskills and drilling endlessly on a series of inherently meaningless subskills (Grubb and Kalman, 1994). While there is evidence that conventional didactic approaches are the least effective methods for teaching many individuals, this approach is likely to be particularly ineffective for the individuals in job training. Most of them have not done well in many years of schooling, using conventional didactic instruction; why they should suddenly be able to learn from this approach in very short programs with bad teaching is unclear.[5]

There are still other reasons for the ineffectiveness of job training. The quality of job training itself is suspect. A great deal of on-the-job training is really subsidized employment, with little or no training going on in the majority of programs (Kogan and others, 1989), and vocational skills training may suffer from the same kind of problems in keeping up with changes in the technology and the organization of production that affect community colleges. The rates of placement in related employment of many job training programs are relatively low; as for the education programs analyzed in Table 3.5, those who find employment unrelated to their field of training earn less than those with related employment (Grubb, 1995d). The operation of job training programs by local organizations has made them vulnerable to local political influence, with community-based organizations sometimes supported because of their political connections rather than their effectiveness. And the concentration of those who have been unemployed and on welfare has created a powerful stigma to having been in these programs, so that many employers refuse to hire from them; for all practical purposes, these programs are invisible to employers. Public job training programs were not used by any of the employers we interviewed, and several employers reported bad experiences. For example, a manufacturing firm in Cincinnati reported hiring an individual who "worked two weeks and was off fifty-two"; the firm was clearly not going to repeat this dismal experience.

My diagnosis then is that the separation of *training* from *education* has been counterproductive. The real economic rewards are to be found in the educational system, not in job training. As Chapter Three pointed out, the rewards to certificates and associate degrees are much more substantial than are the benefits from job training, and sub-baccalaureate education increases earnings over an entire employment history rather than generating benefits that decay after three or four years. The separation has worked to the detriment of the education system too, which could learn from job training about the importance of performance and outcomes rather than enrollments as a measure of success, and about the utility of placement efforts and related support services.

As a result, one way to develop a more effective education and job training *system* would be to recombine them—to link job training with educational programs, using the community college as the conduit between the two. This would create a more continuous system with a greater variety of services for a broader range of individuals than either one now serves. Currently, two-year colleges provide virtually the only links between the two systems: community colleges and technical institutes often provide vocational training for JTPA and welfare clients, and remediation to these individuals as well as their own students. In some areas the community college is the administrator of JTPA programs, and in a few communities the community college is almost the sole provider of all vocational education, job training, and remediation, coordinating the job training and the education system de facto (Grubb and McDonnell, 1991). By participating in both job training and in education, community colleges already have the potential to move individuals from the short-term job training system into the education system. However, it is unclear how often this happens. Even when they administer job training programs, community colleges often establish courses that are independent of the "regular" education programs; and few institutions keep records about the movement of individuals from JTPA (or welfare-to-work programs) into and through certificate and associate programs.

The challenge to creating an overall education and job training system from the two disjointed systems that now exist is therefore to create these links systematically, in ladders of education and training opportunities that can move individuals from their existing levels of accomplishment to higher levels where they are prepared for jobs of increasing skill, earnings, and stability. Furthermore, the consolidation of federal legislation for vocational education, job training, and adult education gives states the ability and incentive to do so, allowing them to develop coherent systems of workforce development.

A Different Vision: Vertical Articulation and "Ladders" of Opportunities

In developing an alternative vision for education and job training, the recently enacted School-to-Work Opportunities Act of 1994 (STWOA) presents a set of principles that could guide federal and state efforts—principles that should outlast the likely consolidation of the STWOA with other education and training programs. While the STWOA was intended to spur reforms in high schools, it can be interpreted as specifying five elements for successful programs of the sort we are interested in:

• Vocational skill training, of varying length to prepare individuals for jobs of different levels of skill, responsibility, earnings, and stability.

• Academic instruction, integrated with occupational education. In job training programs academic instruction could refer to remedial instruction, which proves to be necessary for large proportions of individuals. The STWOA specifies that academic (or remedial) and occupational instruction should be integrated, consistent with the argument in Chapter Five that such integration is a powerful way of providing a context or application for academic subjects to increase student motivation.

• The inclusion of work-based education, coordinated with classroom-based instruction through "connecting activities." The purpose of work-based education is to provide a different kind of learning, complementary to classroom instruction; within the sub-baccalaureate labor market, the importance of experience makes work-based learning particularly important. The purpose of connecting activities is to ensure that the lessons of the two are consistent with one another, rather than generating work placements with no applications of classroom-based instruction, or including academic and vocational education that is not used in work, as currently happens in low-quality work experience programs.

• The connection of every program to the next program in a hierarchy of education and training opportunities. In the STWOA, high school programs are explicitly linked to postsecondary opportunities through tech prep. The analogy in job training programs is that every program would be connected to a further program at a higher level of skill, with enhanced employment opportunities.

• The use of applied teaching methods and team-teaching strategies. By implication, all school-based and work-based instruction should develop pedagogies that are more contextualized, more integrated or interdisciplinary, student-centered, active (or constructivist), and project- or activity-based.

Currently, of course, most federal job training programs violate this vision. For example, adult remedial programs are usually freestanding, unconnected to vocational skills training, work-based instruction, or higher level programs; they usually use the worst kinds of didactic instruction, often because they are driven by the GED. JTPA programs often fund on-the-job training, intended to be a form of work-based learning, but learning on the job is often insubstantial because individuals are being used as low-cost

unskilled labor (Kogan and others, 1989), and it is usually unconnected to remediation or vocational skills training. JTPA and welfare-to-work programs support occupational skill training, but
these efforts are usually short-term. At best they provide limited
training for repetitive entry-level work, such as "electronics" programs preparing individuals for work as assemblers in high-tech
factories or "computer" programs preparing clients to be data
entry clerks with spreadsheet applications. They are also unconnected to any further training or education opportunities, including certificate and associate programs. Furthermore, these job
training efforts are often disconnected from the remedial instruction that many clients need, as well as other support services.

In other cases clients receive job search assistance without remediation, vocational skills training, or work-based learning. This
is a particularly inappropriate program for individuals who lack
both education and labor market experience. The referral mechanisms that might lead individuals from successful completion of
one program into a higher-level program, or from one service (remediation) to another (occupational skills training), are rarely in
place. While it is possible for individuals to create longer programs
by moving from job training into two-year colleges, for example,
doing so requires the individual to take all the initiative and negotiate the movement from one institution to another. The pieces of
more coherent programs may be in place, but currently they are
disconnected from each other.

The overall task of developing a more coherent and integrated
program of education and job training is enormous, and I can only
outline the elements that would be necessary in this chapter. However, if the central vision that emerges from the School-to-Work
Opportunities Act is kept in mind, then many of the elements necessary for successfully realizing this vision could be developed over
time. The most crucial elements include the linking of programs
in vertical ladders, and the provision of integrated instruction and
services.

Linking Programs in Vertical Ladders

A crucial element of a coherent system would be to require all programs to be linked, to create a series of sequential education and

training-related activities that individuals can use to progress from relatively low levels of skill (and relatively unskilled and poorly paid work) to higher levels of skill and (presumably) more demanding, better-paid, and more stable occupations. Figure 4.1 provides an illustration. Individuals with no occupational skills and little experience could enter short-term job training programs, of the kind now provided by JTPA and welfare-to-work programs, that would provide fifteen to thirty weeks of instruction preparing them for the most modestly skilled entry-level jobs. The individuals could then *either* leave for employment, helped by appropriate placement services, *or* they could enter a subsequent job training program, presumably a certificate program leading to more skilled jobs. The individuals needing to support themselves immediately would go into employment, but they would be able to reenter the system when conditions in their lives permit, and to continue up the ladder of opportunities. The linkages among programs would be occupationally specific; for example, a community-based organization or a vocational school could offer a fifteen-week job training program in electronics providing access to entry-level and relatively unskilled assembly-line employment. After working a while, an individual could continue in a certificate program in electronics, probably in a community college or technical institute.

In turn, certificate programs would prepare individuals for employment *or* for subsequent continuation in an associate degree program, depending once again on the life circumstances of individual students. In turn, associate programs are usually connected to baccalaureate level programs, through articulation agreements and transfer centers that are already part of many community colleges. In this vision, the lower levels of job training could be provided in institutions outside of education—in community-based organizations, unions, and companies—as well as in area vocational schools and two-year colleges; but most certificate and associate-level occupational instruction would take place in two-year colleges. In this way two-year colleges would become the point of connection between what is now the job training system and the educational system.

One requirement for creating such a ladder is that every job training program in a community would be required to specify those programs to which it leads, and those lower-level programs which are "feeders" into the program. This would provide information to

Figure 4.1. A Unified Education and Training System.

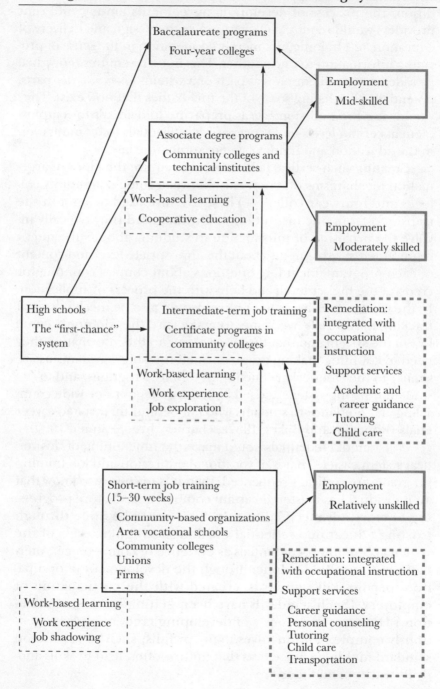

students about the appropriate sequence of programs. But in addition, the process of developing agreements among different providers would require collaboration in the design and delivery of education and training, not merely cooperation in the sense of providing information to one another. This in turn requires individual providers to view themselves as parts of a system—*noncompeting* parts, potentially eliminating some of the turf battles that now exist. They would view their mission *both* as preparing individuals for employment at certain levels *and* as preparing individuals for continuation in the education and training system some time later.

Creating such vertical ladders would require the kinds of articulation mechanisms that now exist between some community colleges and four-year colleges. These are intended to smooth the transition from one institution to another, and they typically involve the provision of information to students about subsequent requirements; agreements about the appropriate level and content of each program, including questions about courses counting for credit at the higher level; and help with the process of application. In the most aggressive systems, there would also be mechanisms of tracking individuals over time, to make sure they do not become lost in the system and that they have access to the information they need to continue making progress. Such tracking mechanisms are similar to the caseworker function in welfare programs, and to the student tracking system devised by some colleges to provide counseling and guidance to students who fall behind their stated career goals (Roueche and Baker, 1987a, chapter three; Palmer, 1990).

A system of credentials would make the functioning of this vertical system easier. That is, if vocational education and job training programs are vertically sequenced, then it is necessary to know that an individual has mastered certain competencies before progressing to more advanced education. This could be done through existing education credentials, as long as higher levels of the system accept lower credentials as evidence of competence. Alternatively, this could be done through the development of occupation-specific skill standards, created with the participation of employers. (Such standards have been getting increasing attention.) However, the process of developing credentials is horrendously complex and involves many pitfalls, such as relying on standard multiple-choice tests that in turn often lead to skills-and-drills teaching methods.

There are several reasons for emphasizing vertical integration and the creating of education and training ladders in place of more conventional forms of coordination:

• The individuals within the education and training system who are in the greatest need require a number of different services: basic language skills and other competencies; job-specific skills; help with personal attributes like motivation, discipline, and persistence; help in conquering drug and alcohol dependencies, or mental health problems; and decision-making skills. It has been difficult for them to negotiate programs on their own and has required counselors or caseworkers. They need so much that it is impossible to think about integrating them into the economic mainstream except in small steps, providing support (via welfare, training subsidies, or unskilled work) in the interim.

• Many of those in need of education and training need to work while they are enrolled in programs. This is true by definition for those seeking retraining, upgrade training, and second-chance training, but it is also true for many individuals seeking initial entry into the labor force. They cannot afford to stop working for one to four years to accumulate a credential; they need instead to accumulate small amounts of education and training, work a while, and return to school (probably part-time) to further improve their skills.

• Even where communities provide a range of services, the pathways through them are unclear, particularly to those who are unsophisticated about finding and using programs. Furthermore, eligibility standards are inconsistent, assessment procedures are varied, and the content of programs is uncoordinated. Thus in practice the range of education and services provided is not a smooth continuum.

• The labor market has certain barriers which can be overcome only through specific education credentials. The labor market for mid-skilled occupations is almost completely closed to individuals without high school diplomas; therefore relatively unskilled individuals—for example, high school dropouts in JTPA or JOBS programs—have a crack at entry-level jobs in the mid-skilled labor market only after they get their diplomas. With experience, ability, and motivation they can advance, but some occupations may require subsequent education (for example, from community colleges or technical institutes, in computer applications, specific business procedures, CAD, or specific electronics training) in order to gain entry. Then too, management positions, accountants, computer programmers, many health positions, and most professional jobs with real advancement require baccalaureate degrees. That is, advancement can be blocked sequentially by the lack of the high school diploma, by certain forms of sub-baccalaureate education, or by the baccalaureate itself, so that continuous advancement requires going back into the education and training system. This is particularly true in cases (as with health occupations) where competencies have been codified by occupational licensing. If the country moves toward skill standards, the need for formal credentials will become routine in other occupations as well.

• Existing programs are hierarchically arranged anyway. (This is one reason that there is not that much duplication.) Individuals on AFDC (Aid to Families with Dependent Children) are typically less well-prepared and experienced than those in JTPA, who in turn are less well-prepared than the typical community college student. In job training, area vocational schools and JTPA programs provide shorter and less sophisticated programs than community colleges. In the world of literacy and remediation, community-based volunteer programs enroll those who are completely non-literate, while adult ed programs typically start at the fourth or fifth grade-level equivalent and lead to a GED, and community college programs aim to prepare individuals for college-level English courses. As long as there are such hierarchies in existing programs, it makes sense to take advantage of them.

• Currently there are few mechanisms for revealing low quality in the system. If programs are linked vertically, and a receiving program finds preparation in the sending program to be inadequate, there is a new incentive for blowing the whistle on ineffective programs.

There are, then, many advantages to linking the existing systems of vocational education and job training. The advantage is not primarily that of eliminating waste and duplication, since there is very little of that. Instead, a unified system has the possibility of being more effective, particularly for the individuals who find themselves in short-term job training programs with small and short-lived payoffs.

Providing Integrated Support Services

In the world of job training programs, the worst-off participants suffer from multiple barriers to employment. Some participants, especially single mothers on welfare, have small children that complicate their efforts to become independent; others are saddled with families and communities that undermine their resolve and independence. They face the same uncertainties as community college students about how to get into the world in a complex, rapidly changing, and often forbidding labor market. These barriers are extremely varied, of course, but they are linked by the fact that the conventional offerings of education and job training, including classroom instruction, work-based learning, job search assistance, and help with job placement, cannot overcome them.

Recognizing these multiple barriers, some job training programs have provided various supportive services in addition to education and training. The Job Corp has provided social services for high school dropouts in residential settings, that is, away from the presumptively harmful families and communities from which these young people come. Other experimental programs have focused on particular groups with multiple problems; for example, the Minority Female Single Parent Demonstration (MFSP) provided an extensive array of services such as child care, counseling, guidance in managing daily problems, and help in finding jobs after the program. Similarly, the New Chance program, also aimed at young mothers (most of them high school dropouts), provided remedial education, preparation for the GED, career exploration, instruction in job-finding skills, health education, family planning, and life skills, as well as child care and some services to children. Finally, some of the most effective programs in the job training system—particularly the Center for Employment Training in San Jose, and the Riverside (California) welfare-to-work program—seem to be effective because they provide a variety of services and help individuals in several distinct ways (Grubb, 1996).

The strategy of providing supportive services is not confined to job training, of course. In K–12 education, the idea of providing

comprehensive services in schools or at school sites has been a popular idea at least since the turn of the century; it has been revived
in the past few years as the students coming to school are more
likely to be poor and in need of health care, food, counseling, hous-
ing, interventions with their parents, or protective services (Kagan,
Goffin, Golub, and Pritchard, 1995; Lewis, Carr, South, and Reed,
1995). In community colleges, provision of counseling, tutoring,
and child care services has become common, in addition to expansion of remedial education; many community colleges also provide
special services to minority students to improve their progress
through the institution. Some states have set up special centers for
support services; in North Carolina, for example, such centers help
the institutions accommodate JTPA and welfare clients as well as
regular students. Four-year colleges also provide an extensive array
of such services even though their students are less likely to be poor
or lacking in parental support. Like the provision of second-chance
programs themselves, efforts to provide more comprehensive services represent one of the most benevolent intentions in American
policy, one that recognizes the varied needs of many students.[6]

Unfortunately, we know very little about what contributes to
effectiveness in supportive services.[7] While systemic information is
lacking, the resources available for guidance and counseling in
community colleges and for the caseworker function in job training programs seem to be limited, aside from a few experimental
programs like New Chance.[8] One might reasonably conclude that
more intensive services, provided with considerable thought to the
ways they will be received by students and clients, are likely to make
some difference; but one could also conclude that most programs
fail to provide enough services, or services of the right kind.

There is, of course, no dearth of recommendations about how
to make supportive services more effective. Many of these merely
repeat bromides that are not particularly helpful; they often
say, for example, that services must be increased, or that services
must be provided by individuals who are "sympathetic" and "supportive" of their students and clients, or that services should be
appropriate to the problems at hand. However, the examples of
remediation and counseling, and the relative success of services
in New Chance, provide a few clues. In general, remedial education has been provided in classes that are divorced from regular
academic and occupational classes, using the skills-and-drills

teaching that is particularly suspect for older students who have already completed many years of conventional schooling. Similarly, guidance and counseling is often provided independently of other elements, by counselors who may not be familiar with the rest of the program and who are usually poorly prepared to provide career-oriented counseling; indeed, complaints about counselors being ignorant about local labor market conditions and about occupational offerings are staples of both high schools and community colleges. The dominant approach to counseling appears to be the "information dump," in which individuals are provided with masses of information about the nature of jobs, regardless of whether they can absorb this information or make use of it in their own decisions. Similarly, education related to personal skills—for example, education about spending and saving, personal relationships in general, sex and contraception, drug and alcohol abuse—very often takes the form of didactic instruction, in freestanding classes unrelated to the other activities of an individual's life.

This suggests that a different approach to supportive services should be incorporated into the early stages of the education and training system, as illustrated in Figure 4.1. Four principles ought to guide such services:

1. They should be integrated with the other elements of a program, rather than provided in freestanding classes or by individuals with little connection with other elements of the program. The integrated provision of remediation, described in Chapter Five, provides one illustration; another is the inclusion of career education and career exploration in the context of work placements, as is done in the Co-op Seminar of LaGuardia Community College (Grubb and Badway, 1995).
2. They should avoid didactic approaches and information dumps, since these are unlikely to be effective. Instead, it is necessary to consider the ability (or lack of ability) of students to interpret or act on such information. Those who lack planfulness or decision-making abilities, for example, who are unable to consider the future consequences of present actions, or who do not understand the complex web of obligations underlying most employment, are unlikely to be able to make good use of information about job opportunities.

3. They should be experience-based, rather than independent of the specific context in which various competencies are exercised. Indeed, the value of incorporating various kinds of work-based learning in programs, as the School-to-Work Opportunities Act recommends, is to provide students with yet another kind of experience from which to view the world, to help them understand in a more direct way the role of formal schooling and the competencies one needs at work.

4. They should themselves be continuous and developmental. That is, just as the occupational and academic skills training depicted in Figure 4.1 becomes increasingly sophisticated, as an individual moves from initial, shorter programs of the current job training system to the longer and more complex associate degree programs, so too should any necessary supportive services provide competencies and information of increasing levels of sophistication.

The details of applying such principles to a variety of efforts to provide counseling, tutoring, and instruction in personal skills are myriad, of course, and cannot be adequately developed in this chapter. In fact the details of operation cannot be determined a priori at all, since they depend on a specific program, a particular work context, and a group of students with known backgrounds and individualized needs. What remains important is that the programs of a unified education and training system treat supportive services in the same integrated and developmental way that they treat occupational and academic competencies.

Implementing a Coherent System

The most important aspect of the coherent system articulating Figure 4.1 is that it provides a consistent vision of what needs to be done in reforming existing programs. The details of these reforms are multiple, and many of them must be worked out at the local level in any case. Even without getting into the nuts and bolts of such changes, such a system requires several distinct changes in state and local policy:

1. *A state agency or council to oversee its development.* (For example, this could be the human resource agency permitted by recent

JTPA amendments.) Such an agency needs sufficient power to improve vertical coordination, oversee the development of better information, and the like. Such an agency must include all relevant participants, be unbiased about the existing range of programs, and be motivated by a principled vision of a system. If the council is viewed as partisan—if, for example, it is simply the existing state Job Training Coordinating Council with a bias toward short-term job training, or is simply the state Council on Vocational Education with its bias in favor of high school vocational programs—then it will fail to pull together all relevant groups.

2. *A local or regional council to oversee its development at the local level.* Its role would be to improve vertical articulation; oversee the local implementation of information and tracking systems; improve information available to prospective students and clients; improve the quality of local programs; and take responsibility for other interprogram problems that arise, including the identification of "holes" in the local system where required programs are unavailable. Like the state-level council, it is crucial that this group be viewed as impartial among education and training programs; for that reason, basing it on local PICs, with their bias toward short-term training, or the Employment Service, with its low reputation among employers, would be inappropriate. At the same time, this local council should be an arm of state policy, rather than a creature of local politics. If the local political manipulations that have hamstrung so many JTPA programs were replicated in these local councils, they would again fail to improve the existing system.

3. *Incentives for vertical coordination, and disincentives to programs maintaining their independence from others.* There are several incentives that state government has at its disposal:

- The bully pulpit of the governor's office and of state agencies (including the state council).
- Federal funds, which can be allocated to provide incentives for vertical coordination.[9]
- State regulation of local programs. These ought, for example, to require that programs referring their students and clients or others develop guidelines for doing so, refer individuals only to programs known to be of sufficient quality, and monitor the progress of individuals referred elsewhere.

- State funding for community colleges, area vocational schools, job training and welfare-to-work programs, which can be made contingent on vertical integration.
- Performance mechanisms, including those required by federal legislation, which can be used as the basis of student tracking mechanisms and can include measures of continuation in other programs.

4. *Information systems.* They should be designed to track individuals through the system so they do not become lost; provide better information on effectiveness of existing programs; and provide information to prospective students/clients about the effectiveness of different programs, so that they can make rational decisions about which to enter.

5. *Decisions about abolishing programs* that are inconsistent with the central vision, *or creating institutions necessary for the vertical system* (like the local or regional councils mentioned above). For example, the adult basic education system in most states is extraordinarily ineffective, and it violates the notion that remediation should be integrated with job training. It should therefore be abolished (as I recommend in Chapter Seven as well) and its responsibilities transferred to community colleges, which provide remediation of their own, often in more creative ways. Because of lax regulation, there are many ineffective proprietary schools that should be closed, and the quality of area vocational schools themselves is so variable that some of their short-term job training responsibilities should probably be transferred to community colleges. A greater emphasis within each program area on outcomes and effects in place of enrollments will result in some programs declining while others expand. However, it has always been difficult to close ineffective programs because they develop political constituencies; doing so will therefore require a coherent state policy, and state power to back it up.

A number of other issues will need to be resolved, of course. However, a vision of vertical integration provides a goal that is more appropriate both to the existing structure of programs, and to the needs that many individuals face in their efforts to make their way into the stable employment of the sub-baccalaureate labor market. This goal will help create a coherent system of education and job training from the quagmire that now exists.

In the process, community colleges and technical institutes will gain a critical role as the linchpin connecting job training programs to the education system. In turn, this means that they will have to be ready to prepare an even broader variety of individuals than many of them now do. The reforms in the next two chapters, as well as the policies articulated in Chapter Seven, are intended to respond both to the requirements of jobs in the sub-baccalaureate labor market, and the need to further develop the community college as a nontraditional institution helping its enormous variety of students in ways different from most educational institutions.

Chapter Five

Integrating Occupational, Academic, and Remedial Instruction

Among the insistent demands of employers over the past decade have been calls for a better-prepared labor force, in the sense that they will have mastered basic competencies *and* the capacity to apply them, not in the sense that individuals will have more years of schooling. As we saw in Chapter One, employers in the sub-baccalaureate labor market are often dissatisfied with the preparation in high schools and community colleges, and their complaints about "atrocious" verbal skills and deficient mathematical preparation reflect a quiet despair that educational institutions cannot do a better job of preparing their workers.

These discussions at the local level mirror national discussions, of course. As the Committee for Economic Development (1985) declared: "Business, in general, is not interested in narrow vocationalism. It prefers a curriculum that stresses literacy and mathematical and problem-solving skills" (p. 15). The Commission on the Skills of the American Workforce portrayed the future starkly in the title of its widely cited report as *America's Choice: High Skills or Low Wages!* (CSAW, 1990), and went on to describe the skills needed for a "third industrial revolution" encompassing "the demonstrated ability to read, write, compute, and perform at world-class levels in general school subjects (mathematics, physical and natural sciences, technology, history, geography, politics, economics and English). Students should also have exhibited a capacity to learn, think, work effectively alone and in groups and solve problems" (p. 69).

The Secretary's Commission on Achieving Necessary Skills (SCANS) of the Department of Labor outlined *What Work Requires of Schools,* complaining that "we are failing to develop the full academic abilities of most students" (p. vi) and arguing that "tomorrow's career ladders require even the basic skills—the old 3 Rs—to take on a new meaning." Among the five competencies and three "foundation skills" advocated as part of "high performance schools," the report illustrated the need for greater competence in the conventional academic capacities of reading, writing, mathematics, and computational skills, as well as "thinking skills" such as decision making, problem solving, and knowing how to learn (SCANS, 1991).

To be sure, there are contradictory messages from the business community. As Chapter One reported, the emphases in hiring requirements on job-specific technical skills (often too job-specific for any educational institution to teach) and the local business or educational institutions for entry-level job preparation are quite different from the national-level commissions calling for "thinking skills." These pressures often lead occupational instructors to argue that there is no room in their programs for academic skills that might violate "the integrity of the occupational curriculum"; some community colleges that are especially intent on "economic development" and narrowly vocational purposes have resisted the suggestion that any technical skills should be sacrificed for academic or higher-order competencies. One way to understand these conflicting pressures is that the demand for technical and job-specific skills reflects the competencies necessary for entry-level jobs, while higher-order skills are necessary for advancement over time—precisely the kind of advancement associated with promotions and with the long-run increases in earnings that distinguish *education* from *training.* Neglecting the more academic or higher-order competencies may not affect employment in the short run, but it is likely to be detrimental to the long-run prospects of students.

This position has recently been seconded by the Commission on the Future of the Community College: "if technical education programs are too narrow, if work cannot be a broadening experience, then the students may achieve only short-term gains." The Commission then went on to recommend "exploring new ways to combine technical and general studies throughout the undergraduate experience" and declared that "[c]ommunity college faculty should take the lead in closing the gap between the so-called 'liberal' and the 'useful' arts," particularly by developing "up-to-date programs that integrate the core curriculum and technical education" (p. 21). Similarly, a 1984 report on the economic roles of community colleges, *Putting America Back to Work*—written well before the current infatuation with "higher-order skills"—stressed that "[t]raining for one job is not going to serve a worker all of his/her life. Foremost in any training program must be instruction that concentrates on *how to learn;* if possible, on *enjoying learning;* and on *making a commitment to learning throughout life*" (American Association of Community and Junior Colleges, 1984, p. 29). The report went on to recommend a two-tiered system, in which the first tier includes a broad background in math, science, communications, analytical and reasoning skills, together with a second tier of more job-specific content (American Association of Community and Junior Colleges, 1984, p. 29).

One way to address these demands from employers and community college reformers both is to integrate greater academic content into occupational programs. Indeed, in searching for ways to nudge the educational system toward more general competencies, Congress included the following prescription in the 1990 Amendments to the Carl Perkins Act, providing federal support for vocational education: "Funds made available . . . shall be used to provide vocational education in programs that . . . integrate academic and vocational education in such programs through coherent sequences of courses so that students achieve both academic and occupational competencies" (Serial No. 103-C, p. 42).

Unfortunately, community colleges have so far made little progress in implementing this provision, partly because the idea has been so unfamiliar (Grubb and Stasz, 1993; Boesel, 1994). In the first section of this chapter, therefore, I present several ways in which innovative two-year colleges have integrated academic and vocational education, in the interest of preparing individuals with a greater range of academic competencies as well as "thinking skills."

A second kind of challenge that the two-year institutions face is associated with remedial or developmental education. In its role as a second-chance institution, open to all individuals who think they can benefit from further education, community colleges and technical institutes have found themselves with more and more students whose academic preparation is inadequate for college-level work. But students who come to these institutions to get into the world and yet find themselves in remedial courses, drilling on sentence completion and simple math problems, often fail to complete these courses. One solution that some two-year institutions have tried with success is to follow the path of integrating academic and vocational education once again, that is, to teach remedial courses in tandem with occupational courses, so that students can see the importance of mastering academic subjects and so that the applications necessary for particular occupations are covered. This approach is particularly important when community colleges include underprepared job training clients and welfare recipients in welfare-to-work programs, or when they serve as the link between short-term job training programs and the education system as recommended in the previous chapter. The second section of this chapter describes these practices in greater detail.

To be sure, there are substantial barriers to the efforts to integrate academic and occupational education, and to teach development education in tandem with occupational courses. But the benefits are substantial as well. Quite apart from the principal benefit of upgrading the preparation of the workforce, these changes generate greater attention to the quality of teaching and to the creation of learning communities. They promote thinking of community colleges in much more flexible ways, as institutions that provide a *range* of teaching practices to meet the *range* of competencies necessary in modern employment, in those institutions that pride themselves on being teaching institutions for nontraditional students. The final section of this chapter clarifies the variety of benefits for students and institutions alike in integrating academic and occupational education.

Integrating Academic and Occupational Education: Innovative Practices

Community colleges and technical institutes in the United States are enormously varied, as befits their status as local, community-serving institutions. Consistent with this pattern, instructors and administrators consider an enormous variety of practices as forms of integrating academic and vocational education.[1] While initially bewildering, the responses fall into several distinct approaches, although there is substantial variation within each of these. A particular approach should not be interpreted as a blueprint, but rather as a general direction which can vary depending on specific fields of study, the interests of instructors and students, and the requirements of employer.

There are, however, two forms of "integration" that are quite widespread but should probably not be considered integration in any meaningful sense. The first is that the course requirements for certificate and associate degree programs in occupational fields generally include a sequence of occupationally specific courses *and* related academic courses (Grubb, 1987). Because of these related academic courses, some individuals respond that postsecondary programs are "naturally integrated." However, most instructors do not consider related academic coursework to be instances of integration partly because such efforts typically require *students* to assimilate material from courses that are otherwise independent, with no help from instructors in making connections among courses. Another limitation of this practice is that it requires students to complete all the courses required within a program, even though many community college students take only a few courses.

Second, many instructors consider the general education requirements of community colleges to be forms of curriculum integration. Such courses are overwhelmingly drawn from academic subjects: of community colleges and technical institutes with general education programs, 96 percent include courses in communications (both writing and speaking), 94 percent in the social sciences, 86 percent in the natural sciences, 85 percent in the arts and humanities, and 67 percent in health, physical education, and family education (Hammons, 1979). Within the institutions we have examined, communications skills, critical thinking and problem-solving abilities, an understanding of civic responsibilities, and appreciation of the arts and humanities are common rationales for general education requirements. However, while general education requirements incorporate academic courses into occupational programs, they have not fostered the integration of academic competencies and occupational content since gen ed courses typically remain independent of occupational courses. Like the inclusion of academic requirements in occupational programs, they require *students* to make the links to occupational concerns or the requirements of employment.

If community college students were adept at integrating different content areas, there might not be any problem with such an approach. However, there is good reason to think that community college students, whose prior academic records have often been weak, who may have been out of school for considerable periods of time, and who may be insecure about academic coursework in particular, are likely to need substantial help with such integration.[2] Instructors often remark that occupational students take academic and general education courses only grudgingly, and that they often fail to see the relevance of general education to their occupational goals. And those who are looking for a route into employment are likely to find general education courses particularly irrelevant, since they assume a purpose that these experimenters do not share.

In a different sense, general education requirements may not be effective ways to integrate academic and occupational content because they generally apply only to students in associate programs, not to those in shorter programs or those enrolled for a few courses. By one estimate, about half of community college students are in vocational programs that do not require general education (Cohen, 1988); many will leave the institution before completing any such requirements. For that reason alone, general education requirements probably reach only a minority of occupational students in community colleges and technical institutes.

There are, to be sure, a few examples where two-year colleges have modified their general education programs to provide some context for occupational programs, or a deeper understanding of the forces affecting occupations. For example, Springfield Technical Community College (Massachusetts) cites "an understanding of the historical basis of our modern technological society" as one of its goals. Nashville State Technical Institute (Tennessee) intends its requirements to prepare students to "use technology and science effectively and responsibly"; it states that "assignments [in English courses] frequently allow students to make use of their job experience or technical background," suggesting an effort to link the "academic" training in writing and communication with occupational knowledge and concerns.

A somewhat tighter link between general education and occupational programs has developed in a few institutions which provide guidance about the particular general education courses that would be most useful to occupational students. One institution, the Pennsylvania College of Technology in Williamsport, developed a general education program around occupational requirements: it asked successful graduates from different occupational areas what capacities individuals need to be successful and used these responses to develop core competencies to be incorporated into general education courses. To be sure, the resulting competencies are not much different from those cited in most general education statements of purpose; they include "comprehensive interrelated skills" including problem identification and problem solving; communications skill; mathematics; computer-related competencies; humanities, social sciences, and arts; science and technology; and competencies labeled "personal" and "career."[3] However, the process by which they were derived was substantially different, and the purposes of general education (in an institution where all students are occupational) are more clearly related to the programs they enter.

But these are clearly exceptions; in most institutions, general education is an incomplete approach to integrating academic and vocational education since it places the burden for integration on students themselves and may not reach the occupational students most in need of such abilities. The most promising approaches to curriculum integration place the responsibility for such integration squarely on instructors and create new courses and groups of courses that are quite different.

Combining Academic and Vocational Content in Individual Courses

The most pervasive approach to integration is the infusion of particular lessons or modules into an existing course. Often this takes the form of academic material incorporated into vocational courses; for example, instructors might provide a quick review of ratios for students learning Ohm's law in an automotive or electronics program, or review proportions when studying the laws of gases in respiration therapy. This kind of teaching or reinforcement of a particular concept is quick and informal; a more extended and formalized approach to infusion is to incorporate longer modules taken from academic approaches. For example, the Introduction to Law Enforcement course at Southern Maine Technical College added a component on the history of law enforcement; and instructors at Nashville State Technical Institute inserted modules on historical, ethical, and aesthetic perspectives into Industrial Engineering, Mechanical Engineering, and Business Technology courses. The inclusion of ethics, normally a topic within philosophy, in a variety of occupational programs is by now a standard recommendation. While infusion is often a vehicle for including particular academic competencies, many instructors have expanded the content of their courses in order to bring broader political and moral perspectives to occupational students, serving the purposes of general education.

In some institutions, the process of infusion has been used systematically to incorporate the skills necessary for high-skills workplaces, sometimes referred to as "SCANS skills." For example, programs at Cape Cod Community College (Massachusetts) added new assignments related to "the efficient use of resources," a critical performance skill identified by SCANS. The modules require students to use criterion-based assessment in selecting nursing equipment and flowcharts to identify productive and nonproductive processes in hypothetical nursing situations, and they teach students to apply a systems approach to a care-giving setting and to apply social audit techniques to resolve ethical dilemmas. As part of transforming the New Hampshire Technical Colleges into comprehensive community colleges, a statewide group of faculty, administrators, and business representatives used a procedure similar to a DACUM (Developing a Curriculum) process to establish core competencies and now incorporate instruction for each of these competencies in every course. Tyler Community College (Texas) conducted a series of field trips for both academic and occupational faculty to identify SCANS and academic skills required by local businesses and industries and then encouraged cross-disciplinary planning based on this information. These are all ways of infusing certain competencies systematically into occupational courses, rather than relying on the idiosyncratic efforts of individual instructors.

In other cases, infusion has been used for purposes of career exploration. At Santa Barbara Community College (California), for example, career exploration activities are incorporated into a number of introductory courses, by including assignments that require research in the Career and Transfer Centers. Counselors assist students in completing interest inventories and computer-assisted labor market research. Following the Career Research Project guidelines, students gain not only research skills but experience using data for further clarification of career goals and the guidance services of career and transfer counselors (Friedlander, undated).

Still another systematic way to incorporate more academic skills into occupational programs has been to adopt cross-curriculum efforts in an entire institution. The best-known example is Writing Across the Curriculum (WAC), in which all instructors, both academic and occupational, are encouraged to incorporate more writing into their courses. Writing Across the Curriculum efforts have been implemented in several different ways. Florida has required WAC of all its community colleges, consistent with its active state role. In the majority of community colleges, however, much more informal methods are used to motivate faculty to participate, including recruitment and outreach by members of the WAC staff (usually from the English department), seminars and staff development efforts to show instructors how to incorporate writing exercises into their courses, and availability of WAC staff to provide help to individual instructors. The best WAC efforts therefore provide instructors with some resources to modify their course content, as well as the rationale and peer support to do so.

WAC is often viewed as a method of improving instruction by helping students think more deeply about their subject, to clarify and organize their thoughts, and to become more active learners (Watkins, 1990); the approach is often labeled Writing to Learn. For example, the WAC coordinator at Cedar Valley College (Lancaster, Texas) stressed that the ability to write different kinds of papers is not as important (especially for occupational students) as is using writing in the service of improved teaching and learning. The head of the air conditioning program notes that his students are "turned off" to writing, and he therefore avoids mentioning writing as an independent exercise; however, he incorporates writing in class exercises as a way of clarifying what students have learned and as a pathway into critical thinking, since the diagnosis of equipment failures requires the kind of troubleshooting and problem solving often incorporated in critical thinking (Eishen, 1991).

Similarly, Prince Georges Community College (Largo, Maryland) instituted a WAC Program with an emphasis on writing to learn. As an example of the emphasis on improving learning (rather than improving writing), writing exercises were introduced into business math classes, to help students move between word problems and mathematical formulations, to identify applications in everyday life, and in other ways to focus on the mathematical content in nonstandard ways. The instructors reported substantial increases in the passing rate among students completing the writing exercises (Stout and Magnotto, 1988). The humanities faculty at Mohawk Valley Community College (Utica, New York) developed a Learning Through Writing program as a way to teach writing in an informal way; the program has been used particularly in the Human Services Technology and Health programs.

Although Writing Across the Curriculum is by far the most common cross-curricular effort, there are a few others. Prince George's Community College initiated Communication Across the Curriculum, which developed materials to enable students and instructors to increase the amount and coherence of discussion—an attempt to shift to a pedagogy where students are more active and questioning. Nashville State Technical Institute has adopted what might be called humanities across the technologies, incorporating some of the humanities in every course to improve student outcomes in communications, the arts, math, and writing. For example, a mechanical engineering technology course now includes components in the history, art, and ethics of the field and a unit on "solving problems related to balancing academics and beginning a technical career," while other technical courses include activities "designed to enhance [student] abilities in communication, critical thinking, and problem solving." A course in Mechanical Equipment provides a good example of how many different perspectives can be incorporated into a technical course. The instructor requires students to give oral presentations, with possible topics including whether the designer of the Tacoma Narrows Bridge (which collapsed in a high wind) should be criminally prosecuted, and whether the third little pig overengineered his house. One paper requires students to clarify what steps technicians can do to "help preserve and/or protect the environment," and other assignments require them to read Petroski's *To Err is Human: The Role of Failure in Successful Design* and then write about the development of Gothic structures, the ambivalence of William Wordsworth toward nineteenth-century technology, and Galileo's error in calculating the yield stress of cantilever beams.

When community colleges and technical institutes adopt a cross-curriculum effort, it is difficult to know how extensively instructors modify their courses. The informal and voluntary nature of most WAC and other cross-curriculum programs is a potential weakness because the incentives for faculty to participate are slight. Not surprisingly, the participation of instructors varies enormously: one director mentioned that "the old guard types say it's impossible," while others are more accepting. In some institutions, WAC has been adopted more by the occupational faculty than the academic faculty; the director of occupational education at Three Rivers Community College (Poplar Bluff, Missouri) claimed that this occurred because of insistence from their business advisory committees about the importance of communication for successful job performance. At Orange County Community College (California) the Writing Consultancy Project focuses specifically on eight technical and allied health occupations (Godwin, 1991; Killingsworth, 1988). However, in other cases deans report that occupational instructors participate in cross-curriculum efforts less than academic instructors because they are less persuaded of the value of writing, because it takes time away from occupation-specific skills, because it requires skills that occupational faculty may not have, and because they may not be included in the networks of academic instructors.[4]

A still more formalized approach to infusion and curriculum integration is the development of applied academics courses, which typically take conventional academic subjects and infuse them with applications from occupational areas.[5] This is clearly the most common form of integration (Grubb and Kraskouskas, 1992; Grubb and Stasz, 1993), and a perusal of course catalogues suggests that virtually every community college and technical institute has several such courses. Examples include Technical Writing, or Writing for the Workplace, or Written Business Communication; Applied Math or Technical Math, sometimes further specialized as in the Technical Math for Nurses course at San Bernadino Community College (California), or Applied Math for Recording Technology (Cedar Valley Community College, Lancaster, Texas); and Agricultural Economics or Business Economics.

While applied academics courses are sometimes generated in response to specific problems, so that an institution may have only one or two such courses, in other cases a community college will take a more systematic approach. For example, Yavapai College (Prescott, Arizona) offers applied math courses for health sciences, for welding, for electronics, and for management, as well as Technical Math I and II; Cedar Valley College (Lancaster, Texas) offers applied math for nursing, veterinary technology, recording technology/music, business, and economics; Johnson County Community College (Kansas) offers several varieties of technical chemistry courses. Boise State College of Technology established a required core of seven applied courses on the advice of industry, partly to enhance their accreditation standing: applied physics, applied math, applied English, applied communications, technical math, teaching writing, and materials science. Broome County Community College adopted a series of applied courses, to serve the middle range of their students, in mathematics, biology, earth science, Principles of Technology (an applied physics course), chemistry, and communications; in all, the college offers twenty-three sections of applied courses.

Applied academic courses generally adapt the content from conventional academic subjects and use practical applications taken from occupations. In many cases, these courses have been developed as a way to serve the needs of occupational students more precisely, sometimes because of the perception that standard academic courses in math or English are too general, too abstract, or too lacking in appropriate applications. Typically, applied academics courses are taught to occupational students only, reinforcing the ability of instructors to mold the content to a particular occupational area. Most such courses are locally developed, although in Alabama centrally developed courses in Technical English and Technical Math are used for all nondegree occupational students; the state curricula occurred as a way of imposing some quality standards and consistency on local institutions.

These hybrid courses may be taught either by academic instructors or by occupational instructors; rarely, because of fiscal limitations, are they team-taught. Occasional battles over who is to teach the course reveal an unavoidable conflict: whether an applied academics course should stress the more abstract, theoretical, "academic" underpinnings of the subject, including disciplinary modes of thinking, or whether it should instead stress occupational examples, "practical" information (including institutional details), and a further socialization into the values of an occupation. Often, academic instructors take the first approach while vocational instructors take the second.

For example, in one community college, a business math course was initially taught by business instructors. The math department thought the course inadequate and refused to assign the course a math department number. Finally, the business and math faculty collaborated in developing a course (taught by business faculty most of the time and by math faculty when their teaching loads are light) worthy of being included among the math offerings. This particular episode reveals the inevitable tension between academic and occupational emphases, and it suggests that collaboration is crucial to reaching some accommodation. The only troubling aspect of current practice in community colleges is that since there is so little team teaching in community colleges,[6] there may not be sufficient opportunities for instructors from different disciplines to hammer out compromises that appropriately balance academic content with occupational applications.

Of course, there is a potential drawback to applied academics courses: they segregate occupational students from others, a form of tracking that could limit their ambitions. As a dean at Bunker Hill Community College (Boston) explained his opposition to such courses, "These [occupational] students need to have broader exposure. It's useful for them to sit in class with students studying different fields."

As another example, an effort in one community college to establish an English course specifically for occupational students failed. The faculty found that "it isolated students and they ended up being too focused on their technical area," a comment that mixing with transfer-oriented students is a valuable aspect of general education requirement. In addition, the courses devised were largely remedial instruction in areas where students were weak; they perceived this as adult basic education, and "students didn't like that approach." Whether the benefits of making the content of applied academic courses occupationally related outweigh the costs of segregation from other students is difficult to answer in general, although the practice is so widespread that most institutions have implicitly decided that the benefits are substantial.

Infusion takes many forms, therefore, from the quick and casual review of academic competencies to the more formalized approaches of Writing Across the Curriculum and applied academics courses. It is thus a flexible approach to integrating the curriculum, adaptable to several purposes, and accommodating a variety of informal and formal changes.

Multidisciplinary Courses Combining Academic Perspectives and Occupational Concerns

A quite different approach to integrating academic and occupational education has been the development of multidisciplinary courses, taking the perspectives and methods of particular academic disciplines but incorporating issues and concerns that are distinctly occupational. The resulting hybrids are often courses that could be included in general education programs, although unlike most general education courses, which tend to have standard academic content, they have subjects of special interest to occupational students. Examples include the following:

• Working in America (Kirkwood Community College, Cedar Rapids, Iowa) is a literature course, in which (according to the syllabus) fiction and nonfiction concerned with work are used to examine attitudes toward work, to understand the "past, present, and future of working," to "develop [student] abilities to communicate about basic human experiences such as work," to "become more competent in the interpretation of stories and other symbolic expressions." This course has also spawned a reader, *Working in America,* that provides students and instructors with readings from various fictional and nonfiction sources about work, with appropriate introductions (Sessions and Wortman, 1992).[7] Culture and Technology, within the same institution, also includes a good deal of literature concerned with work, but also some reading about current ethical issues (such as genetic engineering) and movies and music concerned with work.

Similarly, Science and Technology as Themes of Literature (Northeast State Technical Community College, Blountville, Tennessee) examines various literary works, including science fiction, to explore themes surrounding technology such as hopes for technology, the sense of betrayal as technology fails to deliver on its promises, problems of alienation in the workplace, loss of self as machines have replaced people in production, the effects of industrialization on leisure, and ethical issues. A course titled Changes and Choices: Experiencing Living in the Workplace, the Home, and the Broader Community (Muscatine Community College, Iowa) uses short stories, novels, poetry, essays, and some history to (according to the syllabus) "assist occupational program students in using the humanities to make everyday decisions, to take on the challenges of change, to make major decisions, and to decide to effect change."

• History of Technology (Yavapai College), Society and Technical Change (New Hampshire Vocational-Technical College, Manchester, New Hampshire), Discoveries, Investigations, and Explorations (Northeast State Technical Community College), and Science, Technology, and Society (Pennsylvania College of Technology, Williamsport) are all courses examining technical change in historical perspective, the effects on society, and the conflicts over technical change, allowing students to explore the current issues surrounding technological developments. Such courses are related in spirit, if not in their origins, to the courses in Science, Technology, and Society (STS) that have proliferated in secondary schools (Yager, 1990).

• Humanities and Technology, taught in various forms in several New York community colleges during the mid-1980s, examines technical change and its social effects from the vantage point of several of the humanities including history, philosophy (both inquiry and ethics), and art in various forms.

• Technology and Human Values (Yavapai College) examines the ethical issues generated by advancing technologies, as well as the influence of technology on individual and social values. Ethical Dilemmas in Modern Society (Southern Maine Technical College, Portland) is a general ethics course, but within a technical college; one of its themes is the "intellectual flexibility and tolerance necessary for the workplace."

The common element in these courses is the application of academic subjects—history, literature, ethics and philosophy, the study of culture from sociology or anthropology—and their concepts and analytic methods to technological developments, to working and its consequences, or to other employment-related issues that are presumably more compelling for occupational students. These courses can also serve as vehicles for introducing students to radically different ways of viewing the world. A business instructor teaching a course called Wisdom for the Workplace—using literature together with case studies from business to "teach students that the wisdom of great writers from the past is still pertinent to the solving of contemporary job-related problems"—described the process (Smith, 1990, p. 10): "I have also discovered why my business-career students generally falter when faced with complex problems in their business or technical core courses, especially those that deal with human issues. The juxtaposition between the humanities—which always ask questions about life, happiness, and freedom—and the courses that fill their career programs (always focusing on the absorption of accepted processes or pragmatic applications) is so strong. [My course] is a wild mix that asks students to question first, and then to justify their opinions convincingly, rather than to simply accept" (Smith, 1990, p. 10).

Most efforts to develop interdisciplinary courses have led to one or two such courses. However, a more systematic approach is also possible. At Salt Lake Community College, faculty and administrators were concerned that many students lacked any clear purposes and often treated general education requirements as something to "get out of the way"; the consensus was that gen ed was "helter-skelter" and lacked any control over quality. In an effort to educate all students about their career and academic choices for all students, especially the undirected students, the college obtained a Title III grant to revise general education. The faculty developed the view that all courses should be related to students' present and future lives, including careers, and established the following criteria for general education: "The general education program at Salt Lake Community College has as its fundamental purpose the integration of attitudes, skills and broad abstractions of knowledge. The program will encourage students to be active and creative agents in the life-long process of inquiry, evaluation and decision making. All general education courses will be non-major classes and will provide an introductory overview with no prerequisites. They must also meet . . . six criteria of communication, creativity, critical thinking, esthetics, social web and substance."

As a result, every existing general education course was evaluated, with the result that few continued in their previous form, and the college added a multidisciplinary requirement. The new courses have very different conceptions than conventional general education. Understanding History is subtitled "What history is and what historians do"; it is a study of how to do (rather than merely read) history. Electricity and Modern Living is one of the most popular of the new general education courses, because students not only gain an historical perspective of the development and impact of electrical technology but they also conduct safety inspections, wire circuits, install GFCI receptacles, and do a host of other laboratory activities. Several of the general education courses have led to enrollment increases in vocational programs, as students have made historical and philosophical connections to occupations and gained personal experience in careerlike activities.[8]

Most multidisciplinary courses have come from the humanities rather than the social sciences. This may be due to the fact that these hybrid courses have often been developed with special funding, from the National Endowment for the Humanities and from the NEH-supported project on "Integrating the Humanities into Occupational Programs" (Shared Vision Task Force, 1989; 1991; Sessions, 1992). However, there are other obvious candidates for multidisciplinary courses related to various social sciences. These could include courses examining public policy and political issues related to technological change and employment issues (including unemployment, discrimination, the quality of work, and other unpleasant realities of capitalism); courses examining the sociology and the psychology of work[9] (including the psychology of occupational choice, for students unsure of their direction); and courses in business-government relations, to examine the ethical, political, and regulatory issues surrounding employment. Almost every area of the humanities and social sciences contains issues which are related to employment and which could form the basis for several courses.[10]

The reliance of multidisciplinary courses on special funding is testimony to the resources necessary to develop novel approaches. Every participant in multidisciplinary courses has stressed the need for staff development, since individuals are generally unfamiliar with the range of disciplines required; faculty must have release time to develop new materials, and many hybrid courses have required the collaboration of faculty from several disciplines, at least in the development stage. Some but not all of them are team-taught as well, again increasing their costs.

However, there is a dangerous side to reliance on special funding: when the funding disappears, the courses may disappear too. One clear example arose in New York state, which supported interdisciplinary courses in nine community colleges through a grant from the NEH. The project, starting with planning grants in 1984–85 and ending with a summary conference in 1987, brought together two-person teams from the humanities and occupational fields, and developed several versions of a course entitled Humanities and Technology. However, funding for such efforts subsequently ended, and there appear to be no more than one or two such courses still being taught[11]—and these rely entirely on the initiative and interest of individual faculty without any institutional support. The challenge is to institutionalize such courses, to have them become part of the normal offerings of community colleges and technical institutes from regular rather than special funds, and accepted as legitimate by faculty, administrators, and students alike.

Despite the difficulty institutions have had institutionalizing these courses, they present a promising vision. They represent a fresh approach to curriculum integration, one which creates new courses rather than modifying existing courses in minor ways. The best of them have required the collaboration of both occupational and academic faculty, providing new opportunities for faculty collaboration. The difficulty institutions have had in institutionalizing them is distressing, to be sure, but the current round of courses is relatively new, and with the interest in broader forms of education and higher-order skills they may be able to establish themselves as permanent parts of the community college.

Tandem and Cluster Courses and Learning Communities

The examples of integrated instruction given so far attempt to reshape individual courses. Another approach has been to develop a *series* of courses, both academic and occupational, that students take simultaneously, with each course designed to complement the other. This kind of interaction among courses can happen at several different scales. Two subjects can be linked, creating tandem courses. For example, Chemeketa Community College (Oregon) has developed a Human Services Practicum coupled with Writing 121. The practicum introduces students to various human services placements and requires extensive writing from students about positions they might like, in effect getting them to assess opportunities in human services; the writing course presents various styles of writing and enables students to work more intensively on the papers they prepare for the practicum.

On a larger scale, clusters of more than two courses can be related to one another. LaGuardia Community College (Long Island City, New York) has developed an umbrella called the Enterprise Center for cluster courses related to business. One cluster pairs introductory accounting with basic reading; it is essentially a remediation sequence with a clear focus on business uses of reading and arithmetic. The Introductory Business Cluster includes Introduction to Business, Composition I, and Introduction to Economics. The Advanced Business Cluster includes Principles of Management; Philosophy, Values, and Business Ethics; and Writing Through Literature. The advanced cluster has also articulated four themes—the entrepreneur versus individual rights, the individual within the organization, cultural and corporate values, and the social cost of business—intended to cut across the three courses in the cluster. The choice of themes reveals purposes related both to general education—providing critical perspectives from the humanities, for example—and to broad vocational purposes like introducing students to the personal and social tensions within business.

In addition, basic math is paired with a course called Computer Topics, again at a relatively basic level, while the pairing of Introduction to Business and Introduction to Computers is designed "to explore the impact of computer technology on contemporary business." Other clusters at LaGuardia include the Animal Health Technology Cluster, including Introduction to Animal Health, a chemistry course, and an English course, designed in part to clarify for students the need for good writing; and a pairing of ESL and keyboarding for students new to this country—what the instructors called a "sheltered pair" because it shelters students from the more rigorous pacing of a standard class. Of course, clusters can be developed without a vocational component; for example, Chemeketa

Community College offers a sequence in Evolving American Cultures which includes a course in American literature, one in U.S. history, and one called Understanding Movies.

Another systematic approach to clusters has emerged at San Diego City College, where a set of clusters called City Blocks are advertised as "courses that fit together and make sense." The college offers two very different forms of clusters. History of Technology in the Workplace combines transfer-level history, English, and computer information science to focus on the theme of historical changes wrought by technological advances. Two other clusters, Workplace Ethics and Communications Skills, combine occupational perspectives with liberal arts studies in philosophy and with written and oral communications. Workplace Ethics combines assignments, readings, cross-faculty discussions and joint assessments between an accounting course and a philosophy course. The final examination includes a case study to be analyzed for elements of fraudulent accounting practices, after which students discuss the advice that Mills or Kant would give to an employee involved in this ethical dilemma. College officials report that the linked courses have enticed vocational students to take more academic coursework and allowed academic students to gain knowledge of career pathways.

In several institutions, clusters have been developed in order to simulate workplace conditions. A new program initiated at Macomb Community College (Michigan) addresses several components of manufacturing including internal and external communication, problem solving and scheduling techniques in manufacturing, and technical competencies in machining. A related approach to simulating workplace conditions has been implemented at the College of DuPage (Illinois), where a business professor designed a flow-of-work simulation to link seven business and marketing courses. Students enrolled in these courses attend class at a common location and complete tasks which simulate the interdependence of information and production flow on the job, as well as learning the job-specific and generic technical skills necessary to operate business equipment, schedule output, and complete accounting and marketing tasks.

In clusters, students take all courses simultaneously (or, less often, over two semesters). Instructors report that students within clusters are engaged in deeper ways than are most community college students. They have stronger personal relationships with other students, since they see them more frequently; they tend to work more collaboratively, and to develop study groups and other support mechanisms. (Indeed, some instructors have capitalized on this development by having students work in small groups and using other collaborative teaching techniques.) Students can refer to material from other classes, and they benefit from having connections among classes clarified both by the structure of the courses and by instructors. As one student mentioned,[12] "The topics were interrelated between business and economics, and English brought it together. Also, we were all in the same class and could exchange ideas among ourselves."

For their part, instructors can be more confident about what material students have already learned and can therefore build on earlier material in other classes. The faculty at LaGuardia College report that their regular meetings include discussion of assessment and teaching and learning methods, suggesting another mechanism where teaching can improve. They also claim that students in pairs and clusters are more motivated and less likely to drop out; while there is only a little evidence, the conclusion that students in clusters have closer ties to other students is consistent with the finding that dropout rates are lower among individuals whose social connections within postsecondary institutions are stronger.[13]

To be sure, there may be some drawbacks to clusters. Several instructors mentioned that they never had sufficient time for joint planning. While acknowledging the benefits of greater student interaction, several mentioned that students form cliques and that discipline problems may develop; "familiarity can become too familiar," in the words of one instructor. Several faculty members expressed the feeling that clusters were not worth the effort necessary to coordinate instructors and to cope with discipline problems, though one faculty member considering leaving a cluster still acknowledged the value of clusters: "When it works, it's incredible." Evidently, clusters represent substantial departures from conventional classroom practice for instructors and students alike and place novel demands on instructors; some may be unwilling to spend the time, and some may find themselves unprepared for the cooperation that clusters require.

Of course, tandem courses and clusters can become larger

groupings of courses, sometimes referred to as learning communities (see for example Gabelnick, 1990; Gabelnick, MacGregor, Matthews, and Smith, 1990; Hamberg, 1991; Matthews, 1994). Any number of disciplines can be linked within learning communities, of course, and many examples group conventional academic courses—economics and history, math and science, literature and art—rather than incorporating occupational fields. Whatever the specific disciplines, the most important aspects of self-conscious learning communities are the emphasis on interdisciplinary study, the development of institutional structures (like co-enrollment and team teaching) that overcome the fragmentation of conventional educational institutions, integration of skills from various disciplines and content areas, and development of more active approaches to teaching, with seminars, discussion groups, and projects more common than conventional lectures.

Capstone Courses

Capstone courses are in many ways a kind of hybrid course, like applied academic or multidisciplinary courses, but they serve a different role in the curriculum and have taken on new value as both occupational and academic courses move toward more authentic assessment. Capstone courses require that students plan and execute a project, similar to one in a work setting, that includes planning, finance, technical, and production skills, as well as labor, safety, environmental and community issues. For example, Sinclair Community College (Ohio) has adopted senior projects in several technical fields, in one case requiring students to apply plant layout and material-handling knowledge to project designing manufacturing plants. At Columbus State Community College (Ohio) microcomputer operations students work either independently or in small groups to design and develop appropriate forms, presentations, data entry, and retrieval procedures using various media for a typical small business system, evaluate the hardware and software that might be appropriate. By drawing on material and competencies that arise in several different areas, capstone courses provide another way of integrating coursework from several disciplines; by focusing on a project, this approach provides a more natural and worklike context for such integration.[14]

Teaching Developmental Education and ESL in the Context of Occupational Preparation

The forms of integrating academic and vocational education described so far respond to the demands of employers for a better mastery of academic competencies and for broader forms of occupational education. But two-year colleges face a very different problem because of their role as second-chance institutions, open to all who want to enroll with entrance requirements. A large and increasing fraction of students entering two-year colleges have left high school without mastering fundamental academic competencies and need some form of remedial education, which is often termed developmental education to avoid the stigma associated with remediation and to signal more student-centered pedagogical approaches. Virtually every community college and technical institute now offers some form of remediation (Mansfield and Farris, 1991), with estimates of the fraction of entering students in need of basic instruction varying from 25 percent to 50 percent (Cahalan and Farris, 1986, Table 6; Plisko and Stern, 1985; Roueche, Baker, and Roueche, 1985) to 78 percent in the Tennessee system (Riggs, Davis, and Wilson, 1990). In addition, given the enormous waves of immigration in this country since the 1960s, an increasing number of students enter community college without much knowledge of English, and often specifically seeking instruction in English, particularly in English as a Second Language (ESL) courses. If community colleges serve to link short-term job training and education, then the numbers of such students will only increase.

Students in need of remediation and ESL—who come to the community college like other students, seeking to enter the economic mainstream—often find themselves in remedial courses filling out worksheets, doing standard arithmetic problems, and making little visible progress toward their occupational goals. Many instructors report that students (and occupational students especially) are bored with remedial courses and fail to see their relevance to occupational goals. The result is that dropout rates in remedial courses are high; and students needing remediation but failing to complete the appropriate coursework are unlikely to persist or to complete their programs of study.[15]

One remedy to the problem of how best to provide remedial instruction and ESL is to borrow the method of integrating academic and occupational content, that is, to develop remedial (or developmental) courses and ESL programs with an occupational emphasis, or to teach these subjects in tandem courses or clusters, with developmental English and math clustered with an occupational course. These approaches teach basic academic skills, or English, while introducing students to the concepts, tasks, and job-specific skills required in occupational areas. In addition to providing some sense that remedial courses are connected to occupational purposes, these approaches exemplify the position that learning in a particular context is most effective (Collins, Brown, and Newman, 1989). Some examples follow:[16]

• Springfield Technical Community College (Massachusetts) has developed a course called Introduction to Business, aimed at students contemplating a career in business but needing some remediation. The course itself uses a business text and covers some topics from standard business courses (business practices, business-related vocabulary and concepts, familiarity with different business careers) but uses a variety of materials (including computers, music, and video) for students whose reading levels are not yet adequate for more advanced courses such as accounting and management (Baraldi, 1990).

• Introduction to Technology at Yakima Community College (Washington) provides remediation in math, reading, and writing in the context of an introduction to various technical occupational specialties, including jobs in agriculture, engineering, and auto/diesel mechanics. The proposal for the course states the problem as the separation of remediation from subsequent coursework: "developmental students are physically remote from vocational/technological programs and faculty [and] remain unaware of program opportunities available to them . . . this collaborative learning community will build bridges for faculty and students, and more clearly define a pathway from developmental education to vocational and technological programs."

• The Basic Technology Program at Schenectady County Community College (New York), designed for "students with limited math/science backgrounds or weak basic skills," includes two courses titled Introduction to Technologies which describe technical careers, applied math (for example, measurement and scales), some physical processes, and the equipment used in technical positions. Supporting courses include a remedial math sequence, freshman English, and introductions to chemistry and computers.

• At Chemeketa Community College a program in drafting and study skills has been devised with the collaboration of a drafting instructor and an instructor from developmental education.

• A somewhat more complex program, with a sequence of remedial courses connected to occupational instruction, is the Health Career Community developed at Springfield Technical Community College, for students preparing for one of twelve health programs but needing remediation. A series of three courses focuses on reading skills with practical applications in medical settings (including a great deal of medical vocabulary); study skills (like note taking, outlining, and test taking) using a specially selected text on health; life skills (time management, stress management, nutrition, and self-confidence), again using examples drawn from health; and familiarization with career opportunities in health, with an attempt to convey what is required in different occupations—a kind of career exploration. Simultaneously, students can take the conventional developmental courses in reading, math, and science. When they have passed the introductory courses, they can begin the regular courses of the health occupation they have chosen. The director claims higher retention rates than in the community college as a whole.

• LaGuardia Community College, where learning communities are probably better developed than at any other two-year college in the country, teaches all of its programs for welfare recipients through learning communities. Typically, a remedial English and a math course are combined with an introductory occupational course; one example combined English, math, and an introductory biology course that had previously been a barrier to those attempting to enter health occupations. Another example combined courses in reading, sociology, and Introduction to Social Services for students who wanted to enter various social work positions. In such clusters the content of the developmental courses can be changed to reinforce the specific reading, writing, and math skills necessary in a particular group of occupations. In turn, the instructor in the occupational course can count on certain prerequisites having been learned in the related developmental courses and can have specific competencies (for example, a particular kind of writing) reinforced in the other courses. In addition, such clusters generate a support group among a group of students (in this case, welfare recipients) facing similar problems in making their way through the institution and into employment.

• Winning the award for best course title, a cluster at Palomar Community College (California) called "Reading, Writing, and Wrenches" combines developmental skills courses with an occupational course teaching basic approaches to tools, materials, and technology.

Of course, it is possible to develop developmental courses which use academic rather than occupational courses to develop applications. Schoolcraft College (in Livonia, Michigan) has developed "paired classes" in developmental reading and psychology, and found—in a relatively well-controlled study—that students enrolled in the pair earned higher grades and had lower dropout rates than did a control group of equivalent ability (Gudan, Clack, Tang, and Dixon, 1991). As a result of this success, the college is planning to extend such pairs to business and political science.

A similar approach has been taken in several ESL courses, sometimes labeled English for Special Purposes (ESP) or Vocational English as a Second Language (VESL):

• At Bunker Hill Community College, an ESL program for Allied Health, preparing students to become nursing assistants, lab assistants, and pharmacy technicians, and one for electronics have been developed, based on the belief that "language training is most effective when taught in the context of skill training." The courses aim to improve the English-language reading and writing of students, but they include reading and vocabulary drawn from the related occupation, develop writing assignments that mimic those that will be used on the job, and introduce students to the careers available and the basic tasks and capacities required.

• An approach called technology-specific ESL has been developed at the Applied Technology Center operated by Everett and Edmonds Community Colleges (Washington). ESL instructors are first taught about electronics; then, in consultation with industry supervisors and managers from local high-tech firms, they teach limited English-proficient employees of these firms "the reading, writing, and speaking skills necessary to participate in the problem solving and collaboration required in high technology firms" and to pass the certification tests required by federal contracts.

• Black Hawk College (Moline, Illinois) has developed a machine tool curriculum for new Indochinese students, with vocational instructors and the Laotian and Vietnamese bilingual staff of the college collaborating.

• LaGuardia Community College, committed to teaching in clusters, has paired an ESL course with introduction to computers, where students concentrate in their ESL class on the vocabulary and documentation particular to computer-related fields. While the occupational course remains relatively unchanged, the ESL course has been substantially modified to include occupationally specific vocabulary, reading, and writing in place of the conventional literature-based approach.

Bridge programs, designed to facilitate the return to formal education for particular groups—older adults, for example, or individuals with histories of lackluster preparation, or Hispanic students—often provide preparation in the form of clusters. In a few cases the same goals are met within single courses; for example, Worker Effectiveness Training (Southwest Community College, Minnesota), Workplace Readiness (Broome County Community College, New York), and The World of Work (Philadelphia Community College) all offer oral and written communication, math, keyboarding, and career planning, all in some occupational context. In other cases multiple courses are developed. Indian River Community College (Florida) offers a two-option bridge program, including one or two full semesters of linked courses in applied philosophy, principles of academic success, applied physics, applied math, and applied communications. Students choose between occupational courses in manufacturing and in business technology. High school students who need academic reinforcement are "invited and recruited" to participate in the bridge program and are organized into "production teams" for activities, group projects, and attendance.

In these cases, then, the integration of academic instruction and occupational content involves teaching basic skills (or English) within courses that draw reading, vocabulary, writing exercises, and other applications from a broad occupational area. Each also provides what might be termed career exploration: an introduction to the specific jobs within the occupation and to the concepts, practices, and demands in these positions. These courses, or the longer sequence of the Health Career Community in Springfield Technical Community College, prepare students to enter regular occupational programs, and so their vocational purpose is clear—in contrast to most remedial programs, which prepare students to pass basic skills tests but fail to link remediation to any future ambitions of students. The claims that this approach increases retention, consistent with the complaints of instructors in conventional remedial programs that their students are unmotivated and fail to see the connection to vocational goals, suggest real promise for this particular form of "contextualized" instruction.

The Benefits of Curriculum Integration: The Community College as a Nontraditional Institution

Is the integration of academic and occupational education likely to benefit students, given the need for specialization at the postsecondary level and the substantial job-specific requirements in certain fields? Perhaps the high school should be the appropriate place to learn general and academic competencies, while postsecondary education should be reserved for specialization.

The most convincing response to this question is the one raised by employers, as described in Chapter One. The dominant complaints from employers about their workers—both among the employers we interviewed, and in national reports of the SCANS Commission and others—is not that their job-specific skills are deficient but that they lack more fundamental competencies, including the ability to read and communicate at appropriate levels and various higher-order capacities. These are capacities that can best be taught with a mix of academic and occupational content, appropriately integrated so that students could see how general abilities are necessary in specific occupational settings. The most powerful rationale for integrating academic and occupational education, then, is the reason that first motivated this subject: students will be better-prepared for occupations over the long run, especially in a world of changing requirements and escalating skill demands, if they are broadly rather than narrowly educated.

Another benefit to students of integration stresses the nonvocational purposes of education. While the moral and humanistic rationales for education often seem submerged in our utilitarian age, nonetheless a persistent stream of commentary has urged that occupational programs include these aspects too, lest they produce "technopeasants"[17] who are technically qualified but otherwise unable to participate in society in any but the most primitive ways. To cite the Commission on the Future of Community Colleges again (*Building Communities,* pp. 20–21): "We also acknowledge that the utility of education and the dignity of vocation have important value, not just for those enrolled in general and transfer studies. Only by placing emphasis on both can all students help in the building of community. . . . Students in technical studies should be helped to discover the meaning of work. They should put their special skills in historical, social, and ethical perspective. Those in traditional arts and sciences programs should, in turn, understand that work is the means by which we validate formal education." Such a view lends particularly strong support to the multidisciplinary courses described above.

Yet another benefit to students is related to career choice. Many integrated programs have incorporated modules that can be considered career exploration, sometimes as part of an applied communications course, sometimes as part of an introductory course in remedial programs linked with occupational programs, sometimes in multidisciplinary courses, and sometimes in introductory courses like Introduction to Business or Introduction to Health Careers. As a way of responding to the uncertainty of many community college students about their occupational futures, incorporating career information into courses is a powerful approach since it integrates career information with job-specific skills and contextualizes information about occupational options. This is a conceptually different approach to career exploration than are the decontextualized services provided by counseling and guidance staff, services that some students do not find particularly valuable.

There are still other benefits, somewhat less obvious. One of them, particularly important in teaching-oriented institutions like community colleges, is that efforts to integrate academic and occupational instruction can improve teaching practices. Integrated approaches provide examples of learning in context, in this case the important context of an occupation, that can enhance motivation and learning. They are more consistent with the project- and activity-based approaches of the best vocational instruction and are more student-centered when they use issues and themes of interest to occupational students. Many integrated courses and programs include statements of purpose indicating that they are moving away from the straightforward transmission of facts and figures, towards a form of teaching in which students are more active in constructing meaning and interpreting issues of importance to them. For example, the cross-cutting themes used in LaGuardia's Advanced Business Cluster, the greater use of collaborative teaching methods in pairs and clusters, the introduction of novel content in the air conditioning program at Cedar Valley College, and the statement about general education at Diablo Valley College that such requirements will "help you make meaning from your encounters with the world" are all cases of more active teaching than is conventionally the case. In contrast to long-standing complaints among occupational students about the "irrelevance" of academic courses, instructors in integrated approaches report higher levels of motivation, as students come to see the applicability of academic material.

These approaches to teaching are consistent with the current view that learning in context is a superior method, compared to the conventional practice of teaching reading, writing, math, or science as abstract bodies of skills and facts disconnected from their applications—consistent both with good practice in adult education and the widely cited recommendations of SCANS "that teachers and school must begin early to help students see the relationships between what they study and its applications in real-world contexts," that "the most effective way of teaching skills is 'in context'" (1991, p. 19).

One way to summarize these benefits for students is to see how the various forms of integrating academic and vocational education, and the related practices linking community colleges more closely with employers (the subject of the next chapter) work together to provide students with the *variety* of competencies they need. Table 5.1 lists these competencies, taken from the demands of employers, from the evident needs of students searching for meaningful careers, and from the desire to prepare citizens able to discharge their responsibilities in all spheres of life. The *range* of competencies necessary is quite formidable, going well beyond the job-specific skills of conventional vocational education and the academic skills of academic education. But in a community college that has adopted the innovative practices illustrated in the previous sections, the range of instructional methods is formidable too. In this vision, the community college is not just a random collection of courses, where individuals mill around hoping that the courses they take will prepare them for the future. Instead, the community college becomes a more purposive institution—what I call in Chapter Eight the community college as a learning community—in which a variety of institutional methods are used to develop students in a variety of ways.

There are still other institutional benefits to the efforts to integrate academic and occupational education. One is the collaboration among faculty that integration encourages. Because conventional teaching is often quite isolated, many instructors welcome the contact with other faculty that infusion, tandem courses, clusters, and Writing Across the Curriculum fosters. As a dean responsible for a remedial learning community commented, "It has brought instructors together in a new way. They have to co-plan the program. Assignments are structured so that they build upon one another. The content has been developed to correspond with other work being done. That builds a synergy effect. We get more accomplished and make better progress. The instructors love it. It pulls them away from the isolation they've experienced. They didn't all like it going into the planning, but all have ended up being real fans of the program."

Of course, collaboration usually requires more time and some accommodation to different points of view, since collaborative teaching requires faculty to go outside their fields of expertise. But

Table 5.1. The Educational Content of Occupational Preparation.

Competency	Description	Methods of Instruction
Job-specific skills	Production skills used in particular work tasks	Traditional occupation-specific courses; work-based learning including co-op education, on-the-job training; short-term job training programs
General occupational competencies	Skills used in a variety of occupations: computer applications, business procedures, diagram/blueprint reading, quality assurance techniques	Occupational courses with infusion; linked courses; broadly work-related activities and materials
Generic skills for modern workplaces	"SCANS skills": Decision making, problem solving, communications skills, independent learning, understanding systems, organizing resources	Integrated instruction of all kinds, especially infusion/WAC; linked courses; occupational applications and teaching in context; work-based learning and co-op education
Related academic competencies	"Foundation skills": Reading, writing, and other communications skills; appropriate mathematics, including problem solving; appropriate science and social science, including workplace applications	Applied academic courses; infusion and WAC; linked courses and learning communities

Table 5.1. (*continued*)

Competency	Description	Methods of Instruction
Career exploration and decision making	Determining career interests and abilities; learning about labor markets; decision-making abilities	Introductory occupational courses; bridge programs; infusion; work-based learning, co-op education, and co-op seminars; guidance and counseling
Economic, political, and social aspects of work	Understanding broad economic and political issues; historical perspectives; responsibilities of citizens and community members; traditional goals of liberal education	Infusion; multidisciplinary courses; linked courses and learning communities; revised general education programs

Source: Adapted from Badway and Grubb (forthcoming).

institutions where collaboration is the norm would also be more supportive places to experiment with novel approaches to teaching. For those who have been able to work well with colleagues in developing integrated curricula, there are substantial personal benefits as well as benefits to students.

A final institutional advantage of integrating academic and occupational education is also the loftiest. As the community college has developed, it has added new (and even contradictory) purposes. To the early "academic" emphasis on preparing students to transfer to four-year colleges, occupational education has come to be a critical mission, even dominant in some states; remedial or developmental programs have expanded enormously; community service courses of various kinds constitute important components; customized training and other firm-specific instruction have come to play a crucial role. Some community colleges provide adult education in their states or regions, adding a variety of noncredit programs and new populations; and many provide short-term training for JTPA clients and welfare recipients. Many more would serve such individuals in the integrated system of education and training outlined in the previous chapter. Most community colleges have responded to these responsibilities by adding new divisions, and communication among the various divisions is often quite poor.[18] As a result, the community college often appears to be *an archipelago of independent islands,* each serving one mission but with limited communication among them.

But this obviously need not be the case. The examples of several community colleges that regularly support curriculum integration, learning communities, and collaborative approaches to teaching indicate that a college can establish an atmosphere where faculty regularly collaborate with one another. In this way curriculum integration can help bridge the distinct "islands" of activity within the community college, preventing them from being expedient collections of different purposes that fail to reinforce one another. Curriculum integration is, therefore, one of the most powerful ways of achieving a goal of the Commission on the Future of the Community College, which argued throughout its report on *Building Communities* that community colleges should be not only community-serving institutions but also internally cohesive communities.

In thinking about the institutional benefits of curriculum integration, it is necessary to distinguish between those reforms that
change individual courses—often the responsibility of small numbers of faculty, working independently without much institutional
encouragement—from those that transform the institutional support for teaching as a whole. In the latter cases, a distinct pattern
of innovation has often developed. Effective leadership and a gen-
uine interest in reform among instructors—that is, both top-down
and bottom-up strategies simultaneously—improve the chances for
innovations to survive, as does the provision of institutional resources. At LaGuardia Community College, for example, an early
college-within-a-college failed partly because a top-down decision
was not accepted by faculty members. However, when an administrator then used Perkins funds for staff development programs
focused on active learning techniques, the participants developed
the idea of pairs and clusters and then became the leaders in
generating new ideas and applications. This approach to change—
administrative leadership coupled with the transfer of responsibility to faculty, with institutional resources allocated to innovations
as necessary—is a common pattern in one of the most widely cited
community colleges, Miami-Dade (Roueche and Baker, 1987a).

The need for administrative leadership to support curriculum integration is due in part to a particular barrier to integrating academic and occupational education, cited over and over by
the instructors and administrators who have developed novel
approaches: the disciplinary specialization that affects virtually all
of education. Many instructors are wedded to their own disciplines,
and some are uninterested and unprepared to make links to related fields. The unwillingness to try new approaches is expressed
in different ways: academic instructors often complain about pressures to "water down" the curriculum, occupational instructors
express concern with "the integrity of the occupational curriculum" and with teaching sufficient occupationally specific skills, and
everyone is worried about enough time to cover what they consider
the most important topics—the "tyranny of coverage." The general
problem of fragmentation by disciplines is often particularly serious in the split between academic and occupational faculties, partly
because of the status difference between the two. In one extreme
case—a community college so divided into different camps that
they do not consider themselves a single institution—the dean of

occupational education declared, "We're a vocational school housed in a community college."

It is, of course, difficult for faculty working independently to do much about disciplinary barriers and the split between academic and occupational education. These are systemic and institutional issues rather than individual problems and therefore can be corrected only by changing the culture of an institution. Similarly, the benefits of creating more coherent approaches to the various missions a community college serves are in large part institutional benefits, requiring an institutional perspective to accomplish—that is, administrators who are willing to promote them, encourage faculty in their initial efforts, and pursue innovation beyond the interests of any one faculty member.

A second institutional barrier to curriculum integration is simply the lack of resources for cooperation. Full-time instructors complain that they have no time to spend with their colleagues developing new and difficult courses; and part-time faculty, which group includes many vocational instructors, often don't spend enough time on campus for much collaboration to take place. However, most community colleges and technical institutes can find the resources for initiatives that they find compelling; for example, with the recent alarm over declining transfer rates, many have been able to fund transfer centers and honors programs. And many of the resources necessary for integrating academic and occupational education are already present, within the existing faculty and the teaching that currently takes place. Integrated instruction is a way of reorganizing existing resources and teaching, rather than an addition to existing programs that requires additional resources.

The benefits of curriculum integration are powerful, not only to the students in them but also to the institutions themselves. They work not only by changing the curriculum and how it is taught but also by improving collaboration among faculty and by changing the culture of an institution. The results of such changes take substantial time to accomplish, of course, but the benefits are substantial too. The results would be postsecondary institutions that are coherent learning communities motivating students and teaching them in the most effective ways, that provide a broad education for occupational students, and that prepare flexible individuals able to change as employment and labor markets require.

Chapter Six

Enhancing Connections Between Educational Institutions and Employers

Because the sub-baccalaureate labor market is quite local, the ability of students to benefit from two-year colleges depends on their being able to find employment related to their education in the local area. If they cannot, then they must either find unrelated employment locally—for which the economic benefits are substantially lower, as Table 3.5 clarified—or search outside their local area, where the institution they attended may not have an established reputation. Both alternatives are risky; the most promising outcome is for individuals to find related employment locally.

In a labor market with perfect information, this might not be particularly difficult; students would be well informed about employment alternatives available, and employers would know which individuals are the most qualified. In practice, however, information is hard to obtain, particularly given the uncertainty surrounding the informal hiring practices and the loosely structured careers typical of the sub-baccalaureate labor market. Therefore an important mechanism facilitating the transfer from formal schooling into employment has been the relationship that educational institutions establish with employers. Indeed, community colleges have a variety of such linkages, in keeping with their image as community-serving organizations, including advisory committees, placement offices, informal placement by occupational instructors, student follow-up and tracking mechanisms, contract education, and various work experience and co-op programs.

Unfortunately, in the four communities we examined, these link-ages often work imperfectly.

But since linkages to employers already exist in some form in most institutions, they can be improved. Enhanced connections with local employers would in turn increase the amount of infor-mation about employment alternatives and facilitate the entry of students into employment. The result, visible particularly in Cincin-nati and in the technical programs in Sacramento, would also be to create closer working relations between educational institutions and employers, in place of the independence that often prevails.

Of course, there is substantial variation among community col-leges and among communities, and it is possible that those we have examined are atypical, with weaker connections to employers than prevail elsewhere. As in examining the hiring practices of local labor markets, *there is no substitute for individual community colleges examining the practices linking them to employers.*

The "Two Worlds" of Employers and Education Providers

In the four labor markets we examined, by far the largest group of employers was simply unable to express any opinion about the edu-cational providers in the local area. They were unfamiliar with local institutions; they did not know from which schools and colleges their employees (or their best or worst employees) come; they were unable to venture any opinions about which local providers pre-pared their students the best or about what changes they would make in local educational programs. I interpret this lack of opinion as indifference to educational providers because of the dominant criteria for hiring in the sub-baccalaureate labor market: since expe-rience, informal job tests, and performance during an initial pro-bation count much more than educational qualifications in hiring, and since job-specific skills can be learned in a variety of ways, there is simply no need to be familiar with local educational programs.

A minority of employers in San Jose and Sacramento who did have opinions about community college, and a slight majority of such employers in Fresno, were less complimentary about community colleges. Their criticisms fell into several predictable areas. Many castigated educational institutions for using outdated equipment and methods. In some cases, especially regarding machining and electronics, it is almost impossible for educational institutions to keep up with technological changes. As the manager of a machining company in Cincinnati explained, "We took [our apprentices] to [the local technical college] and they asked about their program, and the instructor down there said, 'Yes, if you come down here we will teach you how to program a three-axis machine,' and one of our apprentices said, 'But I'm already programming a five-axis now.' [The college] can't buy a Consatti 5-axis machine and the Siemens control on that. That machine is a two million dollar machine, and that's what our apprentices end up learning very soon."

However, even programs not requiring expensive equipment can lag behind. For example, a supervisor of computer operators at a large high-tech firm criticized a nearby community college's computer program because it started with an introductory class that was ten years out of date and then shifted to assembler languages that are not widely used.

In some cases, the internal policies of community colleges rather than the pace and expense of technical advancement are blamed for lags. A number of employers noted the long time necessary to establish new programs and to eliminate obsolete programs, blaming the "humungous" educational bureaucracies of colleges and the need for everyone in an institution to approve any changes. In contrast, one reason for the high rating of contract education among employers is that community colleges can usually develop firm-specific programs through their contract education divisions within very short periods of time.

A second criticism is that educational programs are too theory-oriented and lacking sufficient practical or hands-on experience, not specific enough, and not oriented to producing a product. When asked about suggestions for improving electronics programs, a supervisor of a tire manufacturer in Fresno replied, "Get them more on-the-job training while they're in school because when they come to us they think they're ready to go to work, and they . . . realize they're just now ready to learn. They've only got half the prescription for success, and the other half is out here, dealing with people."

Similarly, in talking about the superiority of the firm's apprenticeship program, the manager of a Cincinnati machining company said: "The difference [between our apprenticeship program and educational programs] is that we base our instruction on real-life situations and not on the theory behind it. We bring in actual parts. We bring in actual prints. We talk about real-life situations. I don't think you get that necessarily in a school situation."

Where employers were able to compare various educational providers, they tended to prefer institutions on the basis of their equipment, that is, whether it was up-to-date and comparable to what was being used within the firm, and the similarity of the training to actual conditions on the job. The result was a position that often translated into a preference for educational programs stressing hands-on rather than theoretical training. Indeed, in a few cases employers prefer a shorter, hands-on program to a longer, theoretical program. For example, a personnel manager for one hospital prefers to recruit associate degree nurses from the local community college rather than baccalaureate nurses from the state college "because the A.D.N. at [the local community college] has more hands-on, practical experience, whereas the other side is more theory." Once again, this clarifies that employers are looking for preparation—whether through experience or formal schooling—that is as specific to their own equipment, production methods, and organization as possible.

At the same time, as we saw in Chapter One, other employers criticize the inability of community colleges to keep up with escalating requirements of basic academic skills. The director of human resources for a high-tech manufacturer in the San Jose area stated: "I think applicants have the initial list of basic skills. However, those skills apply to what was required five or ten years ago. But because of the development of automation in the factory, artificial intelligence, and SPC [Statistical Process Control], and the company direction to use that technique to modernize its production capabilities, the expectation level for our technicians has moved up. So the bar keeps going up; therefore, it's more difficult to find the standard graduate out of a junior college that meets these goals because the colleges haven't kept up with the expectation of employers."

Even employers who hire extensively from community colleges find flaws in their programs, most often in various nontechnical capacities such as communications skills.[1] The personnel directors for an employer near Sacramento, one that has established a co-op program with several community colleges, commented on the quality of community college programs: "Taking an overall look at the programs, on the technical side, I think they're very good. However, communications skills, both written and oral, aren't up to the same quality. When students are involved in a technical curriculum, they aren't allowed much time to develop other skills even though the general education courses are required, and so the written and oral communications skills don't get developed as they should."

Thus community colleges are caught in a dilemma that is not of their own making. While many employers stress the kinds of job-specific skills that are necessary for entry-level employment, including skills that are too specific and too machine-dependent for any educational institution to be reasonably expected to provide, others stress the kinds of higher-order competencies necessary for promotion within flexible, high-skilled companies.

Even within specific labor markets, there was substantial variation in opinions about these educational providers. Some employers reported disappointing experiences, while others expressed approval of the local community college. In the Sacramento area, the division of opinion followed occupational lines. Those employing electronics technicians reported that local programs were excellent, and they tended to require an associate degree. Those employing accountants and other business occupations were generally critical and provided no special recognition of community college credentials. The variation in opinion probably reflects the variation in the quality of programs and the extent of their connections with employers. Community colleges are notoriously independent and varied—indeed, proudly so because of their rhetoric about serving local communities. State controls over local colleges are relatively weak (as Chapter Seven clarifies), particularly in the states of our four case studies. Except in health occupations, where licensing requirements govern, there are neither state nor federal standards for occupational curriculum and no mechanisms, such as SAT tests, that help standardize occupational curricula. In this situation, substantial variation in the quality of occupational programs can persist, and this variation shows up in employer responses.

However, there were several striking exceptions to the general lack of opinion about educational providers. This was particularly the case in Cincinnati, where strong co-op programs place employers and providers in close proximity. There, virtually every employer was familiar both with the co-op programs and with the specific participating institutions, and their comments about the quality of education were uniformly positive. Similarly, employers in technical fields in Sacramento tended to have positive opinions about community colleges and other vocational providers; a number of electronics manufacturers have established programs in which they hire directly from the local community colleges, and several have made an associate degree a hiring requirement. These important exceptions aside, the prevailing attitude of employers was indifference and ignorance, once again forcing students to find their own paths into employment.

But the examples of Cincinnati and Sacramento signal that it is possible to bridge the "two worlds" of employers and education providers. The question is why this does not always happen. In part, as I show in the rest of this chapter, the reason is that the potential linkages between education providers and local employers are often quite weak. In addition, as I argue in the conclusion to this chapter, the particular characteristics of sub-baccalaureate employment make it difficult for community colleges and technical institutes to forge a role for themselves. Connecting the two worlds requires facing both of these problems.

Advisory Committees

Every community college maintains at least some advisory committees, with local employers providing most of the members. In theory, such committees can provide information about skill requirements, hiring standards, trends in employment, and so on, which would help colleges change their programs and adjust enrollments as demand waxes and wanes. In practice, however, we found little evidence that these committees are very active. Several community colleges meet with them only annually, and employers who were members of such committees clarified how inactive they had been. Some advisory committees are institutionwide rather than occupation-specific and cannot therefore provide information about the skills requirements or hiring prospects in particular occupational areas. There is nothing to guarantee that advisory committees exist in all areas of the curriculum; for example, a community college in the Sacramento area, a region with considerable demand for office workers from both financial institutions and government, had no advisory committee for its business division. The dean for occupational education reported: "We're going less and less to the individual program advisory and more and more to the overall advisory group, technical advisory groups, strategic planning groups, because we're finding out that the problems are universal."

The trend to institutionwide committees may be an excellent way to ensure that current shibboleths about skill requirements—for example, the need for basic skills—are communicated to educators, but they are a much weaker device for maintaining contact with employers in specific occupational areas.

Furthermore, there is a startling disjunction between the colleges' perceptions of advisory committees and those of employers. While administrators and department heads referred to such committees as establishing strong links to local employers, the vast majority of employers were unaware of these committees. Where employers were knowledgeable about local community colleges (particularly in Cincinnati with its co-op program and in the San Jose area, where several community colleges have high profiles because of their transfer programs), the reasons have little to do with advisory committees.

There is also some frustration among educators about advisory committees since they do not always provide the right information. One community college dean complained about the value of "shiny pea lunches": "Often the folks that the businesses put up to be on the advisory committees are not the decision makers and they aren't even that well informed about what the needs are in the industry. These people have time to go off to the college somewhere and eat shiny peas. So there is a lot of frustration all around about the working relationship and how to reconfigure it in a very different way."

Another acknowledged the problem of conflicting information within firms: "In the PIC [Private Industry Council] groups, industry sends its personnel people, and they are not the ones who ultimately say yes or no. The people in manufacturing, research, sales,

[and] administration have different criteria for hiring people than personnel does. It's hard for education to guess what is needed."

One community college researcher complained that many companies would not provide the right information:

> Many of the industries won't tell you what they will be doing because they are very, very secretive about what's next or what kind of people they'll need next. PIC meetings don't even bring out this information. Business won't say what it will be needing or what they are developing. We sort of have to stick our finger in our mouth, hold it up, and see which way the wind is going. There is opportunity for biological technicians, but the demand isn't there yet; so [my college] won't prepare for it. Industry won't tell education where [employment] will go, so it makes it difficult.

In addition, the timing of information is clearly a problem. A personnel manager of a high-tech firm in San Jose admitted that "long range for us is probably six months" and admitted that most "planning" is concerned with a period three months in the future. Numerous employers complained about the slow place of educational institutions, but employers may be just as much to blame because of their inability (or unwillingness) to forecast employment needs.

Community colleges make the greatest use of their advisory committees in deciding whether to establish new programs. Typically, colleges will respond to requests for a new program by convening a committee of potential employers and asking them about occupational trends and the content of a possible program. However, even in these cases, the information colleges receive from their advisory committees is uncertain. Necessarily, colleges ask whether there will be employment opportunities in an occupational area, not whether local employers will hire graduates (or even noncompleters) of community college programs. The latter is the more precise but more difficult question, especially given the uncertainties of small employers and of firms operating in the sub-baccalaureate labor market. Given the evidence (in Chapter One) that employers in the sub-baccalaureate labor market prefer to hire individuals with specific experience over those with formal schooling only, advisory committees may be giving colleges overly general information about employment opportunities.

Advisory committees, then, are awkward mechanisms for linking employers and educational providers, and there is fault on both sides for the weakness of this connection. The underlying problem is the difficulty of a link that trades only in information where that information is uncertain at best. The powerful advantages of linking providers and employers in joint activities, rather than merely exchanging information, becomes evident when I examine the benefits of co-op programs.

Placement Offices

Virtually every community college operates a placement office, and it too provides a potential source of information for students about employment and an additional connection to employers. However, most placement offices are woefully understaffed, with most institutions having perhaps two or three individuals (or several work-study students) for colleges enrolling up to 25,000 students. Moreover, placement efforts usually concentrate not on employment of students leaving the institution but on part-time work for students to support themselves during their education, or "stay-in-school-type jobs," as one placement director called them. Similarly, a number of employers mentioned that they would post notices of temporary jobs at community college placement offices—"specifically targeting college students for whom these temporary, part-time, or evening jobs would be convenient"—but distinguished such jobs from regular, full-time positions for which they recruited differently. As a result, the quality of jobs available through most placement offices is low; many jobs posted appeared to be barely above minimum wage, often in fast-food restaurants and for other unskilled occupations. More to the point, most jobs handled by placement offices are unconnected to the occupational programs of the college itself.

Some employers routinely send notices of job vacancies to local community colleges as part of their general publicity. But even here, employers and placement officials report discouraging experiences. Several employers reported contacting local community colleges about job vacancies and meeting with little enthusiasm and no action except the posting of notices. That is, there were no efforts to refer well-qualified students. While these incidents might reflect idiosyncratic incompetence, a more likely interpretation is that a placement office that helps continuing students find stay-in-school work is unprepared to execute the screening function that these employers requested. In still another kind of breakdown, a new director of a placement office reported consistent failure in trying to institutionalize connections to vocational departments so that the office could refer appropriate students to employers when they called for referrals. In this case, vocational departments were simply unconcerned with placement, a rational response for any department and institution that is enrollment-driven and whose enrollments are adequate. Many educators stressed that students are responsible for their own placement—a confirmation of the oft-mentioned declaration that community colleges are "educational institutions, not placement bureaus."[2]

In addition, there is an imbalance between the interests of placement offices and those of employers that might limit the effectiveness of this matching function. As the manager of a machine shop for a very large employer in Cincinnati described it, "When we hire for the apprenticeship program, we try to stay away from [community college] people who counsel because their objective is to place people and our objective is to be very careful about selecting people who will be successful in this environment. We believe that we've got a better skill at it, at interviewing and evaluating applicants for our particular needs."

Were placement offices to make more strenuous efforts to link students with employers, they would be placed in a difficult dilemma. To stay credible with employers, they would have to recommend only the most capable students. But that recommendation would make them ineffective in placing weak students. The only solution to this dilemma is to have all students be capable. But in nonselective and noncoercive institutions like community colleges, and in employment situations where many dimensions of ability (such as motivation and persistence) are beyond the capacity of community colleges to affect, this becomes difficult to achieve.

There are some exceptions to the weakness of placement efforts. In Cincinnati, where placement offices are better staffed, we heard many more favorable reports from employers about placement offices. This may be partly a result of a state policy that used to consider closing programs with less than 75 percent placement;

because the placement offices conducted the follow-up surveys necessary for this determination, departments were beholden to placement offices. The co-op programs in Cincinnati also have more strenuous placement efforts partly because of the desire of educational providers to find co-op placements for their students. In another example, the short-term job training center of one community college has a placement office that includes several "job developers": individuals responsible for maintaining regular contact with employers and active in "developing" job opportunities rather than waiting for employers to request students. This program is funded partly though JTPA and JOBS, with their greater emphasis on placement. These exceptions have developed under conditions where there are incentives to increase placement. Otherwise, the placement efforts of community colleges are uncertain ways of strengthening connections to employers.

Placement by Occupational Instructors

A different way to carry out placement is to give occupational instructors the responsibility for placing students. This has the potential advantage of having individuals who are the most knowledgeable about the particular program and about students conduct placement, and it ensures that information from employers gets back to those who teach in occupational programs. In some cases, it is clear that this kind of placement does happen. At the area vocational schools in Cincinnati, instructors are supposed to do placement, and several other instructors gave examples of the ways they place students with former employers and other community contacts.

However, the majority of instructors seem to do little placement. For example, one community college placement director estimated that only 5–10 percent did any placement, and they were largely part-time faculty "working out in the field [who] have connections." Another, commenting on "the line" dividing placement and instructors, went on to blame workloads: "People are just overwhelmed, and something like placement is sort of way in the background."

Even when instructors claim to be sources of employment, their methods of placing students sound haphazard, and they often acknowledged that they place relatively few. For example, a computer instructor in the Sacramento area said, "Because of the fact that we're out in the community, we'll mention positions that we see. And I go to a very large church, and I have a lot of friends who are in the computer field, and . . . yeah, we act as a conduit."

But he also admitted that he placed only three or four students a year—"not a great number." In addition, responses to questions about local employers were often vague. Several admitted virtual ignorance about employment opportunities. One accounting instructor in a well-regarded San Jose community college confessed, "I don't know how firms perceive an accounting degree from [my institution]. People know that a year or two of accounting classes will only get you so far. A community college is a community college, I believe."

Some instructors think that placement is not their responsibility, as do many educational institutions as a whole. Some, not surprisingly, come from outside the area and are unfamiliar with local employers, while others have so little experience in industry that it is unreasonable to expect them to be knowledgeable about the local labor market.

A different kind of structural problem limits the ability of some instructors to be active in placement, a problem that is similar to the one affecting placement offices. Successful placement requires differentiating students, recommending only the best and most motivated. But the best teaching requires that instructors *not* differentiate among students; that they devote as much time to weak students as to the strongest, if not more; and that they concentrate on the strengths of students rather than on their weaknesses. Since the teaching role and the screening role are antithetical, some instructors are reluctant to do more than provide information to students. As one drafting instructor described his placement efforts: "In one of the advanced drafting classes, we have a job board, and . . . I hate picking. That's the first thing the business people want—'Hey, pick me somebody. Who have you got who's good?' And I don't like doing that. So [students] pretty much know, since they're older, they know when they're ready. And so any time there's a job, I'll say, 'Hey, here's the data'—name, rank, serial number, type of job, salary range, etc. And then we'll put it up on the board." As a matter of principle, however, he refuses to engage in "picking."

In general, relying on occupational instructors to provide placement would require a consistency of effort and a level of experience with local employment that would be difficult for community colleges to ensure. Placement is not currently part of the job description for community college instructors; indeed, it is somewhat inconsistent with their roles in motivating and teaching students. The result is that this approach to placement results in only idiosyncratic success.

Student Follow-Up and Tracking

Another mechanism of generating information about the labor market is to follow students as they leave the institution and to collect evidence about their employment and earnings over time. While this does not provide information about specific employers, it does allow instructors and institutions to analyze the patterns of employment among students—whether students in particular occupational areas find employment related to their field of study, whether their employment is stable rather than intermittent, what wage rates they earn, whether they advance over time or not—in ways that are useful to students trying to decide what occupations to enter and useful to institutions trying to identify weak programs.

However, student tracking systems are not well developed in most community colleges across the country. A few states such as Florida, Minnesota, and Ohio have developed tracking systems relying on telephone surveys of former students. Florida requires vocational programs to maintain a 70 percent related-placement rate, based on the information from such surveys. Idaho similarly subjects programs to termination if they fall below 75 percent placement for two years. Ohio has in the past reviewed programs whose placement falls below 75 percent. California has funded a pilot project to follow up vocational students using Unemployment Insurance data (see an example in Tables 3.6 and 3.7), but the project has been carried out only in a sample of community colleges and the results are not yet in general use. While this method of tracking students has been tested in a number of other states, the approach is still in its early stages (see Baj, Trott, and Stevens, 1991; on approaches to student follow-up, see Palmer, 1990).

The result is that, in most institutions, there is little usable information about the subsequent employment of occupational students or the success of particular programs. An accounting instructor at one college, an individual who admitted that community college certificates and associate degrees are "almost useless in private industry" because of their tendency to hire B.A.s, mused, "You know, I've often wondered what happens to two-year students," admitting that most of the students he knew personally had transferred to four-year colleges to earn B.A.s in accounting.

It is possible that student follow-up systems will improve in the future. The 1990 Amendments to the Perkins Act require states to develop performance measures for their secondary and postsecondary institutions receiving federal funds, and most states have adopted some measure of placement for their postsecondary institutions (Rahn, Hoachlander, and Levesque, 1992). While there is no requirement to implement these systems of performance measures or to impose sanctions on low-performing programs, most observers feel that from this federal impetus improved student tracking systems are likely to emerge in most states. One result would be to provide better information to students about the employment consequences of the various programs they could enter, and another would be to alert institutions to programs that have low rates of placing students in related employment. Such information is now almost completely missing.

Contract Education

Virtually every community college now offers contract education: short-term programs ranging from a couple of hours to several days, for employees of specific companies that pay a substantial share of the cost.[3] Because individuals in contract education are already employed, the education is almost always upgrade training rather than initial education or retraining; typical subjects include new computer applications (such as word processing and spreadsheets), TQM (total quality management), statistical process control, communications skills, and human relationships. Remedial English, remedial math, and ESL are also frequently taught, particularly when employers find these skills are necessary for upgrade training or for work reorganization involving communications skills.

Potentially, contract education provides another kind of contact with employers. It allows employers to see the offerings of a particular college, and it enables administrators and instructors to see what skills are required in employment and missing among employees. Indeed, this contact may be more useful than that provided by advisory committees because it requires employers and educational providers to collaborate on a specific task. Contract education also requires employers to be concrete about the skills they require and to back their requests with funding, rather than to provide advice about probable trends in employment that may not be accurate. On their part, educational institutions become responsible for providing precisely what employers request, not what students enroll in or what their faculty wants to teach. Several deans mentioned contract education as a model for relationships with employers that ought to replace the advisory committee approach. Indeed, many community colleges that boast about their connections to employers refer to contract education programs, not their regular vocational programs. Contract education is also the major contact between providers and employers in the San Jose and Sacramento areas.

However, the potential for contract education to strengthen the communication between employers and education providers is unrealized in most community colleges. While contract education may sometimes employ regular occupational faculty and use "off the shelf" the courses normally provided by the college, in many institutions contract education is established as an independent office with its own distinct offerings. In trying to promote contract education, community colleges have often centralized it in independent offices that are more "business oriented"—more entrepreneurial and aggressive and more focused on the needs of business—rather than "education oriented," emphasizing the needs of students. Instructors are often drawn from the large pool of freelance "consultants" that exist in most cities, with few connections to the regular occupational programs (Lynch, Palmer, and Grubb, 1991; Jacobs, 1992). The establishment of an independent office may promote contract education more strongly and give it greater prominence in the business community, but it also isolates contract education from the offerings of the regular vocational program. As a result, the opportunity is lost for contract education to convey information to employers about the regular offerings of a community college and to occupational programs about the skill requirements of employers.

Sensitivity to Enrollment and Student Demand

Another way in which educational institutions can be responsive to employers and the local labor market is through their sensitivity to enrollment patterns. Administrators are quite knowledgeable about the revenues and costs associated with various types of classes and about the enrollments necessary for a class to break even, that is, to generate as much revenue from tuition and state aid as it costs in instructor time and materials. As a manager from the high-tech industry in San Jose who serves on an advisory committee to a local community college commented, "Each class is considered a profit-and-loss center. Each class, not the program, not the college, not the campus, not the district—each class lives and dies on a profit basis."

As a result, community colleges tend to eliminate classes whose enrollments fall below the break-even level, and they may even eliminate entire programs. For example, one community college eliminated a number of their machining classes and a program in the area of numerically controlled machining, and several community colleges in the San Jose area eliminated their electronics programs when the 1990–1992 recession eliminated jobs and student demand for this subject evaporated. Certain vocational programs, particularly those that are capital-intensive such as machining and electronics or health programs, are especially susceptible to being curtailed because their costs per students are so high. A "rational" community college trying to maximize net revenue will therefore eliminate expensive and low-enrollment technical courses and expand low-cost, high-demand classes in such subjects as ESL.[4]

Conversely, community colleges can expand classes when demand increases, and through their advisory committees they generally have a mechanism for developing new programs in emerging occupations. As long as student demand for classes in particular occupations is sensitive to employment, postsecondary providers will be reasonably responsive to labor market conditions.

However, these incentives do not necessarily work smoothly. Since community colleges and area vocational schools are funded according to enrollments, they are enrollment-driven and sensitive to student demand, but they are not generally *outcome*-oriented. They typically lack information about the subsequent placements of their students, and there are no financial disincentives to enrolling students who fail to find related employment. (An exception is in Florida, where programs that fail to place 70 percent of their completers in training-related employment face elimination; Grubb and McDonnell, 1991, 1996.) Therefore, student behavior rather than employer demand is the linchpin in this adjustment process, and except perhaps in extreme cases such as the decline in high-tech employment in the San Jose area, students are not necessarily well informed about employment conditions. The sources of information about local labor market conditions are weak; students seeking initial training and retraining have little information about the occupations they are seeking to enter (as distinct from those needing upgrade training who have experience in the occupation); and by definition the students I have labeled experimenters know little about the alternatives they face.[5] There is so little information about the placement and earnings of community college students that it is hard to know how they can make fully rational choices among the institutions and programs they face. Therefore student behavior is not a precise mechanism for bringing the supply of education into line with the demand for particular occupations.

Furthermore, student enrollments are also subject to manipulation by educational institutions. The rise of "marketing" during the 1980s at all levels of postsecondary education meant that the principles of advertising began to be applied to public and private education; students might be persuaded to "consume" what they otherwise might not want or need. Institutions facing enrollment shortages therefore began to stimulate demand by advertising and outreach. One community college department head mentioned that "students don't know we're here," as a preface to describing her informational campaign to attract more students.

Conversely, because they are enrollment-driven, community colleges do not maintain programs in areas where students fail to enroll, this despite substantial demand from employers or (a special problem in the case of machining and electronics programs as well as in many health programs) where costs are high relative to the state reimbursements and the tuition that students generate. In Cincinnati in particular, employers complained about community colleges and technical institutes reducing their high-cost machining and electronics programs despite demand for graduates. The personnel director of a hospital complained about the finance-driven priorities of the local community college: "It's cheaper to educate unemployed liberal arts majors than it is to train nurses." (In this particular case, local hospitals came up with their own "private" solution to the problem by financing an additional instructor in the local community college program, in effect offsetting the high costs of the nursing program.) While most institutions maintain a variety of programs, the institutional incentives to maintain education and training programs are linked to state reimbursement levels and costs, not to placements or labor market demand.[6]

Furthermore, the response times of community colleges are often slow. A manager of new products in a high-tech firm, an individual who served on the advisory committee of a well-regarded community college in the San Jose area, commented:

> My fear is that the bureaucracy of colleges is so humungous that the lag time between new technology and the implementation of courses about that new technology is vastly delayed, by three, four years in cases. And likewise the other thing occurs: when a technology is obsolete or no longer useful in industry, colleges continue to teach it for many years. . . . Thus you would graduate without having any potential for getting a job in that discipline. Eventually it does get killed, but it takes many years because the bureaucracy is slow to respond to the changing conditions. So it's bad in the beginning and it's sort of bad in the end, but in the middle it's pretty good.

Others complained about the lag in eliminating obsolete skills. For example, shorthand is still taught in many secretarial programs although it is rarely used. A personnel manager in Cincinnati who had served on an advisory committee to the local community college described how her suggestion to eliminate shorthand had been rebuffed. Then she sighed, "We'll catch up sooner or later."

Potentially, the loose link between educational institutions and labor market conditions may change under the pressure of performance measures currently being developed under the 1990 Amendments to the Perkins Act. Indeed, one employer in Cincinnati came up with the idea on his own of making funding contingent upon performance, after discussing the problem of programs closing because of enrollment-driven funding: "Wouldn't it be interesting if you could fund colleges based on the types of jobs the graduates get and how successful they are in their careers, rather than just funding them based on enrollment?"

As funding mechanisms are currently structured, however, there is every reason to be skeptical about how responsive educational providers are to labor market conditions.

Regulated Occupations and the Role of Licensing Requirements

There is one powerful exception to our general observation about the independence of education providers from employers. In the health sector, occupations are subject to public regulation through state licensing requirements. These requirements specify the educational requirements for particular health occupations, including the duration of programs, the skills that must be taught, and the related academic content that must be included. Such requirements, binding on both employers and educational providers, create a congruence between the expectations of employers and the programs in community colleges.

Furthermore, the process of establishing and implementing licensing requirements puts employers and providers in constant contact. Typically, the committees and task forces in charge of establishing licensing requirements are composed of both employers and providers. The enforcement of licensing requirements is also carried out by accrediting committees, again with both employers and providers represented; the scrutiny of each educational program therefore takes place by a committee of both peers and employers. Thus the amount of regular contact between providers and employers around issues that matter greatly is substantial.

The contrast between these *organized* occupations, in which required skills have been carefully codified by committees of

employers and providers, and other occupations that are not codified at all is striking. In the *unorganized* labor markets more typical of sub-baccalaureate occupations, there is much more variation
in the skills required among different types of jobs that are identically labeled, and much less consistency in what employers expect
from their employees and what educational institutions provide.
Moving in the direction of organized occupations would therefore
benefit students; it would also benefit institutions, by providing reasons for regular contacts with employers.

However, there are not many examples of organized occupations in the sub-baccalaureate labor market aside from health occupations. A few other occupations are licensed, for example,
cosmetologists. But such requirements now vary from state to state,
and some industry groups have tried to establish skill requirements
and certificate programs in the areas of auto repair and inventory
control, for instance. These are exceptions, however, and still spo-
radic and voluntary; they have clearly not affected the majority of
occupations in the sub-baccalaureate labor market nor the majority of community college programs. But the current interest in
establishing skill standards (CSAW, 1990; SCANS, 1991), following
the German model, is a potential harbinger of changes in this area.
If skill standards could be developed, *and* if local employers
accepted these standards in hiring decisions, they would act much
as licensing requirements now do, to enhance the connections
between employers and educational institutions to coordinate the
demands of employers with the programs that educational institutions offer. I return to this subject in Chapter Seven.

The Special Case of Co-op Programs in Cincinnati

A different form of connection to employers comes in work experience and cooperative education programs, which combine formal
schooling with on-the-job experience. Apprenticeship programs,
sometimes operated through community colleges or area vocational
schools, often accomplish the same combination of classroom-based
and work-based learning. Often, work experience programs have
made no effort to ensure that the on-the-job component has any
educational value or is connected to the classroom instruction, so
work experience programs have been criticized as little more than

release time for low-skilled work. When appropriately constructed, however, work experience can provide a different and complementary approach to learning. In addition, it can promote connections between education providers and employers through the process of establishing cooperative programs, of determining appropriate employment, and of formulating the right balance of classroom instruction and on-the-job learning.

Despite the advantages of work experience, very few educational providers have established large work-based programs.[7] The notable exception is the Cincinnati area, where well-established co-op programs exist in all of the secondary area vocational schools, the two-year technical institutes, and four-year colleges. Co-op programs in this area that is sometimes described as "the birthplace of co-ops" started in 1906 with a partnership between the University of Cincinnati and a prominent manufacturer of milling machines. They have since spread informally, without much organized structure; they were initiated in community colleges in 1937 when Cincinnati Technical Institute first adopted a formal co-op program. Virtually all the area employers we interviewed have had some experience with co-op programs, and almost all report them to be excellent.[8] Even those that have not adopted co-op programs have nonetheless heard extensively about them; as the personnel director of one valve manufacturer—a firm that had not developed a co-op program—reported, "One thing I've heard from other people is that the schools that have some type of internship or co-op program, whether the school requires it or the students are free to elect it, that seems to make a big difference in how well they do [on the job]. Part of that has to do with just getting out and seeing what it's like to work."

Some co-op programs have minimum GPA requirements for entry, clarifying that they are in part screening mechanisms. More importantly, students whose job performance or schooling performance is substandard are dropped from the program. In one large program, for example, the employer requires co-op students to pay for the schooling component themselves if they go on probation; and the employer generally drops those who fail courses, providing fiscal and employment incentives to keep their grades up. Completing a co-op program successfully does not guarantee a job because so much about placement depends on the state of the economy, the random timing of job openings, the personal qualities of students, and other factors beyond their control. However, firms involved with co-op programs often hire only co-op students for their entry-level positions, so these programs are the only ways into certain jobs.

Well-run co-op programs provide both formal classroom education and specific, hands-on experience and allow students to see the application of classroom instruction. Given the importance of experience to hiring, the specific experience co-op students acquire is critical to their being hired. In addition, the co-op program itself is a screening mechanism, allowing the firm to observe the individual working and to learn about the personal capacities—motivation, diligence, interpersonal skills, and the like—that are so crucial to employment. A personnel manager for a prominent machine-tool company in Cincinnati described the advantage to both the student and the firm:

> One thing that [the local technical college] is doing is to force everybody through an apprenticeship program or an intern program. That's exactly the reason that they have at least some experience and they know the application of what they're learning. . . . Once they graduate, we have a tendency to hire those people. So then, when they're competing [with other applicants], they're competing with other people who have two-year or college degrees, but they have some hands-on experience in the company; we know them and they know us. . . . And at least half of [my company's] motivation [for participating in the co-op program] is to have these people whom we've been able to watch, we've been able to train—and upon their graduation we've got full-time employees.

From the students' vantage, a co-op placement is a screening mechanism in another sense. It allows an individual to see whether an occupation is suitable: "They haven't spent five years in engineering school to wake up one day to find out they don't like the work," says one co-op coordinator. In addition, some co-ops try to place students in a variety of positions so they can get a broad overview of the jobs available in a company.

A rather different advantage of co-op programs is that they generate sustained contact between employers and educational institutions. In most cases, employers initiate the process and establish the terms of the co-op programs. The director of co-op programs for a medium-sized machine manufacturer described the process:

> Before we have a co-op program, we have to define the need for what our potential employee growth is going to be. And once we determine that, then we determine what kind of person do we want and ultimately what kind of position would they have. And then we contact five, six, seven, or eight schools and we narrow our choices down to three, we make a campus visit, talk to their instructors, we interview their students, we audit a class, we examine their curriculum, and then we invite them here to do the same with us. We share our mission statement, the future direction of the company, and then we select one school. For instance, we use [a four-year college] for electrical engineering for their four-year degree program, but we also use [a two-year college] for their mechanical engineering but not [the four-year college]. So it depends on what the curriculum is, what is the kind of education they get, theory versus practical or hands-on.

In fact, this company had co-op programs with eight different educational institutions, including high schools and two- and four-year colleges. The partnership with these institutions is developed in other ways as well:

> We recently had a partnership day with a technical college, and the heads of the departments and the placement officers and some of the teachers came to [the company] for a couple of hours and we had a tour of the company and then we had a brainstorming session on how we can help one another. And we provide tours for classes at these schools, plus we also provide guest speakers. We send our engineers and our machinists over to do a class if they want them to. And then also where the schools are recruiting at the high school level, we send one of our managers and one of our employees that used to be a co-op, and they do high school recruiting with the colleges as well. So we don't take a co-op from college and say we're going to give them a job. We develop the whole partnership aspect. We don't just take their people; it's how can we help you develop your students as well.

In addition, the students in co-op placements provide another source of information about employment. As the director of contract education in one technical college described it, "The co-op program forces us to have closer ties with business. . . . Students will bring back information to class about the ways in which they do a procedure that's very different than the way it's being taught. If we think that it's better, we'll change the curriculum."

The educational institutions with co-op programs also have more active placement efforts than do the community colleges in the other three communities we examined. As one personnel director reported, "If I need a co-op [student] in anything, I can call [the local technical college] and within a half hour they will have begun faxing some backgrounds."

Finally, the co-op programs generate incentives for both education providers and employers to improve the quality of their education and their jobs respectively; otherwise students will not enroll and employers will not provide jobs. A co-op administrator described the incentives for employers to offer decent jobs: "I inform [employers] if they have a low campus image and nobody wants to interview with their company—because students bring this back, too, you know. There's nothing that can kill a program quicker than students coming back and complaining about their co-op job, so the students really talk to one another about these things—how much they make, what they're doing, and so forth. I mean, there's a lot of buzz on campus about different businesses and where the 'good' jobs are. So employers need to know that."

At the same time, the educational institutions have to be sure to send students appropriate for the kind of work involved rather than "clunkers":

> If [employers] got clunkers every time, if they got somebody who couldn't do the job or learn the job, they would, of course, generally be able to deal with that on a once-a-year basis [but they wouldn't put up with it often]. If a coordinator doesn't screen an applicant sufficiently for the job—I mean, if you put a student out on a job, for example, in drafting or in CAD, and the student hates offices and wants to be in a factory or outside—that is not [going to work well]. So there's a certain amount of common sense to make sure that the situation works right.

The process by which community colleges screen students and employers offer "good jobs" creates a "high-quality equilibrium," where able students are matched with promising jobs, where both students and employers have sufficient information and there is an appropriate match. And each side is aware that cheating on this bargain, whether by providing low-quality jobs or students who are "clunkers," might cause a "low-quality equilibrium" to develop.[9]

The consequence of the co-op programs in Cincinnati is that the distance between education providers and employers, so notable in other regions, has been effectively overcome. Employers spoke knowledgeably and positively about specific educational institutions, routinely hired students from the co-op program, and displayed none of the indifference to the educational system that we found in other areas.

Conclusion: The Possibilities for Strong Ties to Employers

While many mechanisms link community colleges and technical institutes to employers in the sub-baccalaureate labor market, most of them work imperfectly.[10] To be sure, specific programs and individual instructors maintain strong ties to employers; the co-op programs in Cincinnati link providers and employers quite well. And in health occupations, licensing requirements and the codification of skills establish close working relations between employers and providers. But institutionally, many educational providers in the sub-baccalaureate labor market are relatively distant from employers and have little knowledge of specific employers, job opportunities, hiring requirements, promotion opportunities in various occupations and with various employers, and other aspects of local employment that are crucial to their students and to the content of their programs. They know almost nothing about where their students are placed and instead rely on hearsay and anecdote rather than direct evidence. Above all, the incentives for educational institutions to be responsive to employers are weak, since the schools are enrollment-driven and not outcome-oriented. The most distinct image is one in which two independent worlds coexist: the world of educational providers, enrollment-driven but relatively disconnected from employers, and the world of employers who are often unfamiliar with educational providers and indifferent to their activities.

One solution to this problem, of course, is to strengthen each of the mechanisms linking employers to educational institutions:

- Advisory committees should meet more regularly, and should be occupation-specific; and rather than confining themselves to interchanges of uncertain information, they could undertake joint projects—for example, the creation of new programs, the development of locally appropriate skill standards, or the survey of local labor market conditions—that would enhance the familiarity of employers with education providers.
- Placement offices need to move beyond offering stay-in-school jobs to more institutionalized connections with local employers, potentially with the help of job training programs that have always had a greater commitment to placement.
- Student follow-up and tracking mechanisms should be improved, particularly based on readily available Unemployment Insurance records, as a way of making institutions more self-conscious about placements and subsequent earnings.
- Contract education could be structured so that it provided regular information to occupational divisions about the demands of employers, rather than being independent of regular programs as it usually is.
- Particularly with the interest in school-to-work programs, co-op programs and work-based learning could be expanded not only to establish close relations between employers and educators but also to provide students with the combination of experience and formal schooling that is so powerful in the sub-baccalaureate labor market.

The sluggish responsiveness of many educational institutions to shifting demand is another problem that merits attention. To some extent, correcting this requires making the internal decision-making processes of community colleges and technical institutes more fluid. This process would be helped enormously by changing the goals and incentives of postsecondary occupational programs away from a preoccupation with enrollment only and toward a greater concern for placements and long-run employment outcomes. Information about students and their subsequent success would help make institutions more self-conscious, and there are state (and federal) incentives that could help as well (developed in Chapter Seven).

However, it is also important for community colleges and technical institutes to recognize which of the problems expressed by employers can be rectified by educational reforms, and which require a different kind of solution. For example, the problem of keeping occupational programs up-to-date—particularly in rapidly changing areas linked to computer developments, including programs in electronics, manufacturing technologies, and other technical fields—is virtually impossible for educational institutions, since they cannot possibly afford complex and ever-changing equipment merely for training purposes. In this case, either they must establish co-operative programs with local employers, or they have to acknowledge a division of labor, with postsecondary institutions providing more general education and firms providing on-the-job training with complex and expensive equipment.

Similarly, the problem of educators being caught between the inconsistent demands of employers, that is, between those who call for intensively job-specific preparation and those who bemoan deficiencies in academic and higher-order competencies, is not a issue that educators can resolve on their own. Only if employers come to realize the inconsistency of their demands—or the differences among firms, and the differences between short-run and long-run requirements for employment—will these criticisms subside. More regular contact between employers and providers may help clarify to each side the nature of skills necessary in employment, but in this process employers must bear as much responsibility as educators.

Finally, many of the basic employment conditions of the sub-baccalaureate labor market are beyond the reach of educational reforms. The chaotic nature of most sub-baccalaureate occupations—with varying (and unclear) skill demands, poorly articulated career ladders, great variation in the sources of skill training, highly informal personnel practices, and cyclical variation in hiring—makes it difficult for students and providers alike to prepare for employment. In contrast, such organized occupations as health resolve some of these problems, and skill standards have the possibility of creating such organized labor markets, but only if local employers accept such standards and use them in their hiring procedures. This suggests that public policies should consider more direct intervention into labor markets, a subject to which I turn in the next chapter.

Chapter Seven

Rethinking Public Policies Toward Occupational Preparation

Preparation of the sub-baccalaureate labor force has been an orphan of public policy, relatively neglected compared to other areas. Other programs at the federal level, especially student aid (which provides relatively little funding to two-year institutions) and short-term job training, have been more pressing, and postsecondary occupational education has not been the target of any particular program. At the state level, traditions of local control and institutional autonomy have prevented the emergence of coherent policy in many (though not all) states. At the local level, community colleges have often been more concerned with their academic image and the transfer function than with workforce preparation. The result is that mechanisms for improving the education and training of this large and growing group of employees have been few and far between, making it hard to know how to reform the system.

In part, the neglect of policy in this area is due to scattered responsibility, since many different institutions prepare the sub-baccalaureate labor force rather than a single type of institution that can be held responsible. This is the principal mission only of technical institutes, which enroll a scant 1.4 percent of postsecondary students, and of proprietary schools, which are both relatively small (enrolling about 8.5 percent of postsecondary students) and remarkably ineffective (Grubb, 1993c, 1994). The other institutions that educate individuals for this segment of the labor force—community colleges, high schools, and four-year colleges focused on the baccalaureate degree—have other goals as well, usually of higher status. There is, then, a mismatch between the needs of the sub-baccalaureate labor market and the institutional structure of education and training institutions, and this mismatch is likely to continue.

In part, too, the lack of effective policy at the state and federal levels has been thwarted by continued rhetoric about "local control." To be sure, local control in the context of workforce preparation is important, since the sub-baccalaureate labor market is usually local rather than regional, statewide, or national; there is considerable truth to the pronouncement that Washington cannot know what is going on in Tuscaloosa or Fresno. But the rhetoric of local control has allowed policy makers and local institutions to avoid the more difficult question of which decisions should be made locally, and which policies should be clearly articulated at either the state or federal levels. This laissez-faire approach to policy has not always been beneficial to either students or employers.

Finally, the relatively undeveloped state of policy in this area may be due simply to the lack of experience. After all, thirty years ago the sub-baccalaureate labor force was dominated by high school graduates, not by those with some postsecondary education (see Table 1.1); postsecondary occupational education, including the sophisticated programs now available in technical subjects, health occupations, and the like, was relatively undeveloped, since its principal expansion came during the 1960s and 1970s; and the vast array of job training programs did not yet exist. In many ways, the programs preparing individuals for the sub-baccalaureate labor are relatively novel parts of the entire education and training system, and it has taken some time for the issues and problems to become clear.

But whatever the reasons for the orphan status of policy, it is time to remedy the situation. The sub-baccalaureate labor force is too large, and growing too rapidly, to leave its preparation to the whims of imperfect market mechanisms. The amounts of public funds in this segment of the education and training system are too large, and the students hoping to get into the world through various postsecondary education and training programs are too numerous. The institutions preparing students for mid-skilled occupations are now mature, and the novelty and strains of growth typical of the 1960s and 1970s have passed. In this chapter, therefore, I draw together numerous strands of analysis from earlier chapters. I articulate a division of labor among federal, state, and local participants, mindful of the need to respect certain local prerogatives while still ensuring other goals such as equity and program improvement.[1] Although the roles of policy should differ at these three levels, a common set of concerns appear time and again:

- A renewed emphasis on completion of coherent programs, in addition to access
- The provision of better information, to allow students to make better decisions and institutions to develop their own improvements
- A shift to outcome-oriented institutions, in place of organizations that measure success simply by their size

Federal Policy: Falling Between the Cracks

At the federal level, education policy has been dominated by funding for student grants and loans. (Table 7.1 provides figures on the federal funding of various work-related education and training programs in 1995. In terms of spending levels, the only federal programs to rival student grants and loans are JTPA.) Originally intended to support low-income students in four-year colleges, student aid was extended to students in two-year institutions and proprietary schools in 1967. But this has been an awkward mechanism for funding community colleges and technical institutes, because student aid assumes attendance patterns—full-time enrollment, advance planning of enrollment, and stable educational goals— that are not true of many community college students, whose attendance and plans are much more erratic. As a result, relatively little federal student aid flows to two-year institutions. Although they enrolled about 37 percent of postsecondary students in 1987 and 41 percent of low-income students, they received only 13 percent of federal funding.[2] Consequently, the enormous political energy devoted to the federal student aid program has been largely irrelevant to the sub-baccalaureate labor force.

To be sure, the federal government has also provided funding for the improvement of postsecondary programs, principally

Table 7.1.   Federal Employment and Training Programs by Agency, Fiscal Year 1995.

Department and Program	Fiscal Year 1995 Appropriation (in Millions of Dollars)
Department of Labor	
JTPA	$4,912.5
Veterans programs	175.1
Employment Service	845.9
Other	910.5
Department of Education	
Vocational education	1,236.2
Adult education	270.6
Literacy programs	38.5
Student grants and loans	4,716.0
Rehabilitation services	2,086.1
Other	638.0
Department of Health and Human Services	
JOBS	1,300.0
Community services block grants	426.3
Refugee assistance	105.0
Other	192.3
Department of Agriculture	
Food stamp employment and training	165.0
Department of Housing and Urban Development	
Youthbuild	50.0
Empowerment Zone and Enterprise Community Program	640.0
Other	47.3
Other departments	1,763.3
Total	$20,413.9

Source: Adapted from U.S. General Accounting Office (1995), Appendix II.

through the Carl Perkins Act supporting program improvement in vocational education. But again, postsecondary occupational education has been a stepchild. The Perkins Act and its predecessors have been focused on secondary rather than postsecondary programs, and its provisions have always applied awkwardly to postsecondary institutions. Federal funding has been small, amounting to roughly 1–3 percent of total funding in two-year institutions, and perhaps 2–4 percent of all revenues for postsecondary occupational education (Grubb and Stern, 1989). These paltry amounts have been valued because they often constitute the only unrestricted funding available, but they have typically been used to fund equipment, update courses, and provide some remedial education—all relatively routine expenditures, only marginally related to "improvement," that should be supported from these institutions' state and local revenues. Finally, the well-regarded Fund for the Improvement of Postsecondary Education (FIPSE) and other programs such as the National Science Foundation fund some curriculum developments in postsecondary education, but this funding is unplanned and uncoordinated. A few institutions here and there benefit from an improved course or two, but the amounts going to two-year institutions are tiny, the innovations are neither evaluated nor well publicized, and the effect on postsecondary institutions as a whole is idiosyncratic.

With relatively little federal funding in two-year institutions, federal policy related to the sub-baccalaureate labor market has tended to be driven by job training programs, where (as Table 7.1 clarifies) federal funding has been much higher and the federal responsibility more obvious. (This is, of course, the Willie Sutton theory of policy: more attention has been paid to job training programs because "that's where the money is.") Consistently, this has resulted in the suggestion that federal funding for vocational education and job training be combined and allocated to states, and then governed by a state council similar to those that govern job training funds. This is quite similar to the plans that Congress is now considering for consolidating various vocational education, job training, and adult education programs and returning control to the states, on the assumption that such consolidation would permit coherent state "systems" to emerge and that they would allow programs to be developed closer to where the clients are. Although it seems politically inevitable,[3] consolidation also has deep flaws. Consolidation does not resolve problems as much as it simply throws them at states to solve. Most obviously, there is nothing in consolidation to guarantee that states will create more coherent programs than the federal government has. The states such as Oregon, Wisconsin, and Massachusetts that have labored hard to articulate relatively comprehensive workforce policies are likely to use the greater freedom to continue devising their own coherent systems. But others, with weak state governments, or political divisiveness, or governors uninterested in the hard and unglamorous work of "good government" and coherent system building, are more likely to allow their current chaotic systems to continue. Consolidation (like vouchers) makes it difficult to enforce any federal purpose at all; when there are goals that only the federal government can pursue, they are simply unaddressed. And the history of consolidation is not particularly comforting: for example, the Reagan block grants tended to reduce overall funding, shift funding away from redistributive programs intended for the poor and those with special needs, and allow states to undermine the quality of programs by reducing costs (Peterson and others, 1986, chapter one). None of these changes would benefit those students now in community colleges and job training programs trying to get into the economic mainstream; none of them would enhance the quality of the sub-baccalaureate labor force.

One other proposal has consistently emerged that again evades the problems the federal government might redress: a voucherlike system of support that students could use in a variety of two-year institutions, job training programs, proprietary schools, and the like. In part, vouchers are attractive because they seem to be a simple extension of the current voucherlike mechanism that funds postsecondary education (student aid), and they are compatible with the free-market orientation and hostility to government bureaucracy that are currently in vogue. Unfortunately, education and training for the sub-baccalaureate labor market lack all the conditions necessary for vouchers to operate well. The knowledge and judgment of the "consumer" (the prospective student) is poor because information is often lacking about economic benefits and because many students simply don't know what avenues are available to them, as we saw in Chapter One. The "commodity" itself, the education individuals receive, is not straightforward or clearly defined and generally varies substantially among institutions and among labor markets; consumers don't always know what they are buying, as has become all too clear with the amount of fraud perpetrated by proprietary schools. Since the costs of attending many postsecondary programs are so low—both the direct costs of tuition and expenses, and the opportunity costs of time and employment foregone—"consumers" may not be individually motivated to make the right choices with public funds, because they don't bear many of the costs (and they are as well unsure about the benefits).[4] Above all, vouchers make it difficult to pursue federal goals other than simple access to programs; they therefore make the various improvements suggested in this volume difficult to carry out. Vouchers may be politically attractive, but they are wildly inappropriate to the challenges.

If these two approaches are deficient, what goals should federal policy pursue that states are unlikely to address? In general, four goals have justified federal intervention in education and training programs:

1. Equity, since individual states are limited in their ability to counter inequality
2. Development of model practices and exemplars, since the federal government enjoys a breadth of information and economies of scale that states do not
3. Collection of information and statistics, since consistency across the nation is important
4. Pursuit of inherently national goals (see also Hansen, 1994, chapter five)

Indeed, the improvement of the sub-baccalaureate labor force is an excellent example of an inherently national goal since the inability of employers to find well-trained, well-rounded workers may cause them to export their employment to other countries or to further divide and deskill employment into jobs of low productivity, low wages, and low satisfaction, to the detriment of the nation as a whole. Turning this task over to states to carry out piecemeal is likely to be ineffective.

More specifically, there are five areas where the federal government could play a vital role.

Equity

Equity implies above all continuing to fund the postsecondary education of low-income individuals who could not otherwise afford to attend. Because the participation of community college students in student aid programs is relatively low, federal policy should examine ways of making grants, loans,[5] and work-study funding more flexible and easier to apply for than it currently is.

But student aid has emphasized providing *access* to postsecondary education, and it reinforces the tendency for institutions to emphasize enrollment since that is what they are rewarded for. As Chapter Two argued in greater detail, *completion* is necessary for the most substantial economic benefits (especially for women), and a shift from emphasizing enrollment to emphasizing completion would help institutions become more outcome-oriented. Unfortunately, student aid itself is an awkward mechanism for enhancing completion since providing penalties for noncompletion may place burdens on the low-income students who can least afford it, and the reasons for noncompletion may have little to do with the financial incentives they face.[6] Therefore it is necessary for other elements of federal policy, particularly those associated with program improvement, to devise ways of enhancing completion.

Program Improvement

Federal policies intended to improve the quality of postsecondary programs have been both limited and relatively ineffective, largely because two-year institutions have not been central to federal legislation. But this need not be the case; legislation parallel to the Carl Perkins Act but concentrating instead on postsecondary occupational education could emphasize program improvement in community colleges and technical institutes. This could then provide seed money and technical assistance, as federal legislation typically does, for such improvements as:

- Integration of academia and vocational education
- Tech prep programs (both now supported by the Carl Perkins Act, which will soon disappear)
- Development of learning communities

- Improvement of remedial education, including its teaching within learning communities
- Development of methods to enhance completion rates, including tracking mechanisms to make sure students know where they are in their programs
- Development of innovative guidance and counseling programs to help students make decisions about their education
- Implementation of student follow-up through Unemployment Insurance wage record data, to provide better local information to students and institutions about the economic consequences of different programs

"Routine" improvements—the kinds of changes that local programs should carry out on their own, such as the updating of courses and the purchase of equipment—should not be supported by federal funds. The program improvements I have outlined are instead new developments, justified by the fact that the federal government has an advantage over states in both developing promising practices and then, once they have been implemented in a number of institutions, evaluating them and publicizing their value to other institutions.

Skill Standards

The federal government has begun to support skill standards, providing a series of contracts to develop such standards in eighteen occupational areas. Standards have been considered ways of enhancing skill levels and providing individuals with "portable" credentials (CSAW, 1990; Wills, 1994; Bailey and Merritt, 1995)—although, given the local nature of sub-baccalaureate labor markets, the value of portability has probably been oversold. But there is a very different way to think of skill standards: like the licensing requirements that organize the labor markets in health occupations, they could be ways of developing standards to which both employers and educational institutions adhere, creating a consistency between the competencies employers need and those that educational institutions provide, and providing a smoother transition from postsecondary institutions into employment. And the process of establishing the standards themselves, if carried out at the state and local levels, could itself bring educational providers and employers into more regular contact, thus enhancing these connections.

However, to serve the role of organizing a particular labor market, certain conditions are necessary. The most crucial is that skill standards must be accepted by *local* employers as the basis for hiring, in place of their current reliance on closely related experience. Otherwise they will serve no role in regularizing the process of moving from school to work; there will be no economic benefit to meeting such skill standards, and over time institutions and their students will have no incentive to meet the standards. Therefore the development of skill standards at the national level is merely a precursor to efforts by states and local institutions to have these standards accepted at the local level, modified as appropriate for local conditions.

Creating an Education and Training System

Chapter Four presented a vision of a consolidated system of occupational education and job training, one that links programs of varying duration and sophistication in ladders of ever-increasing levels of skill and sophistication. Currently, federal legislation provides some encouragement for states to develop such coherent systems, but the difficulties of doing so—the "barriers to coordination" repeated by virtually everyone who has examined the subject—are formidable. Of course, the currently popular proposals for consolidating federal programs and giving them to the states to manage does not resolve this problem; it merely thrusts it onto another level of government and therefore shifts the blame for waste and duplication away from the federal government to the states.

Even if the federal government consolidates education and training programs, or consolidates them and delegates their governance to the states, it should take steps to ensure that the complex of programs it has created can reasonably be coordinated. As the report of the Committee on Postsecondary Education and Training for the Workplace expressed it, "Having helped create the problem, the federal government should help find a solution" (Hansen, 1994, p. 124). The simplest way is to require that every program with federal funding follow the principles established in the School-to-Work Opportunities Act: that they be linked to other programs, both "higher" and "lower" in the ladder of opportunities; that they link job skills training with academic or remedial education, as appropriate for the individuals in the program; and that they search for appropriate forms of work-based education, ranging from the more introductory forms of worksite visits and short-term internships to the fullest forms of co-op education in associate degree programs. The requirement of linking to both higher and lower programs is particularly important, because that begins the process of establishing the ladder of opportunities. In addition, as programs are required to establish such links, they will begin the process of uncovering the gaps in the programs within local communities, the weaknesses in particular programs, the ways in which eligibility requirements or assessment standards or related services are inconsistent. The process of building coherent education and training systems is likely to be time consuming, and it will be done only in the crucible of programs being forced to knit their efforts together. But the result would be a coherent system with a much greater chance of moving individuals from unemployment and unskilled work into the more valued positions in the sub-baccalaureate labor market.

The Special Case of Adult Education

The federal government should exercise some responsibility in yet another area where it has helped create a problem. Publicly supported adult education, funded partly by federal resources, is in serious trouble. Most offerings are of low quality, using didactic and rote methods of teaching with the most stultifying material. The dominant goal of having students pass the GED is one with small and uncertain benefits for employment or subsequent education. Students attend sporadically and usually fail to complete more than a few months of instruction. Their teachers are poorly paid, part-time, and untrained. And there is no evidence that they are effective in improving the basic skills of the adults who come to them.[7] As Diekhoff (1988, p. 629) concluded: "Adult literacy programs have failed to produce life-changing improvements in reading ability that are often suggested by published evaluations of these programs. It is true that a handful of adults do make substantial meaningful improvements, but the average participant gains only one or two reading grade levels and is still functionally illiterate by almost any standard when he or she leaves training. But published literacy program evaluations often ignore this fact. Instead of providing needed constructive criticism, these evaluations often read like funding proposals or public relations releases."

Furthermore, the governance of the "system" is chaotic, with a pastiche of school districts, postsecondary institutions, community-based organizations, and many other organizations all having a hand, varying from state to state and often among communities as well. Thus it is virtually impossible to get a purchase on the system: understanding is impossible, and reform is beyond the pale.

The only way out of this morass, at least from the federal level, would be simply to eliminate federal funding for adult education and to transfer these funds to other programs with greater promise, for example, to the postsecondary educational institutions such as community colleges that are responsible for job training. These institutions already have substantial responsibilities for remedial education; there are many efforts at innovative teaching within community colleges (some of them outlined in Chapter Five); their instructors are better trained and less unstable than those in adult education; federal and state policy could be used to improve the quality of their efforts; and they would be required to link their remedial efforts to job skills training, providing yet other opportunities for the adults enrolling in them. This kind of transfer is possible under the likely consolidation of federal programs; but like the creation of a coherent employment and training system, without federal pressure this may not occur.

These five areas for federal policy provide some supports for the state and local policies that follow. They would not encroach on the ability of states to establish policy; nor would they interfere with the necessary ability of institutions to adapt to the local conditions of sub-baccalaureate labor markets. But they would provide funding for low-income students, as well as some guidance about innovation and alternatives from which states and localities could choose. And they would move toward undoing the damage that has been done by the proliferation of federal programs over the past three decades, by encouraging the development of coherent systems from the fragments that now exist.

State Policy: Balancing Local Control

States are in many ways the most crucial level of policy making because the institutions that prepare individuals for the sub-baccalaureate labor market are creations of states; there is, in effect, not a single system of preparation but forty-nine independent systems, varying considerably in their effects.[8] But almost uniformly, and for some of the same reasons as for federal policy, state policy related to the preparation of the sub-baccalaureate labor force has also been neglected. Elementary-secondary education absorbs considerably more attention, partly because enrollments are much greater, expenditures higher, and political interests more volatile; and four-year colleges and universities usually attract more attention too because of the higher status of baccalaureate education and of research institutions. In addition to their relative anonymity, the community colleges and technical institutes that most explicitly prepare students for these opportunities have enjoyed a great deal of local autonomy, in most (but not all) states. In part, this comes from the background of most two-year institutions in K–14 schooling systems, with their own traditions of local control and community funding. In part, the drive to become "colleges," with the kinds of academic autonomy and freedom from external intervention enjoyed by four-year colleges and universities, has protected community colleges and technical institutes as well.

The result is that most states have done very little aside from establishing the types of institutions that exist, providing state funding in ways that have varying effects on local programs, and requiring state approval of new programs.[9] There has been, for example, almost no control of curriculum (less control than for the K–12 system, for example), much less regulation of instructors through teacher licensing and credentialing, and very few analogues to the kinds of exit exams and competency exams that proliferated in K–12 education during the 1980s. Even in the basic area of statistics, most states have collected information only on enrollment. Only five collect information about any measures of academic achievement; only fourteen have any information about job skills, largely by surveying employers; and only twenty follow completers to ascertain their employment status (McDonnell and Zellman, 1993, Table 3.6). By and large, states lack even the most basic information to know whether local institutions are succeeding in any way.

There has also been relatively little effort to define and promote exemplary practice in these postsecondary institutions. In K–12 education, many states have worked quite hard over the past decade to devise school reforms of great variety and complexity. These efforts wrestle with the problem of how state policy can improve schooling, while schools remain local institutions with a great deal of autonomy and teachers can thwart almost any reform behind the classroom door. But at the postsecondary level this kind of ferment and reform has been largely missing. There is, then, a disjunction between the crucial role of states in creating and funding two-year institutions and the lack of active state policies to improve them.

There are, to be sure, a number of states with more active policies toward their sub-baccalaureate institutions. Florida has developed a complex process of allocating programs at different levels to different institutions, intended to prevent the kinds of turf battles among institutions that are common elsewhere. The state requires occupational programs to maintain a related-job placement rate of at least 70 percent to maintain funding. Idaho similarly subjects programs to termination if they fall below 75 percent placement for two years. Texas requires students to main C averages and to pass state tests in English, math, science, reading, and social studies. Georgia has shifted control for its technical institutes from the local to the state level; Louisiana runs all aspects of technical institutes; and Hawaii has substantial control because it has only state administration (as it does in its K–12 system). But even though most states dominate funding and control many elements of the funding process, they typically exert little control over spending (McDonnell and Zellman, 1993, Table 3.2)—a negation of the political Golden Rule, "He who has the gold makes the rules."

The small number of active states, along with the fact that even active states have influenced institutions in only one or two areas, makes the point: there has been a vacuum in state policy toward the institutions that prepare individuals for the sub-baccalaureate labor force. The result is considerable variation in the quality of programs. Even within a state institutions vary substantially in their connections with employers, in the currency of their offerings, and in their reputation within the community.

To be sure, it is important to distinguish the responsibilities of state government from those of local administration. Particularly because sub-baccalaureate labor markets are local, community colleges need to have sufficient freedom to adjust their offerings to local conditions; and many crucial practices—improvement of teaching, for example, or training of instructors—are necessarily carried out locally. But there remain substantial roles for states to play, particularly in four areas:

1. Encouraging innovative practices
2. Developing indicators that would allow institutions to assess and improve their own importance
3. Encouraging the creation of networks, associations, and communities of interest
4. Basic structuring of postsecondary institutions and creating a system among them

While local institutions can do some of these things by themselves, states (like the federal government) have a broader reach and generally enjoy economies of scale in the development of innovations and in promoting their use; they also play an unavoid-, able role in structuring the kinds of institutions that exist. Most states could be much more active in these.

Encouraging Innovative Practices

I have detailed a number of innovative practices in this volume with the potential to improve the sub-baccalaureate labor force, including integration of academic and vocational education, improvement of remedial education and ESL by teaching them in learning communities, and more generally improvement of remediation (in Chapter Four); development of tracking mechanisms to provide information to students about their progress through the institution (in Chapter Two); and development of more active guidance and counseling mechanisms, including those embedded in programs rather than freestanding efforts, to help students trying to get into the world (also in Chapter Two). Many of these have been developed by innovative institutions, but their spread has been uneven. Others, especially the integration of academic and occupational education, and tech prep programs linking community colleges with secondary schools, have been initiated by federal policy, though in this case an active state role makes a great deal of difference in whether local institutions adopt these innovations (Grubb and Stasz, 1993; Boesel, 1994). Therefore states can play more active roles than they have in collecting information about innovative practices; in clarifying the changes necessary for particular innovations; in evaluating those practices whose effectiveness is unclear; in publicizing these innovations; and in providing seed funding for other institutions to implement them, as well as removing regulatory barriers to their further development.

A particular type of innovative practice that states should promote involves work-based education, specifically co-op programs. As the comments of employers in Chapter One clarified, experience is crucial to entering the sub-baccalaureate labor market; therefore co-op programs provide an enormous advantage to community college students who enroll in them. One important element of state support, according to the active programs in the Cincinnati area, is allowing co-op students to qualify as students for purposes of state aid during their work placements (Villeneuve and Grubb, 1996). This generates the funding necessary for co-op coordinators, the smaller class sizes that are sometimes required for co-op students, and ancillary classes, particularly preparatory classes to ready students for their co-op placements and the kinds of seminars that allow students to examine their work placements critically and thoughtfully (Grubb and Badway, 1995). In addition, states can play a valuable role in promoting the value of co-op. Although most community colleges have some co-op education, and the federal School-to-Work Opportunities Act has promoted the idea of work-based learning, the special benefits of work-based learning and experience are still not widely appreciated. Finally, states often need to ensure that employment regulations are consistent with co-op programs, for example by allowing co-op students to be counted as students rather than regular employees for unemployment insurance purposes. To be sure, the development of a culture that supports work-based learning, including an employer community that understands the benefits of co-op, will take some time; but there are crucial steps that states can take to start this process.

More generally, states could play a more active role in helping all community colleges become the innovative institutions that some of them now are. The pride that many community college educators feel about their institutions often comes from two pillars of the "movement": the fact that these institutions are open to all students, thereby improving the access of nontraditional students to postsecondary education; and the fact that these are essentially teaching institutions, unencumbered by the research missions of universities. But these claims to special status are sometimes simply rhetorical, in those institutions that have taken no systematic steps to address them. Nontraditional students as a group include many individuals who are unsure of their goals, others who are academically poorly prepared, and still others without the personal or the financial resources to make much progress; admitting them and then treating them like traditional middle-class students in selective institutions makes little sense from an institutional perspective. Declaring community colleges to be teaching institutions, but then doing little *as institutions* to promote good teaching, is also contradictory.

Many of the innovations I have mentioned, therefore, would help move community colleges toward greater realization of their role in providing postsecondary education to nontraditional students and to fulfilling their promise as teaching institutions. In fulfilling this promise, they would benefit the entire range of students, including transfer students and not just those preparing for the mid-skilled jobs of the sub-baccalaureate labor market.

Requiring Performance Indicators

It is difficult to know how institutions can improve if they lack basic information about their performance, and it is certainly impossible for states to know which of their institutions are doing well and badly without information that is consistent across institutions. As mentioned above, the information states now collect is generally limited to enrollment data and degree completion; even a refined measure of program completion is missing in most states, and other data are collected by only a few states.

Of the many kinds of data that could be collected, the following are probably the most important:

• Data on student progress and program completion. Many students leave after a few courses, but the economic benefits of completion are much greater than for noncompletion (see Chapter Three). Of course, "completion" is a much trickier concept in community colleges than it is in high schools and four-year colleges, where the high school diploma and the baccalaureate degree are the only measures of success. This in turn implies that community colleges need to monitor intentions much more carefully than they now do, to determine whether individuals have completed their goals or not.[10]

• Data on employment status, from student follow-up. This can now be accomplished by using the unemployment insurance wage record data, as described in Chapter Three. Over longer periods of time, community colleges can start to monitor the long-run performance of their graduates, to see whether they have the academic and other basic skills (like SCANS or generic skills) necessary for advancement.

• Data on the effectiveness of particular practices. These data are especially needed for remedial education, integrated instruction and learning communities, guidance and counseling, and other supportive services valuable not as ends in themselves but as ways of moving students toward their goals. Currently, institutions know little about what practices work, and collecting such information would help make them more self-conscious about the value of such reforms.

Structuring the Postsecondary System

States play a central role in determining which postsecondary institutions are funded—whether comprehensive community colleges, or technical colleges, or area vocational schools and vocational centers limited to short-term programs, or some combination of all of them. Different states have distinctly different configurations of their postsecondary systems (McDonnell and Zellman, 1993, Table 3.1); and these institutions are consistently changing. For example, Minnesota has recently merged its community colleges and technical institutes, and South Carolina has upgraded its technical institutes to comprehensive community colleges. While it is difficult to recommend one configuration over another because of the lack of reliable information, the economic benefits of short-term programs (shorter than a one-year certificate) are small and uncertain (see Table 3.2). This suggests that states should either eliminate institutions that offer only short programs, or make sure they are carefully integrated with institutions providing certificate and associate degrees.

In addition, there is a small amount of information suggesting that the benefits of community college credentials are greater than those from technical institutes (Grubb, 1995g). Comprehensive institutions make it easier to integrate remedial education and academic course taking within one institution; they facilitate the choices of experimenters and other undecided students by providing a greater variety of alternatives; and they reduce the difficulty associated with institutional transitions, since students need not shift to another institution if they change their career goals (Grubb, 1992c). In addition, comprehensive institutions are more consistent with historical preferences in this country for comprehensive rather than specialized institutions, and in many states there has been a steady movement of institutions, away from area vocational schools to technical institutes and to community colleges, partly in search of status. There are then, several reasons for preferring comprehensive community colleges over specialized occupational institutions, and states might consider such shifts.

Funding formulas are another state policy with enormous influence on local programs. There are two troubling aspects of most state financing formulas. The first is that many formulas are based in one way or another on enrollment, for obvious reasons[11]; but this has the effect of reinforcing the goal of increasing enrollment regardless of the consequences and making these institutions enrollment-driven rather than outcome-oriented. States therefore need to search for other ways to make institutions more outcome-oriented, including the development of performance measures and outcome-related statistics mentioned in previous sections. Another way of doing so that emphasizes funding has been adopted in Tennessee, where 5 percent of state funding is contingent on performance. This is not enough to cause institutions to skew their programs inappropriately or to manipulate their data (as JTPA programs sometimes do), but enough to get them to become more outcome-oriented (Hoachlander and Rahn, 1992).

A second problem in most states is that funding fails to consider the varying costs of different occupational programs.[12] Many community colleges make relatively precise calculations of which courses and programs generate "profits"—that is, tuition plus state aid in excess of their costs—and which generate "losses." They tend to restrict those causing such losses—usually high-cost occupational programs, including those with high placements and earnings in medical and technical occupations—in favor of low-cost, high-enrollment courses such as ESL and English 1. But this approach is not in the interests of students seeking employment or of employers with shortages in technical areas, and it does not enhance the overall effectiveness of the institution. One solution is to allow state reimbursements to vary with program costs, reducing the disincentives for the kinds of higher-cost programs that also appear to have the highest economic returns.

Finally, states can—and under consolidation, must—play active roles in developing coherent systems of occupational education and job training. While a few states have been active in trying to create coherent systems, most have been content to follow the lead of federal policy, doing little at the state level to knit together job training and education and doing nothing at the federal level except enforce coordination requirements or create mechanisms by which individuals can move among programs and up a hierarchy of training opportunities.[13] The result is that even where coordination among education and training programs exists at the local level, it often happens because of local incentives to do so, and in spite of the lack of state-level coordination (Grubb and McDonnell, 1996). But consolidation will give states new opportunities to create more coherent systems, along the lines presented in Chapter Four, in which all programs are articulated so that coherent ladders of opportunities are available to individuals at various levels of preparation. To do so requires political will, including the will to restructure job training programs (and the politically powerful community-based organizations that provide many of their services), adult education, and postsecondary educational institutions so that they are more effective, better able to link up with each other, and able to provide the comprehensive services that some individuals require. With consolidation there will no longer be any excuse for states to avoid this responsibility.

Creating Communities and Networks

A final role that states can play is the convening function, the role of organizing groups that have interests in common but that have been unable to get together and articulate these interests. This is, of course, a role that states can play more effectively than local institutions, because states can encompass many more members of a potential interest group than can a local institution. There are potentially many different kinds of interests groups that states could organize; I start with the three that are most relevant to the sub-baccalaureate labor market.

First, many instructors in community colleges do not have a community of practice, unlike instructors in elementary and secondary schools who belong to such groups as the National Council of Teachers of Mathematics, and unlike professors in four-year colleges and universities with their disciplinary groups. Of course, community college faculty usually belong to academic senates, or to faculty unions that represent their economic interests, but there are very few organizations that represent their interests *as instructors,* where members can discuss the issues of teaching, innovation, and standards (including external standards such as licensing requirements or industry skills standards).[14] The result is that there are few forums in which postsecondary instructors can develop the kinds of innovations mentioned in Chapter Five: the integration of academic and occupational education, new ways of providing remediation, the more meaning-centered and active forms of teaching that have been widely discussed in K–12 education. This kind of support proves to be crucial for innovation; in its absence, good teaching is an individualistic and idiosyncratic endeavor rather than an institutional norm. The state agency responsible for community colleges and technical institutes could play a convening role in establishing such communities of practice, simply by sponsoring statewide and regional conferences, creating newsletters, and generating other forms of communication.

A somewhat more complex convening role would involve the organization of small and medium-size employers. One of the problems in the sub-baccalaureate labor market is that many employers are relatively small, too small to have a voice of their own at the state and national level (as such oft-mentioned firms as Motorola and NUMMI do) and too small and often too harried to organize into an interest group. This means that they cannot articulate their education and training needs; for example, the complaints described in Chapter One about the low levels of basic academic skills among community college students, and the preferences for experience over education, were common to a large number of employers we interviewed, but they were unknown to the educators in their local communities. Because employers often have interests in common but do not have the time or resources to organize an interest group to articulate them, several groups have recommended that limited public resources be spent to develop such organizations.[15] Then the employers who are most important in the sub-baccalaureate labor force could articulate their needs more clearly, enhancing the connections between them and educational providers.

Finally, in a sense states would play a convening role in the process of establishing state-level industry skill standards. Creating such standards would require getting employers and education providers together, in much the same way licensing standards are established in medical fields. Then the process of persuading local providers and employers to accept such standards similarly involves convening employers and providers, locally as well as at the state level. In many ways, the process of convening these interest groups may be as important as the skill standards themselves; thus it is consistent with the convening role for states.

The recommendations for state government in this section are lengthy and complex, and I have only barely outlined them. Before any of them could be put into practice, much more detailed recommendations would be necessary. In this period when a political shift to the right has decreased the appetite for active government, such complex recommendations might seem to make little sense. However, the problems of the sub-baccalaureate labor market—the differences between what employers need and what public institutions provide, the difficulty students have in making their way through education and training institutions, the uneven economic benefits, and the confusion employers experience about the alternatives available to them—will not disappear without public intervention. Because states are the creators of most sub-baccalaureate education programs, resolving these problems therefore requires a stronger state role. If the potential of consolidation is to be realized, then states will have to become more active in shaping their education and training systems for the sub-baccalaureate labor market.

Local Institutional Policy: Improving the Status of Occupational Education

The most important level of policy making is of course the local level, because it is here that education and training programs are developed, taught, evaluated (or ignored), and improved (or allowed to go their own way), here that they succeed or fail. Here too, the preparation of the sub-baccalaureate labor force has been a kind of orphan, often neglected relative to the higher-status academic or transfer mission. Except in those states that have technical institutes, or, like North Carolina, that emphasize occupational education as a matter of state policy, the dominant concern everywhere seems to be to improve transfer rates and enhance the academic and "collegiate" status of community colleges. The majority of administrators come from the academic side, the dominant concerns of the national organization (the American Association of Community Colleges) are academic rather than occupational,[16] and at the local level occupational educators often complain that they are second-class citizens within their own institutions. The "institutional drift" from technical institutes to comprehensive community colleges, most recently in Minnesota and South Carolina, is further testimony to the higher stature of "academic" preparation. The problem of status differentials—ubiquitous in our entire education system, of course—means that improving the preparation of the sub-baccalaureate labor force has often had a relatively low priority in community colleges, while there have been few other institutions to perform this role.

In the past, vocational educators have often tried to shore up their status by insisting on the moral value of work, or the crucial role of mid-skilled occupations in growing our grain and building our houses. But these arguments have never had much power because the status differential between academic and occupational education has been based on economic reality and student enrollment, not on simple ideologies subject to principled rejoinder. A different kind of argument on behalf of occupational education for the sub-baccalaureate labor force is more frankly economic, relying on evidence like that in Tables 3.2 and 3.5 (or its equivalent based on local data). For students who cannot or do not earn a baccalaureate degree, or who cannot complete three or four years of a baccalaureate degree, the best economic alternative is to complete an associate degree in an occupational field and then find related employment. At virtually every level of education, occupational education and placement in a related field generate higher average earnings than study in academic fields, although of course finding a related job is important, and the specific occupational and academic fields make a good deal of difference.

More education is always better than less, and so there will always be pressure from students (and from educational institutions seeking status from such upward paths) to move upward. But transfer rates are now as high from occupational fields as from academic fields, particularly because of the rise of such areas as business, health, and technician programs with obvious counterparts in four-year colleges. So there is no reason to downgrade occupational areas in the community college on the mistaken assumption that they do not lead to transfer. Finally, and most importantly of all, students enter community colleges for vocational reasons, as we saw in Chapter One. Many are there to find a career for themselves, and any institution that can help them make this crucial decision and move out into the employment world has performed a great service, whether the specific route into employment involves occupational or academic programs. There are, then, solid economic reasons for granting occupational purposes and programs equal status in the community college.

At the same time, there are numerous improvements suggested by the previous chapters that can only be carried out at the local level. I emphasize four areas of potential improvement.

Enhancing Connections with Employers

As Chapter Six clarified, many two-year institutions have relatively poor connections with their local labor markets. The existing mechanisms of advisory committees, placement efforts, student follow-up, work-based education including co-op education, contract education, licensing mechanisms and other forms of skill standards, and the like are either undeveloped, weak, or operating in ways that fail to connect occupational programs to employers. Each of these merits separate attention from postsecondary institutions, since each has a different influence on the effectiveness of occupational programs.

Some of these improvements would benefit all students, not just a subset who consider themselves to be occupational. Placement offices are used by all students, after all; student follow-up can provide information to the institution about the subsequent success of academic and developmental students too, as the basis for improvement. Co-op programs can be used for liberal arts students as well as occupational students, to provide them with a form of career exploration that is more active and involving than are conventional guidance and counseling. Thinking of reforms in these ways helps soften the boundary between "occupational" reforms and "academic" improvements, since many changes that improve the effectiveness of community colleges will benefit all students.

Supporting Innovative Teaching

Postsecondary institutions can also play a greater role than they now do in supporting innovative teaching. Although community colleges pride themselves on being teaching institutions, in many colleges the institutional mechanisms that might potentially influence teaching—hiring and promotion standards, faculty review, staff development, the leadership of administrators in setting the culture of the institution—are used for other purposes. Good teaching therefore results from individual and idiosyncratic motives, not from institutional intentions, and it is difficult to spread and sustain teaching innovations. As a result certain innovations suffer that are important to the preparation of the sub-baccalaureate labor force, such as integration of academic and occupational education and improvement of remedial or developmental education. Innovation probably cannot become widespread unless these institutions make teaching a more important priority.

As in the case of stronger connections with employers, such reforms would benefit a larger number of students than just those who consider themselves occupational. The consequences of mediocre teaching, largely following the patterns of skills and drills, are almost surely detrimental to the learning of students in remedial courses and to the progress of academic or transfer students. After all, students in community colleges and technical institutes are those who have not performed well in conventional academic settings, which in high school are dominated by skills and drills. Continuing the same kind of stultifying teaching at the postsecondary level makes little sense, particularly since this approach to pedagogy violates all the norms of good adult education (Grubb and Kalman, 1994). Therefore a greater institutional interest in innovative teaching would not only support changes beneficial to the preparation of the sub-baccalaureate labor force, but it would also enhance the education of larger numbers of students in community colleges and technical institutes.

Enhancing Completion

The completion rates in community colleges and technical institutes are quite low, and they seem to be declining. The consequences for economic benefits are distressing, as Table 3.2 clarifies: particularly among women, individuals who fail to complete credentials benefit very little from their postsecondary education. Therefore anything that educational institutions can do to enhance completion will benefit their students. These mechanisms are varied. They include the kind of matriculation process established in California, where entering students are tested, are assigned to remediation as appropriate, and speak with counselors about their plans; the student tracking systems adopted in many institutions (Palmer, 1990); the active tracking and advising system established at Miami-Dade Community College (Roueche and Baker, 1987a, chapter three), where advisers contact students at the first sign of their falling behind their intended goals; tutoring services for students having academic difficulty; and improved financial aid offices, increasing access to grants and loans so that students can work less. (For a comprehensive review of dropout prevention strategies, see Beatty-Guenther, 1994.) Some institutions have also bolstered student activities such as sports and extracurricular organizations because of the view that students who are socially integrated into an institution are less likely to drop out (e.g., Tinto, 1987; Ratcliff, 1995), but nonresidential institutions like community colleges have been limited in their ability to do so. There are, of course, many causes of dropping out that are beyond the control of educational institutions, and some students (the experimenters) will justifiably decide that postsecondary education is not appropriate for them. So none of these efforts can work wonders. However, a commitment to enhancing completion, rather than justifying noncompletion as a sign of students achieving their own limited goals, is essential to developing any of these.

Again, efforts to enhance completion would benefit not only occupational but transfer students as well. The most important reason for declining transfer rates over the past two decades has been the failure of increasing numbers of students to complete the credits and the courses required for transfer (Grubb, 1992c). This problem is internal to community colleges and technical institutes and has nothing to do with the strength or weakness of articulation agreements with four-year colleges. Enhancing completion of coursework and supporting the movement of students through two-year institutions would therefore enhance transfer rates for some and increase employment effects for others, both serving to improve the effectiveness of two-year institutions.

Emphasizing Outcomes over Enrollments

In some ways, two-year institutions have been imprisoned by one of the most generous-spirited aspects of their ideology. The notion of expanding access to postsecondary education, together with the tendency of institutions to become more comprehensive as more roles (or "missions") have been thrust on them, has caused them to measure their success in enrollments. The tendency of funding formulas to reward enrollments, the lack of any state (or federal) performance measures, and the lack of the kinds of reputational "studies" that keep many four-year colleges striving for higher quality have all reinforced the tendency to define success in terms of enrollments. Concern with outcomes has been much less pervasive, whether measured by completion of student intentions, academic achievement, occupational competency, improvement in basic skills, employment in related occupations, subsequent earnings, or general satisfaction levels and individually defined growth. Indeed, institutions and states tend not to collect data about any measures except enrollment; aside from information about degree attainment, the data available about other outcomes is sparse and erratic (McDonnell and Zellman, 1993, Table 3.6). If what they measure is what they value, then enrollment is the dominant concern.

Over the long run, of course, this is not a good way to operate educational institutions, particularly in a period where accountability has become all the rage. Many of the recommendations in this chapter can be interpreted as turning these institutions away from a concern with access and enrollment, and toward a greater emphasis on outcomes. Concerns with completion, enhanced teaching, better information and career-oriented guidance, establishing connections to employers to increase placement rates, and work-based learning such as co-op education are all examples of reforms that operate not by increasing enrollments but by providing different services to those already enrolled so that their learning can be enhanced and their progress accelerated. The concern with creating a more coherent system of education and job training similarly reflects an emphasis on outcomes, in place of simply stuffing underemployed individuals into job training programs of marginal effectiveness. As the proponents of accountability and choice mechanisms (such as vouchers) have repeatedly stressed, anything that can be done to move all public institutions to be more outcome-oriented rather than input-oriented would be beneficial.

This kind of shift will require considerable energy and consistent development. For one thing, the funding mechanisms now in place do not encourage attention to outcomes, and it is foolish to demand that institutions act in ways that are inconsistent with the fiscal incentives they face. For another, the missions that community colleges have accepted are so varied and complex that it is difficult to know how to establish priorities. But these shifts have already started to take place. What is important is that the policies affecting the preparation of the sub-baccalaureate labor force, from the federal, state, and local levels, continue to move consistently in this direction.

Conclusions: The Distinctiveness of Working in the Middle

The vision of two-year institutions that emerges from these recommendations is that of self-conscious, self-renewing institutions—not merely self-promoting ones. It is also a vision of the community college as a distinctive institution, with a crucial role in the middle of the action—not merely a junior college preparing students for continuing on to a baccalaureate, as its advocates have always asserted, but a comprehensive institution that performs many roles and sits astride many crucial transitions. The community college is, of course, the major form of preparation for the sub-baccalaureate labor force, which itself is quite an important role given the size and importance of this segment of the labor market. But it also serves as the transition point between secondary and postsecondary education for those students who are most in need of guidance. It serves as a second-chance institution for those who have not done well in school the first time around and need remedial education. It provides opportunities for those who have, often through no fault of their own, found promising careers shut off and who have to shift to another career. Particularly in cities, it serves as the mechanism for many immigrants to find their way in this country and learn both the language and the mores of a new place. It can serve as the transition point between the shorter-term programs associated with job training and the more intensive programs considered education. And by linking education, job training, and adult education, the community college can become the foundation of a more coherent system.

These are all different ways of working in the middle, and they are all valuable both socially and individually. This vision is more powerful than one that stresses only the academic or collegiate role of two-year institutions. Of course, making good on this vision requires the kind of reforms I have outlined in this chapter, and they are admittedly complex, expensive, and time consuming. But they also help these institutions catch up to their potential role, and they do so in ways that benefit all students at the same time as they improve the preparation of the sub-baccalaureate labor force.

Chapter Eight

Future Trends and Needs of Workers in the Middle

Forecasting is a precarious exercise, especially in economics and in policy. Still, it is unavoidable in analyzing educational institutions, which need to respond to the world around them. A moment's reflection suggests that many changes of the past thirty years are likely to continue, making more urgent the policy initiatives outlined in the previous chapter. The deepest dilemma of the moment is that the social and economic problems requiring government action have become increasingly serious, while the political will to do much about them seems to have weakened.

In this chapter, therefore, I try to forecast the direction of the sub-baccalaureate labor market. I concentrate on patterns in labor markets themselves, the characteristics of students, and trends in the postsecondary institutions that prepare students for this segment of the labor market. I do not try to predict what direction government policy is likely to take, since that truly is a fool's errand; but I do point out where the failure to develop more appropriate and more active policies is likely to exacerbate the problems that already exist.

Long-Run Influences in the Sub-Baccalaureate Labor Market

From the data in Table 1.1 and the long history of increases in education levels, the sub-baccalaureate labor market is likely to grow both in absolute size and in relative magnitude. But this increase has many different causes, some of which stimulate new skill requirements and some of which actually decrease the skills necessary for successful performance on the job. It is therefore necessary to understand the conflicting pressures within the sub-baccalaureate labor market.

The High-Skills Equilibrium and Competing Developments

The past decade of interest in preparing workers for the twenty-first century has rested on a near consensus about changes in employment. As suggested by the title of one influential report, *American's Choice: High Skills or Lower Wages!*, our economic system has been moving from an old Taylorist system of employment—in which most workers were only moderately skilled; work was finely divided; and layers of supervisors provided direction, decision-making ability, and communication with others inside and outside the firm—to one in which hierarchies are flatter, in which front-line workers are more broadly responsible and therefore require decision-making, problem-solving, and communications skills that they didn't previously need to have. Early guesses about the magnitude of high-skill employment were low and imprecise; the Commission on the Skills of the American Workforce stated without a shred of evidence that about 5 percent of employees were in high-skill firms. But a new conventional wisdom about the direction of the economy has developed, promoting the use of education to prepare the workforce of the next century.

More recently, Paul Osterman (1994) has developed better evidence, based on a survey of employers, suggesting that revised employment practices are much more widespread than previously estimated. Only 22 percent of employers have failed to adopt any of the practices associated with workplace transformation; two-thirds have adopted at least one practice relatively thoroughly, and 35 percent have made substantial use of flexible work organization. Based on this evidence, there is reason to think that there is a new day dawning. The kinds of reports from employers presented in Chapter One provide further evidence that there really is a shift taking place that requires workers to have both more skills and skills of a different order (see also Bailey, 1989; Berryman and Bailey, 1992).

But there are two other plausible scenarios about the direction of employment. One is based on the observation that a great deal of unskilled employment persists. Even though the rate of increase of such relatively skilled jobs as systems analyst, medical technician, and computer programmer is projected to be high, the greatest *numbers* of new jobs will be in such conventional low-skilled positions as retail salesperson, cashier, office clerk, and truck driver. This version of the argument that the economy will continue to need garbage men is also consistent with the view that both upskilling (creating new jobs with greater skills demands and education levels) and deskilling (creating jobs of lower skills levels) are taking place simultaneously; it is consistent with evidence of increasing inequality in the distribution of earnings.[1] The implication is that even if more jobs require SCANS skills or higher-order competencies, a great deal more do not.

A third possible scenario, not yet completely clear, points to the recent growth of contingent or temporary employment, and the development of some firms with a substantial fraction of their workers—perhaps 30–40 percent or more—hired from "temporary" job agencies. There is little doubt that many firms are making greater use of temporary help agencies.[2] In our interviews, several employers and other respondents commented on this trend, especially in Silicon Valley, where the use of temporary workers is high because of sharp variation in employment over the past few years. Temporary workers are used as business ebbs and flows, and to cover vacations, medical leaves, and other temporary shortages—what one temporary agency described as the "ideal, true users of temporary services." But they are increasingly used in other ways. Some firms use temporary agencies to hire probationary workers; and some use temp agencies to perform their recruitment and initial screening so that their personnel departments are not "burdened" with such routine work.

A more disturbing trend is the tendency of some companies to hire substantial fractions of their employees as temporary workers. One high-tech manufacturer in the Silicon Valley area typically has about 10 percent of its employees in a "flexible workforce," hired through temporary employment agencies and limited in the hours they can work; another firm of about two thousand employees reported that about one-third of their labor force was hired from a temporary agency for "direct labor" such as operatives and assemblers. In still another case, again in Silicon Valley, a representative of a local temporary agency maintains an office full-time at the headquarters of a high-tech company as an "on-site coordinator" in charge of hiring all hourly employees who are hired through the temporary agency and not through the firm itself. All hourly workers then remain employees of the temporary agency: "They don't sign any contract; they keep working here as long as [the firm] needs them. They could be here for three years and are still our [the temporary agency's] employees; they don't have to be [the firm's employees] to work here."

Not only do companies use temporary help as moderately skilled workers such as retail workers, operatives in light industry, and secretaries and clerical workers, but there is a trend to hire more highly skilled workers in this way. One temporary help agency in Silicon Valley specializes in providing drafters, as does an agency in Sacramento (a "temp agency for technical people"). In another case, an employer laid off a number of engineers who then organized into a firm that does a large amount of consulting with the original employer—in effect converting permanent employees into temporary workers. The practice of hiring temporary workers at lower levels of the occupational structure and the practice of using consultants at the upper levels appear quite similar despite the difference in their status.

The extended use of "temporary" workers has several advantages to the firm. Most obviously, it reduces the benefits employers must pay. It also allows the company to fire individuals if they either demand contracts or prove incompetent, without risking a lawsuit or suffering damage to unemployment insurance ratings. And it eliminates any pretense that the firm might be responsible for the individual's professional development through on-the-job training, promotional opportunities, and the like. A few personnel managers claimed that temporary arrangements allow employers to hire outside of affirmative action regulations, since employees brought into a firm as temporary workers can be hired for permanent positions without being counted in affirmative action reviews. The use of temporary workers also fragments a firm's labor force by creating a pool of employees with rights and benefits and another pool of "temporaries" without that status; to the extent that such divisions help employers avoid unionization or deflect criticism, greater use of "temporary" workers may help employers manage discontent.

Unfortunately, there are negative effects for the employees involved. Obviously, they lack the employment stability permanent employees have, and they may find it difficult to accumulate the kind of experience that employers value. Temporary employees also seem to lack the same legal protections that permanent employees have, making them more vulnerable to violations of health and safety standards and procedural safeguards.[3] The use of large numbers of temporary workers, particularly at low occupational levels, operates to make entry into the firm more difficult since less skilled entry-level positions are filled by temps with no chance of being permanently hired. For the same reason, the greater use of temps shortens the job ladders within firms. A labor market in which an increasing fraction of workers are hired from temporary agencies is one in which employment is more likely to be fragmented and intermittent, in which there will be widening inequalities of earnings between permanent and temporary workers, in which fewer workers enjoy legal safeguards, and in which career ladders are shorter. None of these trends bodes well for individuals in the sub-baccalaureate labor market.

One plausible development is that high-skilled, high productivity firms will retain a core of permanent employees, directing a substantial number of temporary or contingent workers. Contingent workers may require some higher-order competencies, such as communications skills, independence, initiative and motivation, all particularly crucial for contingent workers cycling in and out of new positions. But other competencies, such as problem formulation, problem solving, and initiative in the pursuit of the firm's well-being, may rest largely with the core of permanent employees. With limited prospects for mobility among contingent workers, older notions of careers defined by mobility among jobs of increasing responsibility within a firm may be even less applicable. Instead, individuals may be forced to cobble together "careers" by moving to unrelated jobs as openings occur and by moving among firms. In such a model, upward mobility is unlikely to be steady or predictable, or even comprehensible to those outside specific employment settings. Current discussions about the "demise of the job" and the "virtual firm" (one that puts together work groups for specific projects and disbands them when a project is over, eliminating the concept of stable employment) may be alarmist, but they contain the germ of substantial changes in employment (Bridges, 1994; Rifkin, 1995; Aronowitz and DiFazio, 1994).

On the assumption that economic changes are always slow and incomplete, the most likely future is one in which all three kinds of employment persist:

- A considerable amount of relatively unskilled work exists, unaffected by any of the shifts to high-skilled employment
- Some employment is the kind of flexible, independent work touted by many advocates of the high-skills equilibrium and requiring many of the SCANS skills
- Some individuals with moderate (or even high) levels of skills are essentially fixed in their positions by the immobility associated with contingent work

For educators, one implication is that schools and colleges should not buy wholeheartedly any single vision of the future, since any one is likely to be incomplete. However, a further implication is that all educational institutions, including community colleges and technical institutes, need to continue preparing their students for high-skills jobs because the consequences of being unprepared for such jobs are so dismal; individuals who lack the skills to get jobs in the high-skills end of the market are more likely to spend their work lives either in contingent work, unable to make the transition into more permanent positions, or in jobs with relatively lower skills levels, pay, and stability than they expect. The paradox, then, is that even though many jobs will not become high-skilled jobs, educational institutions need to prepare their students as if they will—with the broad range of academic competencies and the SCANS or generic skills emphasized in many of the current attempts to integrate academic and occupational education.

The Necessity of Constructing Careers

In the development of vocational education, there is a long history of misconstruing the nature of employment. At the turn of the century, the movement for vocational education became caught up in celebrating preparation for careers, that is, for sequences of jobs of ever-increasing skill, responsibility, and pay. This image of careers was appropriate for the emerging professions in medicine, law, engineering, and academic life, for example, where school-based preparation provided an increasingly necessary credential, reinforced in some cases by state licensing. In that sense, the professions promised everything the term *career* connotes. But for the semiskilled jobs for which vocational education prepared students, such careers were not usual. While some workers might become foremen, and others might become owners of small businesses, there was little upward mobility for most workers (Kett, 1982). Later, in sectors dominated by unions, union-enforced systems of seniority created a blue-collar career ladder of increasing real earnings and employment security; but at the time vocational education was incorporated into the high school, the notion of careers applied only to better-educated occupations. Ever since, the image of a career has proliferated despite its uncertain applicability. It is important, then, to be careful about the nature of employment, lest we recapitulate the overly romantic notions of the past.

It now appears that careers are taking somewhat different forms, particularly in the sub-baccalaureate labor market but to some extent in the market for professionals and managers as well. The older idea of ready-made careers seems much less common, where individuals would start in entry-level positions, with a sequence of positions of greater responsibility and higher pay established either by personnel policy, by union rules, or by common practice. The conventional vision of careers constructed by *employers*—what some have called the "industrial" model (Osterman and Kochan, 1990)—has been replaced by a world in which careers are increasingly constructed by *workers* as they respond to notices of vacancies within their own firms in the post-and-bid system of filling vacancies, as they move among companies in the search for advancement, and as they move in and out of education and training when certain opportunities are closed out and others open up. The frequent statement of how often workers are likely to change jobs is a manifestation of this phenomenon, as is the emphasis on "lifelong learning" and the concern for the retraining of displaced workers.

There are, to be sure, several general trends affecting all employment that have contributed to the instability of careers. One is an increase in the instability of companies themselves, as they are bought up, merged, and moved around the country or the world. Another is the decline of unions, since unions tended to create well-defined job ladders. And the growth of part-time and contingent employment has forced individuals to create their own careers, even in some of the quintessential professions like the professorate, law, and medicine.

However, several characteristics of the sub-baccalaureate labor market make it especially necessary for individuals to construct their own careers. Since much of the initial hiring in this labor market is in smaller firms, advancement almost by definition requires changing firms; and smaller companies are more susceptible to going out of business during recessions or being taken over by larger businesses, adding to the instability of employment. In addition, because firms prefer to retain their best-trained workers in recessions, they are more likely to weather downturns by retaining their baccalaureate-level workers—even if they are employed in positions that do not use all their skills—and release their mid-skilled employees.

Another discernible trend is the tendency toward shortened job ladders: the sequence of jobs of increasing responsibility, and the possibilities for on-the-job learning and higher earnings. One cause is the flattening of hierarchies within many firms, including the elimination of layers of supervisory workers that previously represented jobs into which production workers might be promoted. The tendency to fragment employment into lower-level, temporary employees and more skilled permanent employees with higher prerequisites for hiring (and fewer supervisory jobs to be promoted into) also contributes to shorter job ladders. Shorter job ladders within specific companies therefore imply that upward mobility and earnings increases are limited, or that they require a shift to another employer, either one that is larger and has more senior-level positions or one that is more sophisticated in its technology and organization and has greater use for highly experienced or highly skilled workers. But mobility among firms is not necessarily easy, especially given the highly local nature of the sub-baccalaureate labor market and the tendency to promote from within.

For educational institutions, the implications of individuals needing to construct careers are relatively clear, though difficult to achieve. Constructing a career successfully requires a greater breadth of competencies, and therefore programs geared to specific entry-level positions are inappropriate. In addition, certain personal attributes such as initiative, resourcefulness, and planfulness are increasingly necessary, as is deeper knowledge about the labor market and how to find appropriate positions. The kind of bewilderment we saw among both older and younger community college students in Chapter One, as they wrestled with how to go about getting into the world, may be a common experience, but it certainly is not helpful in constructing coherent careers. This suggests that, in addition to developing programs with relatively broad range of competencies, community colleges and technical institutes should prepare students directly for the process of constructing their own careers. While how to do this is unclear, workshops associated with placement offices, co-op education and other forms of work-based learning, the kinds of co-op seminars that allow students to reflect on their past and present employment, and other active strategies may be part of the solution. The challenge for community colleges in their counseling and placement efforts is less to find students specific jobs and more to give them the competencies—the breadth of skills, the initiative and independence, the knowledge of how job markets operate—necessary to understand the chaos of the sub-baccalaureate labor market and to find their own way within it.

Educational Inflation

One reason we can be certain that the sub-baccalaureate employment will continue to increase as a fraction of total employment is that the inflation of educational requirements for occupations has been going on for some time (Archer, 1982). Some part of educational inflation is due to increased skill requirements, of course. However, a staple of the literature on the irrationality of educational requirements is the showing that the educational *qualifications* of individuals in specific occupations have consistently been higher than educational *requirements*—a situation of "overeducation" that results in higher educational requirements than necessary and in declining marginal returns from formal schooling (Rawlins and Ulman, 1974; Rumberger, 1981). The evidence from our interviews suggests that this process is continuing to take place in the sub-baccalaureate labor market, particularly as some jobs come to require baccalaureate degrees and go out of reach of those with a high school diploma and perhaps some postsecondary education. For example, positions as computer programmers, as distinct from positions that involve entering data and using applications like spreadsheets, now require baccalaureate preparation. Most firms require baccalaureate degrees for their managers. And positions that were once filled by electronics technicians now require baccalaureate-level engineers. The result is that some community college programs are simply being bypassed. As the director of human resources for a semiconductor manufacturer in Sacramento explained it, "I can remember hiring people out of [a local community college] twenty years ago and hanging out at the job placement center doing interviews because that was the only place to get [electronics technicians]. Now we're going to Sacramento State College to get the engineers because that is what it takes to keep things going because the sophistication of the equipment has gotten so hot, it takes an engineer to keep it mothered. And the electronics technicians, if they haven't kept up, they just can't compete."

At the same time that some jobs come to require baccalaureate degrees, another tendency is that entry-level jobs that previously required only a high school diploma—for example, positions as secretaries, clerical workers, and accounting clerks—are often filled by individuals with some postsecondary education as employers (particularly in larger firms) demand better qualifications for "entry-level" positions. Examples abound of the tendency to require experience even for relatively unskilled positions like accounting clerks and clerical workers or to require substantial experience among beginning machinists and technicians. As a staff member for one city economic development agency, an individual well placed to observe the developments in the local labor market, commented,

> We've got to get employers to hire more people with *truly* entry-level skills. That's sometimes very difficult to do. They say, "I have an entry-level job, but I want them to do . . . " By the time you get

done, this is not an entry-level position. They require more than entry level. I've gone out to a metal fabrication shop and they say, "I want a welder that can weld to the code and a fabricator that knows how to do this and this." They say, "This is an entry-level job." I say, "No, this is not an entry-level job. An entry-level job is where people don't have this expertise already but may have done some welding." I think it goes across industries. You could take it from accounting or anything else, and they really want them to have a greater level of experience or expertise than what they were willing to pay for.

One consequence for individuals trying to enter sub-baccalaureate positions is simply that it is more difficult to qualify for entry-level positions. Individuals need more education, and in particular more experience; hence we return to the dilemma of how to accumulate experience because most employers demand experience as a prerequisite.

These changes are taking place not as a result of overeducation—educational qualifications outpacing educational requirements—but as a result of changes in work organization and technology requiring more of workers. However, from the viewpoint of individuals, and particularly the nontraditional students (including those in need of retraining) who find their way into community colleges but not four-year colleges, it matters little why educational requirements are escalating. It matters only that the better-quality occupations are increasingly difficult to enter as educational inflation continues to take place.

Thus, educational inflation affecting the sub-baccalaureate labor market takes place in the following way. Some of the best occupations, those with the highest earnings and best prospects for advancement, tend over time to be filled by individuals with baccalaureate degrees. At the same time, lower-skilled jobs replenish the numbers in the sub-baccalaureate workforce as employers come to give preference in hiring for modestly skilled and entry-level positions to individuals with some postsecondary education. This process, operating at both ends of the sub-baccalaureate labor force, is an unavoidable consequence of being in the middle of the highly skilled labor market for baccalaureate-level professionals and managers and the unskilled market occupied by high school dropouts.

From the perspective of educational institutions, educational inflation may be beneficial because it helps expand enrollments. However, for other groups educational inflation may be detrimental. For students, it requires them to stay in school longer and costs them more both in direct and opportunity costs; they may have little choice but to increase their education attainment. It may also cost employers more as they find themselves forced to pay higher salaries for more highly educated workers. Alternatively, the higher wages may cause employers to try to substitute lower-skilled workers, which contributes to the process of deskilling, itself an undesirable outcome. Above all, in a society that supports a high proportion of the costs of postsecondary education, most of the direct costs of educational inflation are born by taxpayers in the form of subsidies for two- and four-year colleges. This is a little-appreciated fact that gets lost in the clamor for greater access to postsecondary education. In many occupations the drive for higher status causes professional organizations to press for higher levels of schooling; for example, the nursing profession has pressed for a shift from associate-degree to bachelor's degree nursing programs, even though there are no economic benefits to earning a bachelor's degree (Spetz, 1994). In a market-driven system, then, the self-interested actions of students and those of educational institutions combine to escalate educational requirements, even if this process is collectively irrational.

The only intervention that could stop this process is one of establishing certain educational requirements and credentials for particular occupations, as Florida has done partially in its "leveling" policy of allocating educational programs of different lengths to different institutions. In addition, skill standards might stop the process of educational inflation if institutions and employers alike accepted certain educational levels as appropriate to particular occupations. But in the absence of a greater willingness to intervene in market operations, educational inflation will probably continue unabated, with mixed results for the sub-baccalaureate labor market.

The Prospects for Reforming Labor Markets Directly

Many of the developments I forecast for the sub-baccalaureate labor market are not especially encouraging. They suggest greater burdens on students and on educational institutions, and continued escalation of the costs of gaining access to good jobs. A reasonable question is whether the labor market itself could be reformed, to avoid some of these problems directly. After all, as many have noted, the United States tends to use supply-side policies exclusively, attempting to reform educational institutions and the supply of educational labor, rather than demand-side or labor market policies. Perhaps a more rational strategy would be to develop *both* demand-side and supply-side policies, coordinated with one another.

However, the prospects for doing so are discouraging. One kind of evidence is that previous efforts to intervene directly in markets—the ideas of developing "industrial policy," popular in the late 1970s—were quickly abandoned at the national level under resistance from employers, Republicans, and most moderate Democrats. Currently, with another wave of interest in deregulation and Republican efforts to dismantle the more activist state existent from the 1930s to the 1960s, the prospects for anything approaching an industrial policy seem remote indeed.

But there are even deeper reasons than current politics for thinking that reshaping labor markets is nearly impossible in this country. The differences between countries like the United States, with market-driven systems of vocational education and relatively unregulated labor markets, and countries like Germany, with highly regulated labor markets and highly institutionalized vocational education systems, are profound and not readily changed. As David Soskice (1994) and others have pointed out, our market-driven system has weak employer organizations, weak unions, and little government intervention into markets; therefore certification for employment is weak or absent (except in a very few occupations, as in health), and there are many different, informal routes into employment. Within the educational system the academic tradition is strong and vocational programs have low status, with equity concerns that preclude directing or tracking certain individuals into particular occupations. Finally, our central government is relatively weak, especially in education with the tradition of local control, and even state governments as the nominal creators of education systems have been inactive in formulating policies.

In contrast, such countries as Germany, with more institutionalized systems of labor markets and education, have strong employer organizations, strong unions, and a strong central government that can establish a coherent policy. These social partners can then work out certification mechanisms that govern entry into employment and regulate the nature of particular occupations, including the hierarchy or career arrangement of jobs. Their schooling systems have much higher-status occupational programs, and there is widespread acceptance of earlier tracking and mechanisms such as high-stakes exams that direct students into various programs. The changes in organizations, attitudes toward government regulation, educational institutions, and equity and tracking necessary to move from our market-driven system to a more regulated or institutional system are so profound, and indeed so contrary to many deeply held American values, that such a shift seems quite unlikely. In the recent infatuation with Germany as a model for our educational system, most advocates have promoted only a small part of the German educational system, the provision of work-based learning in apprenticeships, while ignoring the many other differences in education, regulation, and organization.

Within this framework, certain policies currently being suggested represent initial steps toward a more institutionalized system. Skill standards, mimicking licensing requirements, are one example that could help regularize particular occupations; the proposal to organize small and medium-sized employers is another. Efforts to enhance connections between employers and educational providers, as in Chapter Six, can be seen as ways of establishing "social partnerships" akin to those in some European countries. And the attempts to enhance the economic benefits and stature of postsecondary occupational education can be interpreted as a way of shifting from the single-minded preoccupation with academic disciplines toward systems like Germany's that provide greater stature to occupational programs.

However, comparison of market-driven systems and institutionalized systems clarifies how far this country must go to seriously reshape the sub-baccalaureate labor market directly. Each of the necessary pieces is daunting: strengthening employer and labor organizations, for example, or moderating the exclusively "academic" culture of our schools, or creating even modest skill standards. Creating an institutionalized approach requires having all the pieces of a system in place. In my view this remains a worthy goal, although it is not realistic to think that it will come anytime soon. In the meantime the reform of educational institutions will remain our best recourse. Such reforms must proceed with the expectation that the sub-baccalaureate labor market itself will continue to present special problems to students and educational providers alike.

Trends in Students and Student Needs

The sub-baccalaureate labor market includes a wide variety of individuals, from those having high school diplomas from the most wretched high schools to individuals who have almost completed sophisticated baccalaureate degrees. The institutions that have most directly prepared students for sub-baccalaureate occupations, community colleges and postsecondary technical institutes, are probably the most varied institutions of the entire education system. They include students of a greater age range than all others, students with greater variety in their academic preparation because of their lack of admissions requirements, more minority and lower-income students than other postsecondary institutions, and large numbers of new immigrants. They provide training for initial entry into the labor force, retraining for those seeking to switch careers, and upgrade training, as well as providing a place where experimenters and other students undecided about their futures can gather more information about postsecondary alternatives at relatively low cost. The bewildering variety of students causes its own problems, of course, as instructors cope with students of different levels of preparation and purposes, and as institutions struggle to develop offerings and schedules that can meet such diverse needs.

It would be comforting to think that this diversity might abate. However, the hope seems unrealistic. Each source of increasing diversification seems likely to continue, and only some of them can be moderated by the efforts of postsecondary institutions themselves.

Diversity in Academic Preparation

Many two-year colleges have taken on a large role in remedial education because of the increase in students with inadequate academic preparation. Unfortunately, many observers at the elementary and secondary levels fear that the caliber of preparation is likely to continue falling. We face a likely increase, not decrease, in the social problems that have always created the greatest difficulties for schools: poverty, children from single-parent families, children from non-English-speaking backgrounds. While the resources in the K–12 system have continued to increase in real terms, much of this financial support seems to have gone into new layers of administration, salary increases, special education, and "add-on" programs that leave the basic structure of schools intact. There is now a state of virtually permanent reform, but one with a tendency to lurch among divergent approaches to reform without ever giving one reform a chance.

While the battle over secondary education may seem beyond the reach of postsecondary educators, there are several ways in which they can help. One damaging attitude among some high school students, according to many high school teachers and administrators, is that they need not work hard in high school because they can always "make it up" in community college later on, without needing to meet any entrance requirement. The very existence of an open-door college suggests that there are no permanent consequences of sloughing off. Of course, that attitude is quite wrong: those individuals who enter community colleges with academic deficiencies and have to take remedial courses often do not complete these courses, and even when they do their rates of completion and promotion through postsecondary education are lower.[4] In turn, as we saw in Chapter Three, the economic effects of failing to complete credentials is substantial, especially for women. While community colleges cannot communicate their expectations to high school students through admissions standards and SAT scores, they can clarify the importance of basic high school preparation through tech prep programs and better information to high school students about the dismal consequences of leaving high school unprepared.

In addition, there are now glimmers of a movement to eliminate remediation from postsecondary education, particularly from four-year colleges.[5] This represents a hard view of educational opportunity: students have a chance at economic success through the regular programs of the education system, but if they muff the first chance they do not get a second, or at least not at public expense. (Indeed, this view is consistent with the fear that even offering such second chances will undermine the incentives to work hard the first time.) But eliminating remediation is inconsistent with the role of the community college as the people's college, one that takes students from different backgrounds and provides them access to a variety of goals. The role cannot be abandoned without losing the distinctiveness that two-year institutions now have within postsecondary education.

If the best defense is a good offense, then one remedy to these challenges (apart from clarifying to students early on that the remedial path is difficult) is to improve the effectiveness of remedial programs themselves. As I argued in Chapter Five, that will entail experiments with new approaches to teaching and with new structural arrangements, particularly where remedial courses are taught in tandem with other courses of greater interest to adult students.

The Problems of Getting into the World

Aside from inadequate academic preparation, two-year institutions have large numbers of students relatively unsure of what choices they face and what they want to do with their lives. In part, this is due to a filtering process, in which those individuals who are more certain and more determined end up in four-year colleges. In part, however, the responsibility may rest with the collapse of any career-oriented guidance and counseling at the high school level, and perhaps with greater difficulties in parents and communities providing career orientation to young people, particularly those from low-income communities with weak attachments to the labor force. The consequence is that many students in two-year institutions are not clearly motivated, contributing to instructional problems and dropout rates.

There are now some efforts to reconstruct career counseling in high schools, particularly as part of more comprehensive efforts to focus high schools on broadly defined occupations (for example, McCharen, 1995; Grubb, 1995c), and postsecondary institutions ought to encourage these to the extent that they can. However, the history of such efforts in high schools is relatively dismal, particularly because the counseling fraternity itself has always been in low repute and because it has often been simply a dispenser of information rather than a generator of the kinds of developmentally appropriate, activity- or project-based programs that might help students plan their futures more effectively. In addition, the conditions that generate the need for enhanced counseling and guidance in public institutions—increases in poverty, in parents distant from their children, in low-income communities that cannot support career decision making—are only getting worse. As in the area of academic preparation, postsecondary institutions should probably brace themselves for greater needs in the future.

There are, of course, two approaches to this problem. One has been to declare that educational institutions provide *education*—that is, instruction in academic and occupational areas—and that other forms of preparation are the student's (or the parent's, or the community's) responsibility. This is, in effect, the direction that most community colleges have taken. As a result guidance and counseling, and student development more generally, is a relatively weak direction (Ratcliff, 1995). An alternative vision is of educational institutions as holistic institutions whose educational missions cannot be served as long as they fail to attend to motivational and other noncognitive issues of students; this vision would recognize that the unavoidably occupational role of two-year institutions requires them to provide more active forms of guidance and counseling. But without a direct solution to the guidance and counseling needs of increasing numbers of students, many more individuals are likely to wind up milling around in postsecondary institutions, to the detriment of all.

The Flow of New Immigrants

Even if the current sentiment against immigrants manages to reduce the flow somewhat, immigration is likely to continue at substantial levels because the world conditions that drive immigration—wars, political persecution, and the expanding gap in the standard of living among and within countries—are likely to continue unabated. The largest numbers of these adult immigrants will use two-year institutions (as well as adult education) as their principal entry into the American economic mainstream, because of the institutions' lower cost and open access. While these are often highly motivated students, they also present language problems and

needs for socialization into American ways (or a hopefully benefi-
cent "Americanization") that others students do not. Like the need
for remediation and career-oriented counseling, the particular
needs of recent immigrants place additional strains on postsecondary institutions, although these are strains consistent with the
role of community colleges as open-access institutions, providing
appropriate services to those who come with special needs.

There are, then, many reasons to think that the particular educational challenges facing two-year institutions because of the diversity of their students will continue to become more serious. In the
following section we consider the direction that community colleges and technical institutions take. It is important to remember
that the task of postsecondary education is a moving target, and so
resolving this year's problems is always inadequate by the time next
year rolls around.

Trends in Postsecondary Institutions

Like the sub-baccalaureate labor market itself and the students
entering postsecondary education, some distinct trends in two-year
institutions reflect some of the underlying organizational conditions. One of these, the movement for accountability, has the
potential to improve the effectiveness of these institutions, but the
other trends unfortunately may not.

The Trend Toward Comprehensive and "Academic" Institutions

There has been a long-term trend in this country for educational
institutions to change their missions in order to enhance their status (McDonnell and Grubb, 1991). Thus most teacher's colleges
became comprehensive colleges, and comprehensive colleges have
pressed to become universities offering graduate degrees. Area
vocational schools initially intended for secondary students have
often added programs for adults and then become technical institutes offering associate degrees; in many states, technical institutes
and technical colleges have then become comprehensive community colleges with a transfer function. Most recently, some
community colleges have pressed to become four-year colleges,
sometimes by offering general education courses in junior and

senior years (the "upside down" baccalaureate). This kind of institutional progression has obvious roots in the status differences among types of institutions.

In one sense, institutional drift is beneficial for the preparation of the sub-baccalaureate labor force, because integration of academic and occupational education and teaching remedial subjects within occupational areas are more easily achieved within comprehensive community colleges. In addition, the presence within one institution of varied offerings, academic as well as occupational and transfer-oriented as well as employment-related, provides greater opportunity for those students trying to find a way for themselves, and it facilitates transitions among programs as students change their minds. Comprehensive institutions have also been viewed in this country as more equitable, as less likely to track students into lower-status occupations, relative to specialized vocational institutions; hence comprehensive community colleges are consistent with a larger pattern that can be seen in high schools and four-year colleges as well.

However, as proponents of occupational education and technical institutes have argued for years, the danger in comprehensive institutions is that the so-called academic side, the goal of transferring students to four-year colleges, will come to dominate all other purposes. There are indicators of the danger that this academic bent poses to occupational programs: devotion of greater resources to the academic side, reduction of resources for high-cost but effective occupational programs in subjects like health and technician education, and the problem that ancillary work-oriented programs (such as the co-op programs profiled briefly in Chapter Five) have had in maintaining their funding.

But the academic or transfer strategy isn't especially good for the community college either. It accepts the premise that there is only one kind of highly valued postsecondary institution, defined by the research university. This, of course, is a status battle that community colleges cannot hope to win since they do not offer baccalaureate degrees, they do not carry out conventional research, and they are not selective. It is also a high-risk strategy: if an institution fails in the goal of transferring large proportions of students—and in general only community colleges with middle-class students and suburban locations manage to do so—then its students are left either with academic associate degrees or without any credentials at all, both of which outcomes have uncertain economic value (as Chapter Three clarified).

A better strategy would be to change the terms of battle: to articulate an image of a comprehensive institution working in the middle, providing access to mid-skilled jobs *and* to four-year colleges for those who find that appropriate; providing the mix of academic and occupational skills required in virtually every adult activity; joining the short-term job training system and the larger educational system; and providing education both to conventional students and to the great diversity of students who are older, or underprepared, or new to this country, or unsure of their goals. Allowing a variety of students to establish and attain their disparate goals, and doing so more effectively, would be a worthier goal than emulating the research university, and in the long run it would generate greater public support. This is also consistent with a student-centered institution, rather than one whose goals are specified by a status system that may have little to do with student interests.

Accountability

There is little question that a movement for accountability in government has taken hold, in spheres as different as regulation and environmental protection, education and job training. In response, the federal government has begun imposing performance measures, mimicking those used in JTPA, and states have moved to their own, still fledgling, efforts (Hoachlander and Rahn, 1992).

In one sense, the accountability movement is consistent with the arguments I have made in this volume, because it helps make institutions more conscious of outcomes and thereby potentially more effective. But there are at least two serious problems with accountability, illustrated respectively by K–12 education and JTPA itself. In K–12 education, there are so many externally imposed standards that teachers often feel that they have no room to maneuver: graduation requirements, college admissions requirements, preparation for the SAT exam and various Advanced Placement exams, state-imposed graduation or minimum-competency exams, and now newer proposals for skill standards, certificates of initial and advanced mastery, and national standards. These various standards, sometimes conflicting and largely expressed in the rigid format of multiple-choice exams, have made innovations in teaching and curriculum difficult, thwarting precisely those reforms that might enable schools to meet higher standards.

The warning from JTPA is that performance measures may have little to do with effectiveness. Careful evaluations of JTPA programs using the best statistical procedures show that the effectiveness of job training programs measured by gains in earnings and employment is uncorrelated with scores on performance standards (Doolittle and others, 1993, p. 10). Such results cast doubt on the entire system of performance measures. This can happen because local programs can manipulate their performance measures, because short-term measures of success are not necessarily correlated with longer-term measures of employment, and because the kinds of short and job-specific programs that local JTPA agencies have often devised to meet their performance measures are unlikely to contribute to employability over the longer run. While most JTPA programs are quite mindful of performance measures, sometimes to the exclusion of any other goals, this still does not help make them any more effective. Indeed, a world of performance measures uncorrelated with true measures of effectiveness is the worst one of all, in which innovation is impossible while effectiveness is low.

As others have argued (see Hill, Harvey, and Praskac, 1992), the only solution is to think of accountability not as externally imposed but as internally generated by institutions that are concerned about their effectiveness and monitor their own performance in order to improve it. This kind of accountability is used not for punitive purposes by state governments intent on reducing funding for underachieving institutions, but instead by local institutions interested in diagnosing and correcting problems in accomplishing their mission as they (and their students) define it. To be sure, state government may still be necessary in order to establish elements of an accountability system, and to ensure consistency and accuracy in the data collected, but within certain limits the goals to be met can be specified by local institutions. Indeed, as in many other practices that improve education (such as licensing in health occupations), the process of discussion in determining such standards might be more important than the standards themselves.

Funding and the Responses to Funding "Crisis"

All education institutions including community colleges and technical institutes seem perennially short of funding and are vociferous about their needs for more resources. Complaints about funding seem to dominate the concerns of many administrators, and most political battles concentrate on funding and fiscal control, not on programmatic or educational issues.

In fact, spending in postsecondary education has increased over the past twenty years, not decreased: funding per full-time student in public two-year institutions was $5,292 in 1970–71 (in 1990–91 dollars), increasing erratically to $5,847 in 1988–89, and has been relatively stable since then—a real (inflation-adjusted) increase of about 10 percent. Funding may seem inadequate, either because two-year institutions are funded at much lower levels than four-year colleges,[6] or because the population that might be served in these open-enrollment institutions is so much greater than the one now enrolled, or because "you can't always get what you want" (to cite those great fiscal analysts the Rolling Stones). But real resources have gone up quite steadily, though it is not entirely clear what has absorbed these additional resources.

In the constant struggles over resources, educational institutions of all kinds try to protect their core offerings, which are generally the highest-status classes—transfer courses in community colleges, certain occupational classes in technical institutes. They have done so in many cases by reducing (or failing to expand) services considered "ancillary," including guidance and counseling, tutoring, and other support services, and by shifting from full-time to part-time faculty. In many two-year colleges, the result has been the development of an institution that in many ways resembles an emerging style of corporation, highly dependent on contingent work: a small core of full-time faculty design the curriculum and manage a much larger workforce of part-time and temporary faculty, and institutions concentrate exclusively on money-making activities—in this case, students enrolled in courses generating tuition and state aid. Most part-time faculty play no role in governance, receive no staff development, participate in very few institution-building activities, and have little loyalty to the institution in which they teach. The institution is little more than an agglomeration of courses. The increase in part-time faculty, everywhere lamented (for example, Worthen, in press) but nowhere reversed, suggests a future much like that of adult education, with large numbers of transient part-time instructors, uncommitted to innovation in teaching, too consumed with their own working conditions to worry much about their students or their institution. This is, of course, a vision of slow descent into educational chaos.

The Institutional Alternatives: The "Shopping Mall College" and the College as Learning Community

There are, then, roughly two directions that two-year colleges might take. One we might describe as the "shopping mall community college" (Powell, Farrar, and Cohen, 1985). In this description, the institution offers an array of courses from which students choose, with little constraint or guidance, little concern on the part of the institution with what students do with their "purchases," few institutional goals except the volume of sales, and little concern among staff except to maintain their employment. This is, consistent with the shopping-mall metaphor, a market-driven institution in which *students* bear the responsibility for making their way through, deciding what they want to accomplish, putting together a program, and realizing the benefits once they leave. (In this sense, it is completely consistent with a market-driven system of education and job training and of the sub-baccalaureate labor market generally.) It is, potentially at least, an efficient way of serving students who know what they want and who can make their way through large, impersonal, and bureaucratic institutions. But many others are left behind, whether in the high school, the community college, or large public institutions of higher education.

The alternative would reverse almost all of the practices of the shopping mall college. Although any name is awkward, we might call it the *college as learning community*, a name that suggests its coherence rather than fragmentation and its focus on educational outcomes rather than on enrollments for their fiscal benefits to the institution. This kind of college requires considerably more resources to maintain itself as a community, including full-time faculty who can spend time creating internal linkages and connections to the external communities (including employers), promoting a culture of active teaching, and otherwise engaging in noncourse activities. The institution would try to improve teaching as an institutional priority, not merely allowing good teaching to emerge through the efforts of individual faculty. It would develop coherent *programs* for students, rather than simply providing courses, and it would include the variety of support services that would help students unsure of their directions. It would pay greater attention in all ways to linkages with the external community, including the kinds of linkages with employers analyzed in Chapter Six; for example, co-op programs and placement efforts would be seen as integral to the institution, rather than relatively peripheral as they often are. A greater focus on outcomes would be crucial, and it might lead to the elimination of some programs; but by the same token, effective if expensive programs (in health and technical areas, for example) would be better supported. No doubt novel funding mechanisms would be necessary, to give institutions different incentives than what they now face. In every way, this kind of institution is consistent more with the "institutionalized" approach to education and occupations found in Germany and other northern European countries, in which the passage from school to work is carefully organized. This is the antithesis of the market-driven approach.

It is, of course, silly to think that institutions conform to one or another of these models. In reality, almost every institution has characteristics of both, and some practices of the shopping mall college are desirable. But we have moved in this country toward "shopping mall institutions" without much thought, driven by certain basic values and attitudes toward education, and two-year institutions are moving further in this direction without fully understanding the implications. If our goal as a society is to use education to enhance both individual achievement and social goals such as improving the sub-baccalaureate labor force, and to provide opportunities for the widest possible range of individuals, then this heedless action should be replaced at every opportunity with efforts to institute colleges as learning communities.

Maintaining Our Faith in Education

I began this volume by reminding readers of the long-standing American faith in formal schooling. This faith has sustained the expansion of public education over 150 years, including the development of the high school into an institution that virtually everyone attends and the expansion of postsecondary education in both two- and four-year institutions, particularly since the 1960s. But this faith is not limitless. The critiques of community colleges, the "case against college" which appears every time a journalist finds recent college graduates in subprofessional employment, and the ringing denunciations of education from the business community are all examples of individuals' having felt betrayed by the conventional wisdom surrounding education. Some of these attacks are ill-informed, of course. The *average* benefit of a baccalaureate degree has been high and quite steady in recent years, even if some individuals fail to benefit, and the returns to two-year colleges are substantial if somewhat smaller. But criticisms still reflect a sense that educational institutions have not done what they have been charged to do.

At the same time, our faith in formal schooling sets up expectations that may be too great. As I have outlined in this chapter, the challenges of preparing individuals for the sub-baccalaureate labor market are likely to be even greater in the decades ahead, partly because of changes in the labor markets that we are unlikely to enact and partly because the nature of the students coming into two-year institutions will bring its own educational problems. In a world of moving targets, there is always going to be some disappointment, because institutions are always trying to catch up with conditions that keep developing.

In that world of moving targets, the weak and laissez faire policies that have been typical are especially inappropriate: federal policy designed for other segments of the educational system, inactive state policies, and local institutions that follow the model of the shopping mall college. They allow ineffective practices to continue, and they are inadequate to the task of responding appropriately and flexibly to changes. Particularly given the shifts that are likely to take place in the next few decades, more active policies will be necessary to prepare the sub-baccalaureate labor force, anticipating both the changes in labor market conditions and in students that are likely to take place. Such policies are crucial to maintaining our faith in education by giving it some justification, rather than allowing this faith to continue as a belief without foundation.

Notes

Chapter One: Distinctive Characteristics

1. The BLS projections of educational attainment to 2005 estimate that the group with "some college" will increase only marginally, from 27.2 percent of the labor force to 27.4 percent, while those with high school diplomas will fall slightly from 35.8 percent to 34.9 percent (Silvestri, 1993, Table 9). However, these simulations assume changes in *occupations* but not in *educational attainments* in particular occupations. Given the tendency for educational inflation to take place in specific occupations, the growth in the sub-baccalaureate labor force should be larger than these projections.

2. We did not include any health occupations partly because health occupations have been extensively studied (especially by Hudis and others, 1992) and partly because they are heavily regulated, unlike virtually all the other occupations of the sub-baccalaureate labor market. For more information about the methods used in collecting this information, see Grubb, Dickinson, Giordano, and Kaplan (1992).

3. See also Grubb and McDonnell (1996; in press) for confirmation of the local nature of these labor markets. CPS data on mobility patterns confirm that individuals with less than a B.A. degree are half as likely to move as those with B.A. and graduate degrees and are much less likely to give job changes as reasons for moving (see Bureau of the Census, 1989).

4. If a test is found to have a disproportionate impact on a protected class, for example women or minority employees, then the employer must be able to show that the test is job-related (see Wilcox, Grubb, and Lee, 1995, pp. 41–35 to 41-50.3). The employers we interviewed seem to fear the threat of a lawsuit, rather than thinking they cannot devise a job-related test. However, informal hiring practices as well as formalized hiring tests are subject to the same burden of proof, so relying on informal hiring procedures does not help employers avoid the threat of a lawsuit.

5. Although there has been an increase in companies providing train-
    ing to their sub-baccalaureate employees, firm-sponsored training
    (much of which has firm-specific components) still predominantly
    goes to upper-level managers and professionals (Lynch, 1992; Bow-
    ers and Swain, 1994). In turn, companies are less likely to let go of
    their specifically trained employees since they lose the benefits of
    such training (Becker, 1975, chapter two.)

6. We did uncover other less important mobility patterns. In one, rel-
    atively small and high-tech firms "where scientific knowledge is part
    of the training base" hire individuals from larger firms. In part, this
    allows the smaller companies to use the training that larger com-
    panies can better afford. In addition, initial hiring by firms is a sig-
    nal of ability; as a spokesperson from one mid-sized employer
    remarked, "Employment in larger firms is a sign of employability.
    It is a sign of competency. . . . Small firms look to larger firms to
    screen people for them." In addition, some individuals get initial
    experience in the completely unskilled, routinized work of large
    companies and then work their way up.

7. See, for example, Brown, Reich, and Stern (1992), contrasting the
    new form of employment they describe as *SET* (security, employee
    involvement, and training) with the older *JAM* (job characteristics,
    adversarial relations, and minimal training), and the discussion of
    the high-skills equilibrium versus the current low-skills equilibrium
    in *American's Choice: High Skills or Low Wages!* (Commission on the
    Skills of the American Workforce, 1990). See also Osterman (1994),
    who provides evidence that the shift to new employment practices
    is much more widespread than has been estimated. Yet another
    recent survey of employers reported increases in skill levels among
    production-line workers among 57 percent of companies, with only
    5 percent reporting decreases in skills; employers also report using
    many practices associated with high-skills firms such as TQM, bench-
    marking, and the like (Educational Quality of the Workforce, 1995).

8. Other surveys of firms confirm the importance of competencies other
    than technical skills. See especially McPartland, Dawkins, and Brad-
    dock (1986); Committee for Economic Development (1985); and
    Hudis and others (1992).

9. One educator interpreted the emphasis on certain "foundation
    skills" as a cover for racism, since the stress on communications skills
    works to the disadvantage of nonnative speakers (both Asian-
    American and Hispanic immigrants) and blacks who do not speak
    standard English: "Employers say they want excellent communica-
    tions skills regardless of whether the job really requires it. To me
    it's, in many cases, discriminatory actions." On the other hand, a

placement official in a nearby community college related several stories of limited-English students who were dismissed because of their inability to understand directions. Regardless of which interpretation is more plausible, communications skills are increasingly important job qualifications.

10.   For confirmation of the importance of experience over schooling during the 1960s, see Diamond and Bedrosian (1970). For more recent evidence, employers in the EQW survey (1995) ranked previous work experience and previous employer recommendations third and fifth among recruitment criteria; in contrast, years of completed schooling was seventh, grades ninth, the reputation of the applicant's school tenth, and teacher recommendations dead last among eleven possible responses.

11.   The other ubiquitous way of reducing the uncertainty of new hires is to require a probationary period, commonly of ninety days. Other firms hire workers from temporary agencies for ninety days or longer and decide at the end of this period whether to convert them to permanent employees. Co-operative education programs serve the same role, as I clarify in Chapter Six. A probationary period can be interpreted as an extended job interview: during that period, the workers in a firm can observe a new hire's skills, motivation, ability to work with others, ability to learn new tasks, and adaptability. As a condition of hiring, probation (like experience) emphasizes performance on the job and provides no advantage to educational credentials unless formal schooling has made the individual perform better.

12.   Occasionally an employer will have strong preferences about the source of training. One reported not hiring individuals who were trained in the military because of its rigid approach to work, while another preferred military training because it ensured discipline.

13.   In earnings equations such as those in Chapter Three, earnings differentials between those in moderately skilled positions and those in skilled positions will be variously ascribed to experience, postsecondary education, and military training. However, the individual with postsecondary education will have higher earnings than a high school graduate *without* experience, creating a return to postsecondary education.

14.   Among all the employers interviewed, there was a single exception: A large insurance company in Cincinnati hires high school graduates into Clerk I and Clerk II positions, while individuals with community college education are generally hired into Clerk III and Clerk IV positions. (The next step, to Accountant I, requires a B.A. degree.) The atypical differential for community college graduates

may result from an unusually rigid structure in the accounting department: "That's the way the bean counters are," reported the director of personnel.

15. It is tempting to argue on the basis of these figures that 35.3 percent of college graduates are underemployed, since only 64.7 report that they are in occupations requiring a baccalaureate degree. By this measure, 69.7 percent of those with some college are underemployed, as are at least 85 percent of high school graduates. However, it is quite plausible that many of those with some college are in jobs for which some postsecondary education is not strictly required—since other forms of training are good substitutes—but for which their formal schooling provided them entry to the job.

16. The proportion of workers getting formal upgrade training increased between 1983 and 1991 from 12 percent to 16.8 percent, with increases especially high among those with some college (from 15.1 percent to 20.4 percent), with baccalaureate degrees (from 20.5 percent to 26.1 percent), and with graduate degrees (from 16.7 percent to 23.4 percent). See Bowers and Swain (1994).

17. This is a departure from conventional views of internal labor markets in which job ladders are quite clearly defined (Doeringer and Piore, 1971; introduction to Abraham and McKersie, 1990). The shift to less precise career ladders with more flexibility in the content of specific jobs is more consistent with the "salaried model" of internal labor markets than with the older "industrial model" (Osterman and Kochan, 1990).

18. Kett (1982) has stressed that the movement for vocational education at the turn of the century misappropriated the concept of "career"—which was then developing in professions like medicine, law and academia—in applying it to blue-collar and working-class occupations where job ladders were never ordered in the clear progression associated with "careers."

19. This description is consistent with the view of American labor markets as being poorly structured and complicating the transition from school to work, compared to labor markets in such countries as Germany, which has institutionalized systems to help students navigate the transition (Buechtemann, Schupp, and Soloff, 1993).

Chapter Two: Educational Pathways

1. Tuma (1993), Table 2.1. These figures exclude about 17 percent of the community college students who did not respond to a question about their fields of study. This group probably includes some experimenters who are unsure of their direction, as well as remedial and avocational students.

2. See Grubb (1991). With other definitions transfer rates are higher; for example, if we examine only those students who say they want to transfer, and then eliminate the experimenters who leave with fewer than twelve credits, the transfer rate for the class of 1980 was 39.8 percent instead of 20.2 percent, but still lower than it was (49.7 percent) with this definition for the class of 1972.

3. These results, based on the High School and Beyond sophomore cohort, are not directly comparable to those in Table 2.1. Because this study first interviewed students in tenth grade, thereby eliminating those with less than ten years of formal schooling, the proportion of high school dropouts is relatively low in the HS&B data. In addition, these results do not reflect final educational attainments since some individuals will continue their formal schooling after age twenty-eight.

4. The fraction of those in the sub-baccalaureate labor force with a high school diploma is lower (39 percent) in Table 2.3 than that in Table 1.1 (where 55 percent of those in the sub-baccalaureate labor force had a high school diploma) because of the slow increases in educational attainments, which are higher for the class of 1982 in Table 2.3 than for the labor force as a whole in Table 1.1.

5. See Tuma (1993), Table 2.1 for 1989–90 NPSAS enrollment data, and Tuma and Geis (1995), Table 2.1, for information on the HS&B sophomore cohort. For other information about proprietary schools, see Grubb (1993c; 1994). The results for "other institutions" in Table 2.3 include some public area vocational schools.

6. While it is possible that the increases in noncompletion represent a slowdown in completion rates, rather than a real decrease in completion, this seems unlikely because the conditions conducive to completing college—particularly financial aid, the opportunity cost of attendance, and the availability of supportive services in community colleges—did not markedly improve during the 1980s. In Grubb (1989b) I reject a variety of other explanations including changes in the composition of students, cyclical economic effects, and the deterioration of high schools.

7. In these analyses, credits are standardized to compensate for the differences among institutions on semester and trimester systems, and for a tendency to describe vocational credits in terms of contact hours rather than credits; see Grubb (1989a; 1989b) for technical details. Community college administrators and researchers often distinguish students with fewer than twelve credits from those with twelve or more, considering the former group transitory, casual, or avocational compared with the latter group.

8. Similarly, of the high school class of 1982 who initially enrolled in community colleges (a group that includes only younger students of "traditional" college-going age) 30.3 percent aspired while in high school to a sub-baccalaureate credential, 20.5 percent to a baccalaureate and 12.7 percent to a postgraduate degree; only 22.5 percent wanted a vocational program shorter than a credential, and only 14.1 percent had no postsecondary aspirations while in high school (Tuma and Geis, 1995, Table 2.1).

9. See Grubb (1990), Tables 2 and 3, using the NLS72 data. The size of two-year college systems is measured by the enrollments in two-year colleges as a fraction of the population aged eighteen to thirty, measured for states. The coefficient on this variable in logit equations for the probability of attending a four-year college is positive for both males and females but not significant ($t = 1.62$ for males and 0.58 for females), rather than negative as would be true if cooling out were important. For another, less conclusive attempt to measure the relative importance of cooling out versus educational advancement, see Grubb, 1989c.

10. See Grubb (1990), Tables 2 and 3. The vocational emphasis is measured by the fraction of associate degrees in the state awarded in vocational rather than academic fields. The coefficients on this variable in logit equations for four-year college attendance are positive and significant for men ($t = 2.38$) though positive and insignificant for women ($t = 0.33$). The coefficients in the logits for two-year college attendance are positive but significant only for men ($t = 2.43$), not for women ($t = 1.57$).

11. See, for example, the reviews of students in Cohen and Brawer (1989), chapter two; in Cohen, Palmer, and Zwemer (1986), chapter two; and the chapter on occupational students in Palmer (1988). There have been two ethnographies of community colleges, by London (1978) and Weis (1986); both of them stress the use of community colleges for economic advancement by working class white and black students respectively, but otherwise neither explores the purposes of students attending community colleges. See also the articles in Zwerling and London (1992).

12. The four districts included Contra Costa, with three campuses; the Peralta district, with five campuses; Santa Barbara, with a single campus, and the San Diego district, with three campuses. The campuses range from urban to suburban, from middle-class to heavily low-income and minority, and their reputations vary as well. None of them was rural, so the special problem of rural districts is not addressed, particularly the challenge of preparing students for occu-

pations that do not exist in the area. No student refused our request for an interview, so that aside from undersampling highly mobile students I regard this as a random sample of students enrolled in these four districts. We interviewed a total of forty-one students in spring 1992.

13. It is foolish to treat our sample of forty-one students as a representative sample partly because there are so few of them, partly because of being unable to find many students, and partly because a California sample is nonrepresentative. However, I report rough orders of magnitude because they are some indication of gross patterns. For other efforts to classify students by purpose see Cohen and Brawer (1989, p. 49) citing a 1986 survey by the Center for the Study of Community Colleges that found 36 percent seeking transfer, 34 percent job entry skills, 16 percent job upgrading, and 15 percent personal interest or avocational reasons. Sheldon (1982) concluded that 36 percent of California community college students entering in 1978 could be classified as vocational; of the 16 percent who expected to complete programs, 38 percent were job seekers attending long enough to find a new job, 37 percent were job upgraders looking to move up in a field in which they were already employed, and 9 percent were career changers.

14. Figures on the age distribution of students come from the 1992–93 NPSAS data. Community college administrators routinely cite the average age of students as twenty-nine—a figure that reappears so consistently it seems to have gained the stature of an "urban myth"—to stress how many older students they have. But this figure is misleading. The *median* age of community college students in the NPSAS data is twenty-five, and the median age of full-time students is twenty-one. Similarly, Cohen and Brawer (1989, p. 32) cite a Center for the Study of Community Colleges finding that the average age was twenty-nine, the median age was twenty-five, and the modal age was nineteen. While there are many students over thirty in community colleges, including some in their fifties and sixties that skew the average, most are very much part-time and account for a small fraction of courses taken.

Chapter Three: Economic Perspectives

1. The premise of Pincus's widely cited article is that "vocational education in public community colleges has been touted as an attractive alternative for the bachelor's degree"; but the claim that a two-year college is the equivalent of a program taking twice as long is difficult to believe, and he fails to cite a single source. The studies he uses,

largely those conducted by states following up community college students, are subject to the many flaws cited in the section below on local case studies; in particular, they cannot compare the employment of community college students with that of high school graduates, which is the most relevant comparison.

2. Brint and Karabel rely on several studies in addition to Pincus (1980). Breneman and Nelson (1981) examined wages, occupational status, and weeks employed four years after students left high school, which is too short a period of time for the benefits of postsecondary education to materialize. Their measure of postsecondary education was initial postsecondary attendance in a two- or four-year-year college, not a measure of completion. Work by Monk-Turner (1983; 1990) again compares students from two- and four-year colleges. And the research of Wilms (1974) compares the experiences of students in public and proprietary institutions, implying nothing about the benefits of attending either of these types of institutions relative to earning a high school diploma only.

3. For technical details see Grubb (1995d). The SIPP data have several advantages: they include individuals of all ages, rather than including just one cohort or a few relatively young cohorts, and they have better information about postsecondary education than most surveys; but school attainment is self-reported, with inevitable biases, and information is unavailable about the types of institutions individuals attended. The information about other characteristics of individuals aside from their education, such as race, family background, and labor market experience, is adequate, although some desirable information is missing, particularly on measures of ability and academic achievement. Because of these disadvantages it is critical to supplement information from the SIPP with that available from other data sets, summarized in Grubb (1995h), comparing the results of Grubb (1993a; 1995b; 1995d), Kane and Rouse (1995b), Lewis, Hearn, and Zilbert (1993), Hollenbeck (1993), Groot, Oosterbeek, and Stern (1995), and unpublished Current Population Survey (CPS) results performed for me by Lew Oleinick.

4. The detailed results are provided in Grubb (1995d). The other independent variables include those describing race and ethnicity; the education of the individual's head of household and whether the head of household was female; whether the individual is still in school; whether the individual is married, or disabled, covered by a union contract, or still in school; the number of children (for women only); and measures of tenure on the current job, in prior jobs related to the current job, and in other unrelated jobs, includ-

ing squared terms to capture the nonlinear effects of experience. The regressions also include a series of dummy variables to compensate for various imputations necessary because of incomplete data. The figures in Tables 3.2, 3.3, and 3.5 are coefficients from the conventional semilog functional form, with the log of earnings as a linear function of independent variables. These coefficients are percent changes only for relatively small changes.

5. The problem of statistical significance appears throughout these results. Many of the coefficients in Table 1.2 are statistically significant at the conventional 5 percent level, but *differences* between coefficients are often not significant, even when they are part of a clear pattern. In general, I report results that are part of a general pattern even when some of the underling differences are statistically insignificant, recognizing that individuals who are harder-nosed than I about statistical significance will be uncomfortable with some of my conclusions.

6. Even in 1984, when the effect of less than one year of college is significant, it is significant only for those aged forty-five to fifty-four, indicating that men would have to wait a considerable period of time to realize any benefits from small amounts of postsecondary education.

7. These results confirm earlier findings based on NLS72 data, which indicate that associate degrees in technical subjects and health occupations have the most substantial returns, while in other subjects the returns were essentially zero (Grubb, 1992b; 1995g).

8. For evidence that gender segregation has been declining more in higher-level occupations than in middle- and lower-level jobs, see Blau and Ferber (1992).

9. The matching algorithm was developed from Medrich and Vergun (1994), with a few changes: I added matches for education programs, and I have categorized individuals with "other" education as having an unknown match. Because there are relatively few, broad fields of study, if anything this matching algorithm errs on the side of overinclusiveness, or declaring that a program of study and an individual's occupation are related when they are not.

10. These results are consistent with the findings of Wilms (1974) that roughly 50 percent of students found employment related to their field of study, and to the state studies cited by Pincus (1980), reporting a median figure of 60 percent of students in jobs related to their training. In trials using the NLS72 data, 38 percent of students with certificates and 33 percent of those with associate degrees were in related employment; see Grubb (1989c, Table 16).

However, differences in the definitions of relatedness make comparisons with these data sets difficult. In the NLS72 results it was clear that individuals leaving without credentials and individuals completing fewer courses tended to have fewer courses related to their present employment, indicating that individuals with small amounts of coursework are more likely to be experimenters than individuals who know what area of employment they intend to follow.

11. Response rates have typically been low, often in the range of 10–25 percent. Given the suspicion that only the most successful students and those most satisfied with their education return these questionnaires, the results are likely to be biased upward. Second, these questionnaires are typically sent to students who have enrolled in an institution; at best, then, they can compare the earnings of those who completed credentials with those who enrolled but failed to complete, or compare earnings in different occupational fields, but they do not allow comparison with the earnings of those without any postsecondary education. Third, such follow-up studies have typically surveyed students soon after leaving college, and this is likely to be well before the benefits of postsecondary education show up (typically when individuals enter their thirties). Finally, follow-up studies generally do not collect much information about the other characteristics that might affect employment and earnings, such as measures of ability, indicators of family background, labor market experience, and other personal characteristics such as those mentioned in endnote 4 in this chapter. With a combination of positive and negative biases of unknown magnitude, it is difficult to put much faith in such studies.

12. For a similar diagnosis of the failures of federal postsecondary education policy, see the report of the Committee on Postsecondary Education and Training for the Workplace (Hansen, 1994).

Chapter Four: Creating a Unified "System"

1. These have been reported in Grubb, Brown, Kaufman, and Lederer (1990); Grubb, Kalman, Castellano, Brown, and Bradby (1991); Grubb and Kalman (1994); McDonnell and Grubb (1991); Grubb and McDonnell (1991); Grubb and McDonnell (1996); Grubb and Bailis (1993).

2. For the three annual reports on coordination, see Grubb, Brown, Kaufman, and Lederer (1989), Grubb, Brown, Kaufman, and Lederer (1990), and Grubb, Kalman, and others (1991). For a comprehensive literature review on coordination, see Trutko, Bailis, and Barnow (1989), Grubb and Bailis (1993), and the National Assessment of Vocational Education (Hollinger and Harvey, 1994).

3. For a comprehensive review of job training programs, see Grubb (1995f) or Grubb (1996); see also the review of education and job training programs in *What's Working (and What's Not)* (Office of the Chief Economist, 1995), the review by LaLonde (1995), and the meta-analysis by Fischer and Cordray (1996).

4. For evidence that job keeping is a substantial problem, see Quint, Musick, and Ladner (1994).

5. Since the job training world is so large and varied, there are almost surely a few exceptions. For a description of some of them, see Grubb and Kalman (1994); another one may exist in San Diego (Martinson and Friedlander, 1994).

6. The provision of support services represents yet another manifestation of basing public action on the failure of what would otherwise be familial responsibility; see Grubb and Lazerson (1988). From the larger perspective of social policy, a more effective approach might be to reduce poverty, reduce gender and racial discrimination in employment, and prevent the social pathologies (homelessness, urban decay, crime) that afflict low-income communities. But from the viewpoint of education and training programs without the power or resources to make these more fundamental changes, providing supportive services is the best that can be done.

7. While job training programs have been evaluated using some of the most sophisticated methods available, components of these programs have typically not been evaluated. However, analyses of the Learning, Earning, and Parenting (LEAP) program for high school dropouts showed that the combination of enhanced services (including neighborhood outreach and enriched GED preparation) and the incentives embedded in the LEAP program increased the rate at which individuals received a high school diploma or GED from 13.5 percent to 22 percent, a difference of 8.5 percentage points, of which 2 percentage points were attributed to enhanced services (Long, Wood, and Kopp, 1994, Table 6.7). An evaluation of different approaches to supportive services is now being conducted in Columbus by the Manpower Development Research Corporation, though results will not be available for several years. Finally, Reid and others (1994) found that an experimental program providing case management to at-risk adolescent women was more effective than either monetary incentives or no services.

8. The provision of supportive services in the New Chance program is particularly interesting; see Quint, Musick, and Ladner (1994). The average response to a question about staff caring about clients was 8.0 on a scale of 0 to 10; the average response to a question about

case managers providing services was 7.6; see Quint, Polit, Bos, and Cave (1994, Table 3.8). While the program did increase school retention and GED completion, its effects on earnings, employment, and pregnancy after eighteen months were insubstantial. Clearly there were large numbers of individuals who were "derailed" from more successful paths by circumstances beyond the control of the program, and which case managers were unable to counter.

9. In the past, these have included program improvement funds through the Carl Perkins Act, the 6 percent governor's incentive funds, and the 8 percent coordination funds through JTPA. By the time of publication, these federal funds are likely to be consolidated into a new education and training block grant; but there will still be federal funds to allocate to localities, probably at the discretion of the governor, that can be used to enforce a coherent state vision.

Chapter Five: Integrating Instruction

1. My initial research on integration practices took place in 1991 and 1992. It began by asking a sample of 294 community colleges to indicate whether they were doing anything to integrate academic and vocational education; their responses are summarized in Grubb and Kraskouskas (1992). A survey of postsecondary integration practices was undertaken by the National Assessment of Vocational Education, with the results reported in Grubb and Stasz (1993) and by the National Assessment of Vocational Education (Boesel, 1994). Finally, Norena Badway has surveyed community colleges and technical institutes again in 1994 and 1995, with the results to be analyzed in Badway and Grubb (in press).

2. Cross (1976, chapter five) has argued that the nontraditional students in community colleges (including many occupational students) are more likely to be field-dependent, and therefore to have trouble applying a concept from one area to another. It is important to note that students in even the best four-year colleges are likely to need guidance in integrating material from different courses. The movement for interdisciplinary courses within four-year colleges, the efforts to teach from case studies, and the movement to adopt capstone courses reflect the difficulty all students have with fragmented courses.

3. See "DACUM Profile: Core Competencies, Associate Degree of Applied Arts and Sciences," Pennsylvania College of Technology, October 29–30, 1987.

4. A national survey of WAC programs provided no evidence about its use by occupational versus academic faculty (Stout and Magnotto,

1991). In no WAC program that we observed was there any effort to determine the extent of course changes in response to WAC. A recent special issue of *New Directions in Community Colleges* about WAC (Stanley and Ambron, 1991) contained many articles on how to do it, but only one on measuring effects (Hughes-Weiner and Jensen-Cekalla, 1991).

5. These applied academics courses are locally developed; they are not the same as the Applied Academics courses (Applied Math, Applied Communications, and Principles of Technology) developed for high school students by the Council for Occupational Research and Development (CORD) and the Agency for Instructional Technology (AIT). We have found that most community college instructors are disdainful of these off-the-shelf courses, particularly Applied Math and Applied Communications: their academic content is too basic, the occupational applications are too trivial, and they fail to encourage initiative and collaboration.

6. With the exception of courses supported by special funding, such as the National Endowment for the Humanities, we have found no examples of team teaching; and administrators uniformly reported that fiscal constraints make team teaching rare.

7. On sources for incorporating the literature about work, see also Koziol (1992), and Koziol and Grubb (1995).

8. Personal communication, Elwood Zaugg, dean of vocational education, Salt Lake Community College, July 13, 1995.

9. South Seattle Community College (Washington) does offer a course in The Psychology of the Workplace, described by the division chair as "not really integrated" but still more responsive to the needs of occupational students than is the conventional psychology course.

10. See also Koziol and Grubb (1995) for ways in which occupational issues could be incorporated into courses in the social sciences.

11. Personal communication, LaVerna Fadale, Two-Year College Development Center, SUNY/Albany, who was the project coordinator.

12. This quote is taken from flyers advertising the business cluster to all students. The flyers promote the clusters in similar terms: "Clusters help you learn better by showing you how ideas connect across different courses. Students in clusters tend to do better in their courses."

13. One ESL instructor reported that the pass rate in the ESL/keyboarding pair was 90 percent, compared to 70 percent in nonpaired ESL. Those associated with clusters in LaGuardia Community College contend that the pass rate is higher for cluster students than for noncluster students in the same English courses (85 percent versus 70 percent), and that students in the business cluster have

higher retention rates by 10 to 24 percentage points from the first year to the second. (Of course, self-selection of highly motivated students into clusters might be responsible.) In Tinto's (1987) model, which dominates the empirical literature on persistence, academic integration (essentially, academic success) and social integration (the participation of students in the social life of the institution) are crucial to decisions about continuing. Clusters facilitate social integration, which is otherwise difficult for students in community college because so many of them are part-time and have substantial demands outside of their education.

14.   Capstone courses appear to be the community college equivalent of senior projects in high schools, described in Tsuzuki (1995).

15.   The data about remedial courses in community colleges are not very good, and so it is generally impossible to compare completion rates in remedial courses and "college-level" courses. However, instructors uniformly report completion rates in remedial courses to be low (Grubb and Kalman, 1994). Evidence from Miami-Dade Community College indicates that only 26 percent of students who tested below standard levels completed all the appropriate remedial courses, with the proportion falling as the number of subjects in which a student is deficient increases; see Losak and Morris (1985), reprinted in Grubb and Kalman (1994), and more recent results in Morris (1994).

16.   In addition to these examples, the Two-Year College Development Center at SUNY/Albany sponsored a project in the early 1980s to develop materials for faculty about the integration of basic skills into postsecondary occupational programs. The result was a series of monographs with titles such as *Reading in Postsecondary Occupational Education* and *Basic Skills in Postsecondary Occupational Education*. However, like most projects supported by grant funds, this effort seems to have vanished once the funding (from federal vocational education funds) ended.

17.   On the devastating image of the "technopeasant," see Hersh (1983) and Finn, Ravitch, and Fancher (1984, p. 6).

18.   I know of no systematic analysis of the organizational independence of community college missions. However, in addition to the clear split between academic and occupational faculty, my colleagues and I have previously identified a split between the remedial or developmental faculty and the rest of the institution (Grubb, Kalman, and others, 1991), and between customized training and the rest of the institution (Lynch, Palmer, and Grubb, 1991). The programs serving JTPA and welfare clients are often distinct from regular

courses (Grubb, Brown, Kaufman, and Lederer, 1990); and credit and noncredit courses are often organized in different divisions.

Chapter Six: Enhancing Connections

1. This corroborates a finding of Hudis and others (1992), who discovered that employers in health occupations complained about communications skills although the technical skills taught in community colleges are adequate.

2. For other examples of this view, particularly in contrast to the greater efforts within JTPA and the JOBS program to fund placement efforts, see Grubb, Brown, Kaufman, and Lederer (1990).

3. In the survey conducted by Lynch, Palmer, and Grubb (1991), 94 percent of community colleges reported providing some form of contract education; employer funds averaged 42 percent of total funds supporting contract education. See also Doucette (1993), who found that 96 percent of community colleges offer contract education, with employers contributing a mean of 35.5 percent of costs. However, the enrollments in such programs are typically quite modest—for example, in the latter study 57 percent of institutions served one thousand individuals or fewer—and, especially given the duration of most contract training, are therefore small compared to regular occupational enrollments. For other evidence that contract education has expanded at the sub-baccalaureate level, see Bowers and Swain (1994): the fraction of individuals with "some college" who received formal on-the-job training increased from 15.1 percent in 1983 to 20.4 percent in 1991.

4. From the perspective of economic theory, colleges eliminate courses and programs whose marginal costs exceed their marginal benefits to the institution. Marginal costs vary in obvious ways: technical programs with small class sizes and equipment expenses cost more than classes with high pupil-teacher ratios. Marginal benefits normally include tuition and state aid per student, but they vary in other ways: some states pay different amounts for credit and noncredit courses, some have caps or limits on the numbers of students they support, and job training programs often provide additional resources for JTPA clients and welfare recipients.

5. In addition to the information about community college students in Chapter Two, see Parnes and Kohen (1975) for some older research on the extent of student knowledge about employment. This study found that knowledge about the world of work was highly correlated with general academic ability. Since community college students generally come from the middle rather than the top of the

distributions of ability and high school achievement, it seems likely that their knowledge about employment conditions is less sophisticated than that of students completing baccalaureate degrees. Some indirect information about student motives comes from enrollment studies like those of Betts and McFarland (1995) and Grubb (1988), which indicate that enrollments in two-year colleges are more sensitive to costs than to benefits, that is, to the long-run employment consequences. More recent theoretical work acknowledges the possibility that incorrect information, especially among individuals in low-income communities without educated role models, causes inappropriate decisions, although direct evidence about information is still sparse; see Manski (1993) and Streufert (1991).

6. This is a source of potentially substantial inefficiency. In economic terms, education and training are worth providing when the total social benefits—to those educated, to employers, to coworkers, and to consumers in the form of lower prices—outweigh the total social costs. But community colleges provide education slots when the marginal institutional revenue, or state reimbursements plus tuition, outweighs the marginal institutional costs. Since there is no necessary relationship between the total benefits to society and the marginal institutional revenues, or between the total social costs and the marginal institutional costs, educational institutions provide the socially optimal amount of education only by chance.

7. In Sacramento, San Jose, and Fresno, we uncovered only one co-op program, operated by a local Air Force base near Sacramento for machinists and electronics technicians. Those responsible for this program describe its advantages in terms similar to those of the Cincinnati co-ops. While almost nine hundred colleges report having some sort of co-op program, it appears to be relatively small in most institutions; see especially Stern and others (1995) and Bragg, Hamm, and Trinkle (1995). The only other community college I know with extensive co-op enrollments is LaGuardia Community College, described in Grubb and Badway (1995).

8. Of the thirty-five different employers we interviewed in the Cincinnati area, only one was dissatisfied with the co-op programs and had terminated its participation. For considerably more information about the Cincinnati co-op programs, see Grubb (1995a), Villeneuve and Grubb (1996), and Grubb and Villeneuve (1995). See also Grubb and Badway (1995) on the co-op program at LaGuardia Community College.

9. A low-quality equilibrium would develop where the least able students are matched with the worst kinds of jobs; this has happened,

for example, with the Employment Service, with job training programs, and with many work experience programs. Co-op programs
in Cincinnati have managed to establish high-quality equilibria
informally, without any regulatory mechanisms to enforce quality.
10. For a similar conclusion about poor "alignment" between community colleges and high-tech employers based on research in the early
1980s in Silicon Valley and the Route 128 area near Boston, see
Useem (1986).

Chapter Seven: Rethinking Public Policies

1. The framework for this division of labor is that of fiscal federal-
ism, an offshoot of public goods theory in economics. For a similar effort to articulate a coherent rationale for federal policy in this
area, see the report of the Committee on Postsecondary Education
and Training for the Workforce of the National Research Council
(Hansen, 1994).
2. See Grubb and Tuma (1991). This pattern of lower utilization of
federal aid still holds once the differences among students in two-
and four-year institutions are considered. For more recent results
confirming the same pattern see Malizio (1995, Tables 5 and 6).
3. This manuscript was completed in November 1995, when it seemed
most likely that legislation sponsored by Sen. Nancy Kassebaum and
similar legislation in the House would determine the precise nature
of consolidation.
4. These conditions for the operation of vouchers are taken from a
much fuller discussion in Hansen (1994, chapter seven).
5. Loans are less appropriate for individuals pursuing sub-baccalaureate
credentials, since the earnings increases from which loans are repaid
are lower than for those with baccalaureate degrees. In addition,
advocates for low-income students have emphasized a greater use of
grants compared to loans, and this would clearly help students in two-
year institutions.
6. For example, Fischer (1987) has proposed completion-contingent
loans, which are converted into grants (that is, forgiven) when students complete the appropriate credentials. However, not only does
this reduce the effective subsidy, as Manski (1989) has pointed out,
but it also burdens with the obligation to repay loans those noncompleters who have the lowest ability to repay.
7. For more detailed analyses of the failures of adult education, see
Grubb and others (1992); Solorzano, Stecher, and Perez (1989);
and Chisman (1990). Because the adult education system is so large
and unregulated, there is room within it for individuals to create

innovative programs with powerful teaching methods and some dramatic results. However, these innovations tend to be idiosyncratic and unconnected to other programs, and so the system as a whole must be considered a failure.

8. Fountain and Tollefson (1989). South Dakota has neither community colleges nor technical institutes.

9. McDonnell and Zellman (1993, chapter three). Even the program approval process, the area where states are more active, is relatively toothless in many states: based on case studies in four states (California, Florida, Iowa, and Pennsylvania) Grubb and McDonnell (1991) concluded that state approval processes are weak because enforcement is lax and state officials lack the information to know what is happening at the local level.

10. Many colleges give entrance questionnaires on which they ask students their goals. However, as I stressed in Chapter One, the answers to such questions are not reliable if students literally have no idea what they want to do. More continuous measures of intentions are necessary, hopefully as students progress through an institution and become more certain about their goals; see, for example, the description of Miami-Dade's student tracking system in Roueche and Baker (1987, chapter three).

11. While McDonnell and Zellman (1993) state that only thirteen states directly fund these postsecondary institutions based on enrollment or FTE, at least twenty states in their Table 3.5 consider enrollment directly in setting funding. For those that negotiate funding in other ways, it is likely that enrollments affect funding in substantial ways.

12. Only eight states make funding contingent on varying costs, though a few others may do so indirectly through negotiated funding; see McDonnell and Zellman (1993, Table 3.5).

13. The one exception comes in the area of welfare-to-work programs, where many states have required their programs to work with JTPA and adult education; see Grubb and McDonnell (1996) and Lurie and Hagen (1994). This is, however, largely motivated by fiscal concerns: such coordination is often a way of shifting costs from one program only partially supported by federal funds (welfare) to others that are fully federally supported (JTPA).

14. While there are national associations of community college English and humanities instructors, their memberships appear to be low and most other subjects (and almost all occupational areas) lack such associations.

15. See, for example, the organization of employers and unions in Milwaukee, the Milwaukee-Waukesha Training Partnership, described

in Rogers (1994), Rogers and Streeck (1992), and Parker (1992); and the recommendation that California's Employment Training Panel (ETP) support such organizations, in Grubb and others (1993). The problem is a kind of market failure since the transaction costs of forming an employer organization (or a training consortium of employers and unions) prevent demand—in this case, demand for the appropriate kind of education—from being expressed in the market. Therefore small amounts of resources to organize employers can be interpreted as a market-making device.

16.   If an institution's publication is testimony to its priorities, then the content of the AACC's journal, the *Community College Journal,* is illuminating. From the December–January issue of 1994–95 to the October–November 1995 issue, only two of thirty articles were directly about occupational education: an article on skill standards, and one reporting a survey of work-based learning (such as co-operative education). A third described Florida's accountability system, in which standards for occupational programs are prominent. Occupational education fared slightly better in 1993–94, when six of thirty articles covered occupational subjects, including two on technical institutes.

Chapter Eight: Future Trends

1.   This view is often associated with Henry Levin and Russell Rumberger; see, for example, Rumberger (1987). For the most recent occupational projections, see Silvestri (1993). For a review indicating that both upskilling and downskilling are taking place, see Spenner (1983); on the inequality in wages see Levy and Murnane (1992) and Grubb and Wilson (1992).

2.   For statistical evidence, see Abraham (1990). See also U.S. Department of Labor (1988) for a collection of preliminary papers on contingent work, and the special issue of *The Labor Lawyer,* Vol. 10(2), Spring 1994, for articles about legal problems.

3.   The legal rights of temporary workers are a murky area in employment law. If a firm hires a temporary worker for a relatively long period, then courts have sometimes construed this to be a permanent employment relationship with all the usual legal rights; but this is now being decided on a case by case basis. See Wilcox, Grubb, and Lee (1995), Section 30.04, pp. 13-B to 13-19.

4.   The best evidence is from Miami-Dade; see Morris (1994).

5.   See Traub (1994), who has critiqued the remediation efforts of the City University of New York. The California State University system has recently proposed eliminating all remedial courses. Some supporters of community colleges have tended to downgrade remedial

education in favor of more "collegiate" work; see Eaton (1994) and Cohen and Brawer (1987).

6. Expenditures per full-time equivalent student in public two-year colleges in 1990–91 were $5,763, compared to $16,186 in public four-year institutions and $23,277 in private four-year institutions. See *Digest of Educational Statistics* (National Center for Educational Statistics, 1993, Table 326). The equivalent table for 1994 (Table 325) has some evident errors in the series of two-year college expenditures.

References

Abraham, K. G. (1990). Restructuring the employment relationship: The growth of market-mediated work arrangements. In K. G. Abraham & R. B. McKersie (Eds.), *New developments in the labor market* (pp. 85–118). Cambridge: MIT Press.

Abraham, K. G., & McKersie, R. B. (Eds.). (1990). *New developments in the labor market.* Cambridge: MIT Press.

Alba, R., & Lavin, D. (1981). Community colleges and tracking in higher education. *Sociology of Education, 54,* 223–247.

Amendments to the Carl Perkins Act, 1990. *A Compilation of Federal Education Laws. Volume IV: Vocational Education, Job Training, and Related Statutes as Amended through December 31, 1992,* 103rd Cong., 1st sess., 1993, Committee Print.

American Association of Community and Junior Colleges. (1984). *Putting America back to work: The Kellogg leadership initiative: A report and guidebook.* Washington, DC: Author.

Anderson, K. (1981). Post-high school experiences and college attrition. *Sociology of Education, 54,* 1–15.

Archer, M. S. (1982). *The sociology of educational expansion: Take-off, growth, and inflation in educational systems.* Rohnert Park, CA: Sage.

Aronowitz, S., & DiFazio, W. (1994). *The jobless future: Sci-tech and the dogma of work.* Minneapolis: University of Minnesota Press.

Badway, N., & Grubb, W. N. (forthcoming). *Reshaping the community college: Curriculum integration and the multiple competencies for career preparation.* Berkeley: National Center for Research in Vocational Education.

Bailey, T. (1989). *Changes in the nature and structure of work: Implications for skill requirements and skill formation.* Berkeley: University of California, National Center for Research in Vocational Education.

Bailey, T., & Merritt, D. (1995, December). *Making sense of industry-based skill standards.* Berkeley: National Center for Research in Vocational Education.

Baj, J., Trott, C., & Stevens, D. (1991). *A feasibility study of the use of unemployment insurance wage-record data as an evaluation tool for JTPA* (Research Report No. 90-02). Washington, DC: National Commission for Employment Policy.

275

Baraldi, C. G. (1990). Since dark is what brings out your light. *Innovation Abstracts, 12*(19), 10.

Beatty-Guenther, P. (1994). *Retention strategies at community colleges: Diffusion, legitimacy, and effectiveness.* Unpublished doctoral dissertation, University of California, Berkeley.

Becker, G. S. (1975). *Human capital: A theoretical and empirical analysis, with special reference to education* (2nd ed.). New York: Columbia University Press.

Berryman, S., & Bailey, T. (1992). *The double helix of education and the economy.* New York: Columbia University, Teachers College, Institute on Education and the Economy.

Betts, J., & McFarland, L. (1995). Safe port in a storm: The impact of labor market conditions on community college enrollments. *Journal of Human Resources, 30*(4), 741–765.

Bird, C. (1975). *The case against college.* New York: David McKay.

Blau, F., & Ferber, M. (1992). *The economics of men, women, and work.* Englewood Cliffs, NJ: Prentice-Hall.

Bloom, H. S., Orr, L. L., Cave, G., Bell, S. H., Doolittle, F., & Lin, W. (1994). *The national JTPA study. Overview: Impact, Benefits, and Costs of Title II-A.* Bethesda, MD: ABT Associates.

Boesel, D. (1994). Integration of academic and vocational curricula. In *Program improvement: Education reform. Vol. III, Final report to Congress, National Assessment of Vocational Education.* Washington, DC: U.S. Department of Education, Office of Educational Research and Improvement.

Bowers, N., & Swain, P. (1994). Recent trends in job training. *Contemporary Economic Policy, 12*(1), 79–88.

Bragg, D., Hamm, R., & Trinkle, K. (1995). *Work-based learning in two-year colleges in the United States.* Berkeley: National Center for Research in Vocational Education.

Breneman, D., & Nelson, S. (1981). *Financing community colleges: An economic perspective.* Washington, DC: Brookings Institution.

Bridges, W. (1994). The end of the job. *Fortune, 130*(6), 61–74.

Brint, S., & Karabel, J. (1989). *The diverted dream.* New York: Oxford University Press.

Brown, C., Reich, M., & Stern, D. (1992). *Becoming a high-performance work organization: The role of security, employee involvement, and training* (Working Paper No. 45). Berkeley: University of California, Institute of Industrial Relations.

Buechtemann, C. F., Schupp, J., & Soloff, D. (1993). Roads to work: School-to-work transition patterns in Germany and the United States. *Industrial Relations Journal, 24*(2), 97–111.

Bureau of the Census. (1989). *Geographical mobility: March 1986 to March 1987* (Current Population Reports, Series P-20, No. 430). Washington, DC: U.S. Department of Commerce, Author (available from U.S. Government Printing Office).

Cahalan, M., & Farris, E. (1986). *College level remediation* (FRSS Report No. 19). Washington, DC: U.S. Department of Education, Center for Statistics.

Chisman, F. P. (1990). *Leadership for literacy.* San Francisco: Jossey-Bass.

Clark, B. R. (1960). *The open-door college: A case study.* New York: McGraw-Hill.

Clark, B. R. (1980). The cooling-out function revisited. *New Directions for Community Colleges,* no. 8. San Francisco: Jossey-Bass.

Cohen, A. (1988). *General education and the community college.* (ERIC Document ED 304 196).

Cohen, A. M., & Brawer, F. B. (1987). *The collegiate function of community colleges: Fostering higher learning through curriculum and student transfer.* San Francisco: Jossey-Bass.

Cohen, A. M., & Brawer, F. B. (1989). *The American community college* (2nd ed.). San Francisco: Jossey-Bass.

Cohen, A., Palmer, J., & Zwemer, K. D. (1986). *Key resources on community colleges.* San Francisco: Jossey-Bass.

Collins, A., Brown, J., & Newman, S. (1989). Cognitive apprenticeship: Teaching the craft of reading, writing, and mathematics. In L. Resnick (Ed.), *Knowing, learning, and instruction: Essays in honor of Robert Glaser* (pp. 453–494). Hillsdale, NJ: Erlbaum.

Commission on the Future of Community Colleges. (1988). *Building communities: A vision for a new century.* Washington, DC: American Association of Community and Junior Colleges.

Commission on the Skills of the American Workforce. (1990). *America's choice: High skills or low wages!* Rochester, NY: National Center on Education and the Economy.

Committee for Economic Development. (1985). *Investing in our children: Business and the public schools.* New York: Author.

Cross, P. (1976). *Accent on learning.* San Francisco: Jossey-Bass.

"DACUM profile: Core competencies, associate degree of applied arts and sciences." (1987, October 29–30). Pennsylvania College of Technology.

Diamond, H., & Bedrosian, H. (1970). *Hiring standards and job performance* (Manpower Research Monograph No. 18). Washington, DC: U.S. Department of Labor (available from U.S. Government Printing Office).

Diekhoff, G. M. (1988). An appraisal of adult literacy programs: Reading between the lines. *Journal of Reading, 31*(7), 624–630.

Doeringer, P., & Piore, M. (1971). *Internal labor markets and manpower analysis.* Lexington, MA: Lexington Books.

Doolittle, F., Bell, S., Bloom, H., Cave, G., Kemple, J., Orr, L., Traeger, L., & Wallace, J. (1993). *A summary of the design and implementation of the National JTPA Study.* New York: Manpower Development Research Corp.

Doucette, D. (1993). *Community college workforce training programs for employees of business, industry, labor, and government: A status report.* Mission Viejo, CA: League for Innovation in the Community College.

Dougherty, K. (1987). The effects of community colleges: Aid or hindrance to socioeconomic attainment? *Sociology of Education, 60,* 86–103.

Dougherty, K. (1994). *The contradictory college: The conflicting origins, impacts, and futures of the community college.* Albany: State University of New York Press.

Eaton, J. (1994). *Strengthening collegiate education in community colleges.* San Francisco : Jossey-Bass.

Eck, A. (1993). Job-related education and training: Their impact on earnings. *Monthly Labor Review, 116*(10), 21–38.

Educational Quality of the Workforce (EQW). (1995). *The EQW national employer survey: First findings.* Philadelphia: University of Pennsylvania, National Center on the Educational Quality of the Workforce.

Eishen, T. E. (1991). Writing to learn: A vocational teacher's perspective. *Texas Junior College Teachers Association Messenger, 1,* 6–8.

Finn, C. E., Jr., Ravitch, D., & Fancher, R. T. (Eds.). (1984). *Against mediocrity.* New York: Holmes & Meier.

Fischer, F. (1987). Graduation-contingent student aid. *Change, 19*(5), 40–47.

Fischer, R., & Cordray, D. (1996). *Job training and welfare reform: A policy-driven synthesis.* New York: Russell Sage Foundation.

Fountain, B. E., & Tollefson, T. A. (1989). *Community colleges in the United States: Forty-nine state systems.* Washington, DC: American Association of Community and Junior Colleges.

Friedlander, D., & Burtless, G. (1995). *Five years after: The long-term effects of welfare-to-work programs.* New York: Russell Sage Foundation.

Friedlander, J. (1993). *Using wage record data to track the post-college employment and earnings of community college students.* Santa Barbara, CA: Santa Barbara City College, Office of Academic Affairs.

Friedlander, J. (undated). Incorporating career development activities into the curriculum. Unpublished paper. Santa Barbara, CA: Santa Barbara City College, Office of Academic Affairs.

Gabelnick, F., MacGregor, J., Matthews, R., & Smith, B. (1990). Learning communities: Creating connections among students, faculty, and disciplines. *New Directions for Teaching and Learning,* no. 41. San Francisco: Jossey-Bass.

Godwin, C. M. (1991). The writing consultancy project. In L. Stanley and J. Ambron (Eds.), Writing across the curriculum in community colleges. *New Directions in Community Colleges*, no. 73. San Francisco: Jossey-Bass.

Gordon, M. S., & Thal-Larsen, M. (1969). *Employer policies in a changing labor market: Report of the San Francisco bay area employer policy survey.* Berkeley: University of California at Berkeley, Institute of Industrial Relations.

Groot, W., Oosterbeek, H., & Stern, D. (1995). *A sequential probit model of college choice and wages.* Berkeley: University of California, National Center for Research in Vocational Education.

Grubb, W. N. (1987). *The postsecondary vocational education of 1980 seniors.* LSB-87-4-10. U.S. Department of Education, MPR Associates for the Center for Education Statistics.

Grubb, W. N. (1988). Vocationalizing higher education: The causes of enrollment and completion in public two-year colleges, 1970–1980. *Economics of Education Review, 7*(3), 301–319.

Grubb, W. N. (1989a). *Access, achievement, completion, and "milling around" in postsecondary education.* Berkeley: MPR Associates, for U.S. Department of Education, National Assessment of Vocational Education.

Grubb, W. N. (1989b). Dropouts, spells of time, and credits in postsecondary education: Evidence from longitudinal surveys. *Economics of Education Review, 8*(4), 49–67.

Grubb, W. N. (1989c). The effects of differentiation on educational attainment: The case of community colleges. *Review of Higher Education, 12*(4), 349–374.

Grubb, W. N. (1990). *The causes of enrollment in postsecondary education: Evidence from the national longitudinal study of the class of 1972.* Unpublished paper.

Grubb, W. N. (1991). The decline of community college transfer rates: Evidence from national longitudinal surveys. *Journal of Higher Education, 62*(2), 194–222.

Grubb, W. N. (1992a). The economic returns to baccalaureate degrees: New evidence from the class of 1972. *Review of Higher Education, 15*(2), 213–232.

Grubb, W. N. (1992b). Postsecondary vocational education and the subbaccalaureate labor market: New evidence on economic returns. *Economics of Education Review, 11*(3), 225–248.

Grubb, W. N. (1992c). *Finding an equilibrium: Enhancing transfer rates while strengthening the comprehensive community college.* Working Papers, Vol. 3, No. 6. Washington, DC: National Center for Academic Achievement and Transfer.

Grubb, W. N. (1993a). Further tests of screening on education and observed ability. *Economics of Education Review, 12*(2), 125–136.

Grubb, W. N. (1993b). The varied economic returns to postsecondary education: New evidence from the class of 1972. *Journal of Human Resources, 28*(2), 365–382.

Grubb, W. N. (1993c). The long-run effects of proprietary schools on wages and earnings: Implications for federal policy. *Educational Evaluation and Policy Analysis, 15*(1), 17–33.

Grubb, W. N. (1994). The long-run effects of proprietary schools: Corrections. *Educational Evaluation and Policy Analysis, 16*(3), 351–356.

Grubb, W. N. (1995a). The sub-baccalaureate labor market and the advantages of co-operative education. *Journal of Cooperative Education, 30*(2), 6–19.

Grubb, W. N. (1995b). Response to comment. *Journal of Human Resources, 30*(1), 222–228.

Grubb, W. N. (1995c). *Education through occupations in American high schools. Vol. I: Approaches to integrating academic and vocational education. Vol. II: The challenges of implementing curriculum integration.* New York: Teachers College Press.

Grubb, W. N. (1995d). *The returns to education and training in the sub-baccalaureate labor market: Evidence from the Survey of Income and Program Participation, 1984–1990.* Berkeley: University of California, National Center for Research in Vocational Education.

Grubb, W. N. (1995e). The economic returns to baccalaureate degrees: Corrections. *Review of Higher Education, 18*(4), 483–490.

Grubb, W. N. (1995f). *Evaluating job training programs in the United States: Evidence and explanations.* Training Policy Study No. 17. Geneva: International Labor Office.

Grubb, W. N. (1995g). Postsecondary education and the sub-baccalaureate labor market: Corrections and extensions. *Economics of Education Review, 14*(3), 285–299.

Grubb, W. N. (1995h, November). *The economic benefits of sub-baccalaureate education.* Paper prepared for the Association for the Study of Higher Education Conference.

Grubb, W. N. (1996). *Learning to work: The case for re-integrating education and job training.* New York: Russell Sage Foundation.

Grubb, W. N., & Badway, N. (1995). *Linking school-based and work-based learning: The implications of LaGuardia's integrative seminars for school-to-work programs.* Prepared for U.S. Congress, Office of Technology Assessment.

Grubb, W. N., Badway, N., Dickens, W., Finkelstein, N., Hoynes, H., & Stern, D. (1993). *Choosing wisely for California: Targeting the resources of the employment training panel.* Berkeley: University of California, National Center for Research in Vocational Education and the Center for Labor Research and Education.

Grubb, W. N., & Bailis, L. (1993, April). *Coordination between vocational education and other federal programs: A status report.* Paper prepared for the National Assessment of Vocational Education, U.S. Department of Education.

Grubb, W. N., Brown, C., Kaufman, P., & Lederer, J. (1989, April). *Innovation versus turf: Coordination between vocational education and Job Training Partnership Act programs.* Berkeley: National Center for Research in Vocational Education.

Grubb, W. N., Brown, C., Kaufman, P., & Lederer, J. (1990). *Order amidst complexity: The status of coordination among vocational education, Job Training Partnership Act, and welfare-to-work programs.* Berkeley: University of California, National Center for Research in Vocational Education.

Grubb, W. N., Davis, G., Lum, J., Plihal, J., & Morgaine, C. (1991). *"The cunning hand, the cultured mind": Models for integrating vocational and academic education.* Berkeley: University of California, National Center for Research in Vocational Education.

Grubb, W. N., Dickinson, T., Giordano, L., & Kaplan, G. (1992). *Betwixt and between: Education, skills, and employment in sub-baccalaureate labor markets.* Berkeley: National Center for Research in Vocational Education.

Grubb, W. N., & Kalman, J. (1994). Relearning to earn: The role of remediation in vocational education and job training. *American Journal of Education, 103*(1), 54–93.

Grubb, W. N., Kalman, J., Castellano, M., Brown, C., & Bradby, D. (1991). *Readin', writin', and 'rithmetic one more time: The role of remediation in vocational education and job training programs.* Berkeley: University of California, National Center for Research in Vocational Education.

Grubb, W. N., & Kraskouskas, E. (1992). *A time to every purpose: Integrating academic and occupational education in community colleges and technical institutes.* Berkeley: University of California at Berkeley, National Center for Research in Vocational Education.

Grubb, W. N., & Lazerson, M. (1988). *Broken promises: How Americans fail their children* (Rev. ed.). Chicago: University of Chicago Press.

Grubb, W. N., & McDonnell, L. M. (1991). *Local systems of vocational education and job training: Diversity, interdependence, and effectiveness.* Santa Monica and Berkeley, CA: RAND Corp. and University of California at Berkeley, National Center for Research in Vocational Education.

Grubb, W. N., & McDonnell, L. (1996). Combating program fragmentation: Local systems of vocational education and job training. *Journal of Policy Analysis and Management, 15*(2), 252–270.

Grubb, W. N., & Stasz, C. (1993). *Integrating academic and vocational education: Progress under the Carl Perkins amendments of 1990.* Berkeley: U.S. Department of Education, National Center for Research in

Vocational Education, for the National Assessment of Vocational Education.

Grubb, W. N., & Stern, D. (1989). *Long time a'comin': Options for federal financing of postsecondary vocational education.* Berkeley: MPR Associates, for National Assessment of Vocational Education.

Grubb, W. N., & Tuma, J. (1991). Who gets student aid? Variations in access to aid. *Review of Higher Education, 14*(3), 359–381.

Grubb, W. N., & Villeneuve, J. (1995). *Co-operative education in Cincinnati: Implications for school-to-work programs in the U. S.* Prepared for U.S. Congress, Office of Technology Assessment.

Grubb, W. N., & Wilson, R. (1992). The effects of demographic and labor market trends on wage and salary inequality, 1967–1988. *Monthly Labor Review, 115*(6), 23–39.

Gudan, S., Clack, D., Tang, K., & Dixon, S. (1991). *Paired classes for success.* Livonia, MI: Schoolcraft College.

Hamberg, R. L. (1991). Learning communities: Needed educational re-structuring. *Leadership Abstracts, League for Innovation in the Community Colleges, 4*(9).

Hammons, J. (1979). General education: A missed opportunity returns. In A. Cohen, (Ed.), Shaping the curriculum. *New Directions for Community Colleges,* no. 7. San Francisco: Jossey-Bass.

Hansen, J. S. (Ed.). (1994). *Preparing for the workplace: Charting a course for federal postsecondary training policy.* Washington, DC: National Academy Press.

Hauser, R., & Featherman, D. (1976). Equality of schooling: Trends and prospects. *Sociology of Education, 49,* 99–120.

Hersh, R. (1983). Are Americans turning out technopeasants? *Instructor, 92*(9), 27–29.

Higher Education Research Institute. (1994). *The American freshman: Twenty-five year trends.* Los Angeles: University of California at Los Angeles, Author.

Hill, P., Harvey, J., & Praskac, A. (1992). *Pandora's box: Accountability and performance standards in vocational education.* WD-5799-NCRVE/UCB. Santa Monica, CA: RAND Corp.

Hillocks, G. *Research on Written Composition: New Directions for Teaching.* Urbana, IL: ERIC Clearinghouse on Reading and Communications Skills and National Conference on Research in English, 1986.

Hoachlander, G., Choy, S., & Brown, C. (1989, March). *Performance-based policy options in federal vocational education policy: A feasibility study.* Berkeley: MPR Associates for the National Assessment of Vocational Education, U.S. Department of Education.

Hoachlander, E. G., & Rahn, M. L. (1992). *Performance measures and stan-*

dards for vocational education: 1991 survey results. Berkeley: University of California, National Center for Research in Vocational Education.

Hollenbeck, K. (1993). Postsecondary education as triage: Returns to academic and technical programs. *Economics of Education Review, 12*(3), 213–232.

Hollinger, D., & Harvey, J. (1994). Coordinating vocational education and federal job-training programs. In L. Muraskin, D. Hollinger, & J. Harvey (Eds.). *Final report to congress: Vol. 1. Funding and administration issues.* Washington, DC: U.S. Department of Education.

Hudis, P. M., Bradby, D., Brown, C. L., Hoachlander, E. G., Levesque, K. A., & Nachuk, S. (1992). *Meeting the personnel needs of the health care industry through vocational education programs: A study of the San Francisco bay area* (Vol. I). Berkeley: University of California, National Center for Research in Vocational Education.

Hughes-Weiner, G., & Jensen-Cekalla, S. K. (1991). Organizing a WAC evaluation project: Implications for program planning. In L. Stanley & J. Ambron (Eds.), Writing across the curriculum in community colleges. *New Directions in Community Colleges,* no. 73. San Francisco: Jossey-Bass.

Jacobs, J. (1992). *Customized training in Michigan: A necessary priority for community colleges.* Prepared for Michigan Department of Education, Advisory Board of the Partnership Project.

Kagan, S. L., Goffin, S. G., Golub, S. A., & Pritchard, E. P. (1995). *Toward systemic reform: Service integration for young children and their families.* Falls Church, VA: National Center for Service Integration.

Kane, T., & Rouse, C. (1995a). Comment on W. Norton Grubb, The varied economic returns to postsecondary education: New evidence from the class of 1972. *Journal of Human Resources, 30*(1), 205–221.

Kane, T., & Rouse, C. (1995b). Labor market returns to two- and four-year colleges. *American Economic Review, 85*(3), 600–614.

Kett, J. F. (1982). The adolescence of vocational education. In H. Kantor & D. B. Tyack (Eds.), *Work, youth, and schooling: Historical perspectives on vocationalism in American education* (pp. 79–109). Stanford, CA: Stanford University Press.

Killingsworth, J. (Ed.). (1988). *Designing writing assessments for vocational-technical courses.* Lubbock: Texas Tech University. (ERIC Document ED 298 331).

Kogan, D., et al. (1989). *Improving the quality of training under JTPA.* Berkeley Planning Associates and SRI International, for U.S. Department of Labor.

Koziol, K. (1992). *Novels and short stories about work: An annotated bibliography.* Berkeley: National Center for Research in Vocational Education.

Koziol, K., & Grubb, W. N. (1995). Paths not taken: Curriculum integration and the political and moral purposes of schooling. In W. N. Grubb (Ed.), *Education through occupations in American high schools. Vol. II: The challenges of implementing curriculum integration.* New York: Teachers College Press.

LaLonde, R. (1995). The promise of public sector-sponsored training programs. *Journal of Economic Perspectives, 9*(2), 149–168.

Lazerson, M., & Grubb, W. N. (1974). *American education and vocationalism: A documentary history, 1870–1970.* New York: Teachers College Press.

Leslie, L., & Brinkman, P. (1988). *The economic value of higher education.* New York: Macmillan and American Council on Education.

Levesque, K. A., & Alt, M. N. (1994). *A comprehensive guide to using unemployment insurance data for program follow-up* (Grant No. E-9-4-2-40-59). Berkeley: Institute for the Study of Family, Work, and Community.

Levy, F., & Murnane, R. (1992). U.S. earnings levels and earnings inequality: A review of recent trends and proposed explanations. *Journal of Economic Literature, 30*(3), 1333–1381.

Lewis, A., Carr, B., South, L. A., & Reed, T. (1995). *School-linked comprehensive services for children and families: What we know and what we need to know.* Washington, DC: U.S. Department of Education, Office of Educational Research and Improvement.

Lewis, D. R., Hearn, J. C., & Zilbert, E. E. (1993). Efficiency and equity effects of vocationally focused postsecondary education. *Sociology of Education, 66,* 188–205.

London, H. (1978). *The culture of a community college.* New York: Praeger.

Long, D., Wood, R. G., & Kopp, H. (1994). *The educational effects of LEAP and enhanced services in Cleveland: Ohio's learning, earning, and parenting program for teenage parents on welfare.* New York: Manpower Demonstration Research Corp.

Losak, J., & Morris, C. (1985). *Comparing treatment effects for students who successfully complete college preparatory work* (Research Report No. 85-45). Miami: Miami-Dade Community College, Office of Institutional Research.

Lurie I., & Hagen, J. (1994). Implementing the JOBS program: An assessment in ten states. Unpublished paper, Nelson A. Rockefeller Institute of Government, State University of New York, Albany.

Lynch, L. (1992). Private sector training and the earnings of young workers. *American Economic Review, 82*(1), 299–312.

Lynch, L. (1994). *Training and the private sector: International comparisons.* Chicago: University of Chicago Press.

Lynch, R., Palmer, J. C., & Grubb, W. N. (1991). *Community college involve-*

ment in contract training and other economic development activities. Berkeley: University of California, National Center for Research in Vocational Education.

Malizio, A. (1995). *National postsecondary student aid study: Estimates of student financial aid, 1992–93.* NCES 95-746. Washington, DC: U.S. Department of Education, National Center for Education Statistics (NCES).

Mann, H. ([1842] 1971). Fifth annual report of the secretary of the board. Reprinted in M. Katz (Ed.), *School reform: Past and present* (pp. 140–149). Boston: Little, Brown.

Mansfield, W., & Farris, E. (1991). *College-level remediation in the fall of 1989.* NCES 91-191. Washington, DC: U.S. Department of Education, Office of Educational Research and Improvement.

Manski, C. (1989). Schooling as experimentation: A reappraisal of the college dropout phenomenon. *Economics of Education Review, 8*(4), 305–312.

Manski, C. (1993). Identification of endogenous social effects: The reflection problem. *Review of Economics Studies, 60,* 531–542.

Martinson, K., & Friedlander, D. (1994). *GAIN: Basic education in a welfare-to-work program.* New York: Manpower Demonstration Research Corp.

Matthews, R. (1994). *Notes from the field: Reflections on collaborative learning at LaGuardia.* Long Island City, NY: LaGuardia Community College, Office of the Associate Dean for Academic Affairs.

McCharen, B. (1995). Guidance and counseling: An essential component for effective integration. In W. N. Grubb (Ed.), *Education through occupations in American high schools. Vol. 2: The challenges of implementing curriculum integration* (pp. 141–155). New York: Teachers College Press.

McDonnell, L., & Grubb, W. N. (1991). *Education and training for work: The policy instruments and the institutions.* Berkeley and Santa Monica, CA: National Center for Research in Vocational Education and RAND Corp.

McDonnell, L. M., & Zellman, G. L. (1993). *Education and training for work in the fifty states: A compendium of state policies* (N-3560-NCRVE/UCB). Berkeley: University of California, National Center for Research in Vocational Education.

McPartland, J. M., Dawkins, R. L., & Braddock, J. H., II. (1986). *The school's role in the transition from education to work: Current conditions and future prospects.* Baltimore, MD: Johns Hopkins University, Center for Social Organization of Schools.

Medrich, E., & Vergun, R. (1994). *Earnings and employment outcomes for postsecondary degree holders in vocational subject areas.* Berkeley: MPR Associates, for U.S Department of Education, National Assessment of Vocational Education.

Monk-Turner, E. (1983). Sex, educational differentiation, and occupational status: Analyzing occupational differences for community and four-year college entrants. *The Sociological Quarterly, 24,* 393–404.

Monk-Turner, E. (1990). The occupational achievements of community and four-year college entrants. *American Sociological Review, 55,* 719–725.

Morris, C. (1994). *Success of students who needed and completed college preparatory instruction (Report No. 94-19R).* Miami: Miami-Dade Community College.

National Center for Educational Statistics. (1993). *Digest of educational statistics.* Washington, DC: U.S. Department of Education.

National Center for Educational Statistics. (1994). *Digest of educational statistics.* Washington, DC: U.S. Department of Education.

National Commission on Excellence in Education. (1983). *A nation at risk: The imperative for educational reform.* Washington, DC: Author.

National Council for Occupational Education and the American Association of Community and Junior Colleges. (1990). *Productive America: Two-year colleges unite to improve productivity in the nation's workforce* (Grant No. 99-9-3513-75-013-02). Washington, DC: U.S. Department of Labor.

Office of the Chief Economist. (1995). *What's working (and what's not): A summary of research on the economic impacts of employment and training programs.* Washington DC: U.S. Department of Labor, Author.

Osterman, P. (1994). How common is workplace transformation and who adopts it? *Industrial and Labor Relations Review, 47*(2), 173–188.

Osterman, P., & Kochan, T. A. (1990). Employment security and employment policy: An assessment of the issues. In K. G. Abraham & R. B. McKersie (Eds.), *New developments in the labor market* (pp. 155–182). Cambridge: MIT Press.

Palmer, J. (1988). Bolstering the community college transfer function: An ERIC review. *Community College Review, 14,* 53–63.

Palmer, J. (1990). *Accountability through student tracking: A review of the literature.* Washington, DC: American Association of Community and Junior Colleges.

Parker, E. (1992). *Work reorganization and vocational training: The Milwaukee-Waukesha training partnership.* Madison: University of Wisconsin, Madison Center on Wisconsin Strategy.

Parnes, H., & Kohen, A. (1975). Occupational information and labor market status: The case of young men. *Journal of Human Resources, 10*(1), 44–55.

Pascarella, E., & Terenzini, P. (1991). *How college affects students.* San Francisco: Jossey-Bass.

Perkinson, H. (1977). *The imperfect panacea: American faith in education, 1865–1976* (2nd ed.). New York: Random House.

Peterson, G. E., Bovbjerg, R. R., Davis, B. A., Davis, W. G., Durman, E. C., & Gullo, T. A. (1986). *The Reagan block grants: What have we learned?* Washington, DC: The Urban Institute.

Pincus, F. L. (1980). The false promises of community colleges: Class conflict and vocational education. *Harvard Educational Review, 50*(3), 332–361.

Pincus, F. L. (1986). Vocational education: More false promises. In S. Zwerling (Ed.), The community college and its critics. *New Directions for Community Colleges,* no. 54. San Francisco: Jossey-Bass.

Plisko, V. W., & Stern, J. D. (1985). *The condition of education: A statistical report.* Washington, DC: National Center for Educational Statistics.

Powell, A., Farrar, E., & Cohen, D. (1985). *The shopping mall high school.* Boston: Houghton Mifflin.

Quint, J. C., Musick, J. S., & Ladner, J. A. (1994). *Lives of promise, lives of pain: Young mothers after New Chance.* New York: Manpower Demonstration Research Corp.

Quint, J. C., Polit, D. F., Bos, H., & Cave, G. (1994). *New Chance: Interim findings on a comprehensive program for disadvantaged young mothers and their children.* New York: Manpower Demonstration Research Corp.

Rahn, M., Hoachlander, G., & Levesque, L. (1992). *State systems for accountability in vocational education.* Berkeley: National Center for Research in Vocational Education.

Ratcliff, T. (1995). *The evolution of student affairs and its implications for community colleges.* Unpublished position paper, University of California at Berkeley, School of Education.

Rawlins, V. L., & Ulman, L. (1974). The utilization of college-trained manpower in the United States. In M. Gordon (Ed.), *Higher education and the labor market* (pp. 195–236). New York: McGraw-Hill.

Reid, W., Bailey-Dempsey, C., Cain, E., Cook, T., & Burchard, J. (1994 December). Cash incentives versus case management: Can money replace services in preventing school failure? *Social Work Research, 18*(4), 227–236.

Rifkin, J. (1995). *The end of work: The decline of the global labor force and the dawn of the post-market era.* New York: Jeremy P. Tarcher/Putnam.

Riggs, R., Davis, T., & Wilson, O. (1990). Impact of Tennessee's remedial/developmental studies program on the academic progress of minority students. *Community/Junior College Quarterly of Research and Practice, 14*(1) 1–11.

Rogers, J. (1994). The Wisconsin regional training partnership: A national model for regional modernization efforts? In *Proceedings of the 46th*

Annual Meeting of the Industrial Relations Research Association. Madison: IRRA.

Rogers, J., & Streeck, W. (1992). *Recommendations for action.* Madison: University of Wisconsin, Center on Wisconsin Strategy.

Roueche, J. E., & Baker, G. A., III. (1987a). *Access and excellence: The open-door college.* Washington, DC: The Community College Press.

Roueche, J. E., & Baker, G. A., III. (1987b). Excellent teachers. In J. E. Roueche & G. A. Baker III (Eds.), *Access and excellence: The open-door college* (pp. 145–179). Washington, DC: The Community College Press.

Roueche, J. E., Baker, G. A., III, & Roueche, S. D. (1985). Access with excellence: Toward academic success in college. *Community College Review, 12*(4), 4–9.

Rumberger, R. (1981). *Overeducation in the U.S. labor market.* New York: Praeger.

Rumberger, R. W. (1987). The potential impact of technology on the skill requirements of future jobs in the United States. In G. Burke & R. W. Rumberger (Eds.), *The future impact of technology on work and education* (pp. 74–95). Philadelphia: Falmer Press.

Rumberger, R., & Daymont, T. (1984). The economic value of academic and vocational training acquired in high school. In M. Borus (Ed.), *Youth and the labor market: Analyses of the national longitudinal survey.* Kalamazoo, MI: W. E. Upjohn Institute for Employment Research.

Rumberger, R., & Thomas, S. (1993, March). The economic returns to college major, quality, and performance: A multilevel analysis of recent graduates. *Economics of Education Review, 12*(1), 1–19.

Secretary's Commission on Achieving Necessary Skills (SCANS). (1991). *What work requires of schools: A SCANS report for America 2000.* Washington, DC: U.S. Department of Labor.

Sessions, R. (1992). Humanities and career education: Bridging the great divide. *Community, Technical, and Junior College Journal, 62*(3), 35–40.

Sessions, R., & Wortman, J. (1992). *Working in America: A humanities reader.* Notre Dame: University of Notre Dame Press.

Shared Vision Task Force, National Council on Occupational Education and the Community College Humanities Association. (1989). *Integrating the humanities into associate degree occupational programs: Final report.* Washington: DC: American Association of Community and Junior Colleges.

Shared Vision Task Force, National Council on Occupational Education and the Community College Humanities Association. (1991). *Successfully integrating the humanities into associate degree occupational programs: An implementation manual.* Washington: DC: American Association of Community and Junior Colleges.

Sheldon, M. S. (1982). *Statewide longitudinal study: Report on academic year 1978–1981.* Part 5, Final Report. Woodland Hills, CA: Los Angeles Pierce College. (ERIC Document ED 217 917)

Silvestri, G. (1993). Occupational employment: Wide variations in growth. *Monthly Labor Review, 116,* 58–86.

Smith, E. (1990, Nov. 16). *The humanities in business: A team-taught course.* Panel presentation, Eastern Regional Meeting, Community College Humanities Association.

Solorzano, R., Stecher, B., & Perez, M. (1989). *Reducing illiteracy in California: Review of effective practices in adult literacy programs.* Report for the California State Department of Education, Adult Education Division. Pasadena, CA: Educational Testing Service.

Soskice, D. (1994). Reconciling markets and institutions: The German apprenticeship system. In L. Lynch (Ed.), *Training and the private sector: International comparisons.* Chicago: University of Chicago Press.

Spenner, K. (1983, December). Deciphering Prometheus: Temporal change in the skill level of work. *American Sociological Review, 48*(12), 824–837.

Spetz, J. (1994). *Compensation for nursing: Is the baccalaureate better?* Unpublished paper, Palo Alto: Stanford University, Department of Economics.

Stanley, L., & Ambron, J. (Eds.) (1991). Writing across the curriculum in community colleges. *New Directions in Community Colleges,* no. 73. San Francisco: Jossey-Bass.

Stern, D., Finkelstein, N., Stone, J., Latting, J., & Dornsife, C. (1995). *School-to-work: Research on programs in the United States.* Bristol, PA: Falmer Press.

Stout, B. R., & Magnotto, J. (1988). Writing across the curriculum at community colleges. In S. McLeod (Ed.), Strengthening programs for writing across the curriculum: *New Directions for Teaching and Learning,* no. 36. San Francisco: Jossey-Bass.

Stout, B. R., & Magnotto, J. N. (1991). Building on realities: WAC programs at community colleges. In L. Stanley & J. Ambron (Eds.), Writing across the curriculum in community colleges. *New Directions in Community Colleges,* no. 73. San Francisco: Jossey-Bass.

Streufert, P. (1991). *The effect of social isolation on schooling choice.* Institute for Research on Poverty, Discussion Paper No. 954-91.

Tinto, V. (1987). *Leaving college: Rethinking the causes and cures of student attrition.* Chicago: University of Chicago Press.

Traub (1994, September 19). Class struggle. *New Yorker, 70*(29), 76–90.

Trutko, J., Bailis, L., & Barnow, B. (1989). *An assessment of the JTPA role in state and local coordination activities. Vol. I: Draft final report. Vol. II: Case studies.* Washington DC: James Bell Associates and Lewin/ICF, for U.S. Department of Labor, Employment and Training Administration.

Tsuzuki, M. (1995). Senior projects: Flexible opportunities for integration. In W. N. Grubb (Ed.), *Education through occupations in American high schools. Vol. I: Approaches to integrating academic and vocational education.* New York: Teachers College Press.

Tuma, J. (1993). *Patterns of enrollment in postsecondary vocational and academic education.* Prepared for the National Assessment of Vocational Education. Berkeley: MPR Associates.

Tuma, J., & Geis, S. (1995). *Educational attainment of 1980 high school sophomores by 1992: Descriptive summary of 1980 sophomores 12 years later.* NCES 95-304. Washington, DC: U.S. Department of Education, Office of Educational Research and Improvement.

U.S. Department of Labor. (1988). *Flexible workstyles: A look at contingent labor. Conference summary.* Washington, DC: U.S. Government Printing Office.

U.S. Department of Labor. (1992). *How workers get their training: A 1991 update.* Bulletin 2407. Washington, DC: Bureau of Labor Statistics, available from U.S. Government Printing Office.

U.S. General Accounting Office. (1995). *Multiple employment training programs: Major overhaul needed to create a more efficient, customer-driven system.* Washington, DC: Author.

Useem, E. L. (1986). *Low tech education in a high tech world.* New York: Free Press.

Velez, W. (1985). Finishing college: The effects of college type. *Sociology of Education, 58,* 191–200.

Villeneuve, J. C., & Grubb, W. N. (1996). *Indigenous school-to-work programs: Lessons from Cincinnati's co-op education.* Berkeley: National Center for Research in Vocational Education.

Watkins, B. T. (1990, July 18). More and more professors in many academic disciplines routinely require students to do extensive writing. *The Chronicle of Higher Education,* pp. 13–16.

Weis, L. (1986). *Between two worlds: Black students in an urban community college.* Boston: Routledge and Kegan Paul.

Wial, H. (1991). Getting a good job: Mobility in a segmented labor market. *Industrial Relations, 30*(3), 396–416.

Wilcox, M. K., Grubb, E. B., & Lee, B. L. (1995). *California employment law.* Oakland, CA: Matthew Bender.

Wills, J. (1994). *An overview of skill standards systems in education and industry.* Washington, DC: Institute for Educational Leadership, Center for Workforce Development.

Wilms, W. W. (1974). *Public and proprietary vocational training: A study of effectiveness.* Berkeley: University of California, Center for Research and Development in Higher Education.

Worthen, H. (in press). The problem of part-time faculty. In K. Kroll & B. Alford (Eds.), *Two-year colleges and the politics of writing instruction.* Portsmouth, NH: Boynton//Cook.

Yager, R. E. (1990). The science/technology/society movement in the United States: Its origin, evolution, and rationale. *Social Education, 54*(4), 198–201.

Zwerling, L. S. (1976). *Second best: The crisis of the community college.* New York: McGraw-Hill.

Zwerling, L. S., & London, H. (1992). First-generation students: Confronting the cultural issues. *New Directions for Community Colleges,* no. 80. San Francisco: Jossey-Bass.

Index